LIVERPOOL
&
MANCHESTER
RAILWAY

1830–1980

LIVERPOOL
&
MANCHESTER
RAILWAY
1830–1980

Frank Ferneyhough

Foreword by
Sir Peter Parker MVO
Chairman,
British Railways Board

ROBERT HALE · LONDON

Photoset, printed and bound
in Great Britain by
REDWOOD BURN LIMITED
Trowbridge & Esher

Contents

Acknowledgements

The author acknowledges with gratitude the generous advice and assistance he has received from many friends, former colleagues and organisations, especially the following:

Glenda Ferneyhough; John Rushton Ford; Owen French; Capt. Peter Manisty, RN (Retd); Alex Murray; Tony Quirke; Michael Satow; Lyn Wilson
British Rail; Association of Railway Preservation Societies; Science Museum; Victoria & Albert Museum; National Portrait Gallery; House of Commons Library; St Albans and Marshalswick public libraries; *Manchester Evening News*; *Daily Telegraph* Information Service

He is particularly indebted to the staff of the Liverpool and the Manchester public libraries and museums for facilitating his inspection of Acts of Parliament, directors' board minutes, share certificates, original letters, old newspaper cuttings and other contemporary documents associated with the Liverpool & Manchester Railway. He is indebted also to his wife, Joan, for sharing the research, typing and proof reading.

Illustrations

PICTURE CREDITS

Liverpool Public Libraries: 1, 3, 5, 8, 11, 12, 13, 15, 20, 26, 33, 35, 36, 44,
45, 48, 50, 51, 52, 53, 54; The Science Museum, London: 2, 6, 7, 9, 10, 16,
18, 23, 24, 25, 55, 57; British Rail: 4, 17, 38 and 39 (photo: Bob Bird), 56,
58, 60 (photo: Bellass), 61, 62 (photo: Bob Bird), 64, 65; *Manchester
Evening News*: 14, 21, 27, 34, 37, 40, 42, 46, 47; Manchester Public
Libraries: 19, 29, 30, 31, 49; Victoria and Albert Museum, London: 22, 28,
41, 43; British Transport Hotels: 32; Author's collection: 59; Joma Enterprises: 63; *Evening Sentinel*: 66; *Daily Telegraph*: 67

MAPS

Foreword

By Sir Peter Parker, MVO
Chairman, British Railways Board

As the *City of Liverpool*, with its train of comfortable, air conditioned, Inter-City coaches, picks its way carefully through Edge Hill and drops gently down to Lime Street, it is impossible to realise that, 150 years ago, steam-hauled trains were about to run from Liverpool to Manchester over the first passenger railway in the country, the first indeed, to join two industrial cities.

One autumn day in 1970, Sir John Betjeman left the Inspection saloon, in which he was touring the Liverpool Division, at the remains of the famous Moorish Arch at Edge Hill and, followed by a respectful, and assorted collection of railwaymen, declaimed, hat in hand, on the marvels of the great engineers of the past, as he walked down to the original Wapping tunnel mouth, too small to take a main line locomotive and carriage. Of the group, perhaps only he could have recreated the wonders of the past or realised that, in a few years, we should be celebrating the 150th Anniversary of the Rainhill Trials and of the opening of the Liverpool & Manchester Railway. That same evening, after rejoining his train, Sir John entered Liverpool through what he chose to call "those great hewn cliffs of red sandstone into Lime Street station, the perfect awe-inspiring end for the drama". Earlier, he had visited the Huskisson Memorial at Parkside, scene of the first fatality to a member of the public, passed under the famous Skew Bridge at Rainhill, and then up to Edge Hill, through the Olive Mount cutting, almost untouched by history. The train had stopped quietly and, as a matter of course, in the station.

It is easy to say that the Liverpool & Manchester Railway was opened on 15th September 1830, that the *Rocket* made history at

Rainhill and that it was the direct antecedent, however crude and small, of the steam locomotive which, for over a century, was the greatest instrument in the industrial and social development of the country. But close your eyes for a minute and look back over the years.

The Stephensons, father and son, had yet to make their collective name and most of the greatest names in railway engineering and management were still relatively unknown. The immediate successors to the _Rocket, Northumbrian, Phoenix_ and _Majestic_ had no brakes, no protection for the crew, the crudest of springs; the enginemen and guards had little or no experience, the power of steam under high pressure was barely understood and fortunately only occasionally realised by explosion whilst the signalling system, as we know it, was non-existent. But the engineers and leaders of commerce were men of tremendous courage and foresight whilst the men who ran the railway, uneducated and uncouth by our standards, shared the excitement, involvement and frustration and difficulty of railway work, the first of a breed, which still exists in full measure to this day.

So, as _City of Liverpool_ drops smoothly and safely into Lime Street through the great cutting, cast your mind back to those far off days when the first enginemen, in peak caps and white overalls, took their little charges into Edge Hill station, whistled for assistance from the brakemen, reversed their engines, if they could, whilst their trains of dimly lit, swaying, jolting carriages, ground to an uncertain stand.

Thus the Liverpool & Manchester Railway was born and, a century and a half later, with the age of the High Speed and of the Advanced Passenger train, of the electric locomotive, of safety, comfort and reliability, we shall pay homage to the great pioneers of the past.

Frank Ferneyhough tells this story with all the authority and verve of a life-time of devotion to railways. His timing, just at the moment of the 1980 reconstruction of Rainhill race, is as impeccable as his knowledge of the great Act of Creation in the Industrial Revolution. The world is, in a real way, a branch line of the pioneering Liverpool Manchester run.

Chairman,
British Railways Board

CHAPTER 1

Towards the Railway Concept

The odyssey of the world's first steam locomotive railway to carry regularly both passengers and goods, stands as a tribute to a handful of men – men of incredible courage and vision. Foremost among them were those great protagonists William James, Joseph Sandars, Henry Booth and George Stephenson. By dedication to such a revolutionary project, some of those to be deeply involved worked themselves literally to the grave. Lacking technical equipment as we know it, pioneering engineers with little professional knowledge and home-made tools chalked rough patterns on the workshop floor, and risked limb and life on crude and dangerous locomotives whose steam boilers not only might explode, but often did. In those far-off days of daring in the dark unknown, countless good men were maimed and killed.

Surveyors were brutally beaten up by thugs hired by the landed gentry, and even threatened by shot guns as they measured their lengths and checked with theodolites, sometimes at night, across virgin soil. Promoters staked their capital and fought bitter battles in Parliament, to prevail over the natural fears of an alarmed public, and against powerful and bigoted businessmen holding vested interests in canals, turnpike roads, stage coaches and land.

Looking back from the contemporary scene of Concorde and silicon chip, satellite and colour television, and 125-mph air-conditioned inter-city trains, it is challenging to the imagination to forget for a moment our modern technology, and to think about those tenacious pioneers who virtually changed the paradigm of industrial progress and shattered a social and economic way of life that had barely altered for centuries. At the throbbing heart of the Industrial Revolution which Britain led, lay the Liverpool & Manchester Railway. Of only thirty miles, created in an uncharted environment, it formed the catalyst for many inventions and technical developments, and set the pace for the rapid introduction of railways throughout the civilised world.

Of the several pioneers of recognised engineering genius in that fascinating period, one character towers supremely as the Father of Railways – George Stephenson, the uneducated colliery worker from the bottom of the social strata. He, his talented son Robert, his ardent young acolytes, and experienced engineers who learnt from him on this and other pioneering railways, travelled Britain stoically by pony and stage coach to set up new railways on the proved Liverpool & Manchester pattern. They journeyed through primitive terrain overseas to build new railways in the industrially awakening world. And within two incredible decades, this revolutionary system of inland transport had been established, to inaugurate a new way of life for all classes and races of people.

Seldom is any great technical metamorphosis the work of one man; he is usually sustained by a talented team, he himself arriving at his revolutionary invention on the strength of centuries of accumulated knowledge. And so it was with the steam locomotive railway. Even so, it was the Stephenson *Rocket* and the Liverpool & Manchester Railway which, a century and a half ago, proved to be the watershed in the progress of transport inland. Of the many men who were at the heart of it, few names now remain in the memory. One has to search the records for characters such as Sandars, James, Booth and Lawrence. Yet ask any bright schoolboy two questions: who is the greatest engineer in history and which is the most celebrated locomotive? Most likely the replies would be George Stephenson and the *Rocket*. Both would be right. But ask him to name the inventors of the stationary steam engine, and the steam locomotive, and he would almost certainly say James Watt and George Stephenson. Both would be wrong, which shows how half-true legends so often assume the mantle of authenticity.

As in all great technical revolutions throughout man's history, there were various starting points. Progress along many routes by creative minds in several spheres, not necessarily connected and over many centuries, will finally converge at a point where all the integral components meet and coalesce into a splendid new entity. For the slow progress which culminated in the entity of railways – tracks to take wheels and power to drive them – the earliest motivations must naturally be found in the dawn of man and his need to move stones, timber and earth to build shelter against the elements, roaming wild animals and marauding tribes.

Such work became easier with the invention of the wheel the origins of which are all but lost in antiquity, and to which modern transport owes its beginnings. In time, the chariot developed by the Greeks and Romans was introduced to England during the Roman invasion, but it had faded from the English scene by the time of the Norman invasion in the eleventh century. For centuries the common transport for mixed merchandise consisted of pack-horses and lumbering waggons drawn by oxen or horses. To convey important passengers, a good horse-drawn coach came on the scene when Elizabeth I was Queen; in the early 1600s, London saw its first horse-drawn carriages plying for public hire, and Samuel Pepys noted in his diary the large numbers in service. For longer distances, stage coaches came into increasing use and created their own colourful traditions. Up to the early nineteenth century they were the apogee of elegance, comfort and speed for ladies and gentlemen of the realm. A stage coach network had been encouraged by the improved roads of Telford and Macadam. In reality, an eighteenth-century journey galloping at 12 miles an hour from, say, Liverpool to London in the extremes of weather and in mortal fear of armed highwaymen of the Dick Turpin genre must have been a feat of human endurance.

Wheels were now rolling, but when quarries, mining and iron industries began to take shape, especially in the sixteenth and seventeenth centuries, a new need arose: special 'ways' or tracks to take the wheels of heavily loaded waggons. Even in ancient Rome, flat blocks of stone had been laid to diminish the friction and avoid obstructions impeding the free movement of vehicle wheels on the roads they traversed.

In dawning industrial England, both stone and timber waggonways were laid, that at Wollaton Colliery in Nottinghamshire about 1600 being an early example. They were soon followed elsewhere, notably in the coalfields of Shropshire, Durham and Northumberland. Within about two hundred years, large numbers of waggonways had been laid, especially in collieries and quarries, in England, Wales and Scotland. Improved 'ways' enabled horses to haul several waggons hooked together as a train. From about mid-eighteenth century, many colliery waggon-ways were effectively carrying coal to the new canals built by the Rennies, Brindley and others, and to rivers and estuaries for coastwise boats.

To prevent waggon wheels from sinking axle-deep in the surrounding earth, a wooden guiding flange, L-shaped in profile, was added; sometimes, the wooden 'rails' were laid on cross members, known as 'sleepers', for rigidity.

Iron was now coming into use, and iron ways were introduced as early as 1738 in Cumberland and soon became more common. Because the iron was cast in plates, the tracks were known as plateways, hence the term 'platelayer' still current. In 1776, John Curr laid a cast iron plate-way at the Duke of Norfolk's colliery near Sheffield. For some reason, now obscure, militant colliery workers furiously resisted the new track, tore it up and raised a riot. Terror-stricken, the hapless Curr fled to a nearby wood and hid there for three days and nights. Such was the price the pioneers paid. In 1789, William Jessop introduced a unique and promising innovation on a track he constructed at Loughborough; instead of a guiding flange on the plate-way, he fitted flanges on the waggon wheels to prevent them slipping off the metals. It was quickly copied and remains the rail-wheel principle today.

Plate-ways were known variously as tram-ways, tram-roads, rail-roads and rail-ways. Between 1745 and 1775, as more canals came into use and the extractive industries expanded, large numbers were laid. In the Newcastle-on-Tyne area, wooden rails were made with a rounded top surface; and waggon wheels were cast with concave rims, pulley-wheel fashion, for smooth running. They were noted by a French traveller named Saint-Fond on his visit to Newcastle in 1791. His writings were published under the title, *Travels in England, Scotland and the Hebrides*. Back home, the Frenchman urged his fellow-countrymen in colliery districts to follow the English example of carrying coal to ports; he described the tracks as superior to anything he had seen on his travels.

While progress was being made with ways for waggons, power other than animals and men for their haulage still lagged behind. Yet, astonishingly, steam power had been the dream of man not so long after the time of Christ. The earliest recorded device for using steam power to create rotative mechanical movement is traced to Hero of Alexandria, *circa* A.D.100; steam rose from a boiling cauldron into a hollow sphere to rotate it by means of outlet jets. Down the centuries, Hero's idea doubtless aroused the interest of philosophers, scholars and travellers. Somerset-born Roger Bacon (1214?–1294), a scholar of both Oxford and Paris, wrote: "One day we shall endow chariots with incredible speed without the aid of any animal."

A jet-powered carriage with a passenger seat was outlined in 1680 by Sir Isaac Newton (1642–1727), renowned for his scientific investigations into the force of gravity. A spherical generator would be used. The apparatus would be "mounted on little wheels, so as to move easily on a horizontal plane, and if the hole or jet pipe be opened, the vapour [presumably steam] will rush out violently one way, and wheels and the ball will at the same time be carried to the contrary."

A country doctor named Erasmus Darwin (1731–1802), grandfather of the great naturalist Charles Darwin, was inspired by an idea for a "fiery chariot". In 1791, he published a short poem about steam power that was illuminated by the prophetic lines:

> Soon shall thy arm, unconquered steam! afar
> drag the slow barge, or drive the rapid car;

> or on wide-waving wings expanded bear
> the flying chariot through the field of air.

Now to the more practical: in eighteenth-century agricultural England, mining for tin, coal and other minerals presaged the industrial innovations to come. Flooding quickly presented serious problems, and teams of horses and men, with simple windlasses for pumping out water, were slow and costly, and men of ideas turned their creative gifts to mechanical aids. Thomas Savery (1650?–1715), an English military engineer of Devon, registered a patent for a steam pump in 1698. About that time, Thomas Newcomen (1663–1729) of Dartmouth, Devon, began to develop the first known piston-operated steam engine; and by 1712, the Newcomen engine was doing practical work.

Newcomen's suction pump was to be described later by a writer as a "clumsy and apparently a very painful process, a heavy sigh . . . a creak, a wheeze, another bump, and then a rush of water as it was lifted and poured out". It did the job despite the noises off. This "atmospheric fire engine pump" continued in commercial work long after better engines had been introduced.

Apart from the wheel, Newcomen's steam engine was probably the greatest invention that mankind has ever seen, and a direct lead towards the steam locomotive that gave birth to the Liverpool & Manchester Railway. For the first time, it proved the use of combustion of fuel in generating mechanical power. Undoubtedly catalystic, it played a leading role in the Industrial Revolution. In later years, a verse was to encapsulate a steam power theme:

> In fitness for the urgent hour,
> Unlimited, untiring power,
> Precision, promptitude, command,
> The infant's will, the giant's hand,
> Steam, mighty steam ascends the throne,
> And reigns lord paramount alone.

Now, man was no longer dependent for power on the elements, animals and his own muscles – as long as he could find peat, timber and coal as fuel.

After Newcomen, the next mechanical genius to stride across the workshop floor was James Watt (1736–1819), an instrument maker of Glasgow. Fascinated by the Newcomen engine, with his own considerable skill he set about improving it. He built his own steam engine with high pressure and condensing unit and in 1769 protected it with a patent registration. His friend, Dr Small of Birmingham, urged Watt to build a steam locomotive carriage to run on roads and wrote, "I hope soon to travel in a fiery chariot of your invention". Watt's comprehensive patent in 1784 did, in fact, include a specification for a steam carriage. Meanwhile, he had teamed up with Matthew Boulton who had a small factory at Soho, Birmingham. A Scottish mechanic there named William Murdock, in 1786 built a model, about a foot high, of a steam locomotive for roads; but Watt scorned it; let others "throw away their time and money in hunting shadows". °

Most Boulton & Watt steam engines were massive and cumbersome, many with large timber beams and enormous flywheels, but they were effective. By the end of the century, the partners had sold some five hundred. Many went overseas which must have sparked off other inventors in the direction of a 'travelling engine'. Incidentally, Watt measured the energy of his engines against the power of a horse, originating the term 'horse power'; and an electricity measure later took his name.

In France in 1769 and America in 1804, inventors built experimental steam carriages to run on roads, but they were failures.

Towards the end of the century, another remarkable inventor was thinking up ideas. Richard Trevithick (1771–1833) of Illogan, near Redruth in Cornwall, worked in the tin mining area and he was enraptured by the water-pumping engines and mining machinery. Many Boulton & Watt engines were in use and he became a pupil of William Murdock who encouraged the young man's interest in travelling engines. Trevithick went into business at Camborne with a partner to build stationary steam engines, daring to encroach on exclusive Watt territory. In 1802, he registered a patent for an improved engine and "the application thereof for driving carriages". The engine he built ran successfully along the road and while he was celebrating at a local inn, the machine caught fire in its shed and was destroyed.

His next commission was to build a stationary engine at Pen-y-darran Ironworks near Merthyr Tydfil in South Wales; and while there, he constructed his first 'travelling engine' to run on rails. It had a huge flywheel similar to those on stationary engines and looked a dangerous machine. On 15th February 1804, it was tested on the local plate-way. A few days later it hauled a train of five waggons loaded with ten tons of iron and seventy people, for a distance of nine miles at speeds of up to five miles an hour, a venture which was bitterly resented by the great Watt. This was during the long reign of King George III and it is certain that few of those present on this momentous occasion realised the full implications, for this was consummately the world's first successful steam locomotive capable of hauling a train of waggons along rails at a practical speed. It proved conclusively that a smooth wheel could grip a smooth rail with the adhesion needed to haul a load; it also demonstrated mechanical power in a compact and portable form. However, it proved too heavy and damaged the crude, flanged plate-way. Thus, the basic fault lay not with the locomotive, but with the track.

Feeling that he might have more success in the coalfields of the north-east, Trevithick took a locomotive to Newcastle in 1805, the first of several visits during the next three years, where he met George Stephenson, then aged twenty-four. Stephenson and other young engineers who worked with stationary steam engines in the colliery areas were inspired to follow Trevithick's lead.

Wide public attention was earned by Trevithick's experiments when, in 1808, he exhibited in London his new locomotive and a carriage carrying passengers round an enclosed circular tram-way. Somehow the event was not taken very seriously and Trevithick closed the show in a typical tantrum.

Moody and volatile, the inventive Trevithick strayed from project to project and neglected his invention of the age, the locomotive. Like Watt, he built stationary steam engines for use in Britain and overseas. Some went to Peru which he visited in 1817 with the promise of great wealth. Revolution there sent him home in 1827, dejected and penniless, where he spent his remaining six years pursuing other inventions.

Early in the century, improvements to waggon-ways led promoters to plan services for general public use. The first Act of Parliament for a public railway in Britain was passed in 1801 for a horse-drawn system of six miles between Wandsworth on the River Thames and Croydon, the Surrey Iron Railway Company, to carry goods. Fare-paying passengers were first conveyed in South Wales on 25th March 1807; it was a horse-drawn service between Swansea and Oyster-mouth known as the Swansea & Mumbles Railway.

The year 1812 was set in a period of wars, the year of Napoleon's famous retreat from a wintry Moscow, of Britain's declaration of war against the United States of America and the occupation of Washington. It was also the year in which the first commercial use of a steam locomotive was inaugurated; Matthew Murray's rack and pinion loco-motive with flanged wheels rattled along on Blenkinsop's rack rail between Leeds and Middleton Colliery. Their locomotives were unsteady; one splayed the track and exploded. At Wylam Colliery near Newcastle-on-Tyne, Thomas Waters built a locomotive with a huge flywheel. When it refused to budge, he threatened, "Either *she* goes or *I* go!" On starting, it blew into pieces, fortunately without any personal injury. In Durham, William Brunton's locomotive, which was propelled by two ingenious iron legs "walking along the track", exploded in 1815; several people were killed and injured in this first serious railway disaster.

Strongly influenced by Trevithick's designs, others in the north-east took up the locomotive. Among them were William Symington,

William Chapman, Timothy Hackworth, and William Hedley of *Puffing Billy* fame. So, too, did George Stephenson (1781–1848). Born at Wylam near Newcastle-on-Tyne, the young boy watched horse-drawn waggons hauled along the track. After farm labouring, he worked at Black Callerton Colliery, operating horses and the colliery gin. At fifteen, he fed fuel into the engines and did minor repairs. His natural mechanical skill gained him the compliment among his workmates as "a good engine doctor", and when machinery broke down, the call went out, "Send for George!" In the absence of schooling he was illiterate, and in his teens he took lessons in reading and writing to learn about Watt, Newcomen and other great engineers. He married in 1802 and the following year his only son Robert was born. His wife Fanny, twelve years his senior, died in 1806 shortly after having a daughter who died in infancy. As a widower of age twenty-five he sadly put Robert in the care of the family and in 1807 walked all the way to Montrose in Scotland where he tended a Boulton & Watt stationary steam engine. On returning to Killingworth, he undertook similar work, and every Saturday he took an engine to pieces to study its operations. In 1812, he repaired a Newcomen steam pumping engine which brought him promotion to enginewright at £100 a year, more than twice a labourer's wages. His next promotion gave him responsibility for all the machinery at several collieries in the district.

During this period he became engrossed in steam locomotives, for he could see their value in collieries. He studied the locomotives designed by Murray and Hedley, and, backed by his employers, built his first, the *Blücher*, in 1814. One feature he had noticed in engines, stationary or travelling, was that the fierce exhaust steam escaped wastefully into the atmosphere. A strong and continuous fire was essential to keep a good head of steam, always a problem; so he directed the waste steam through the chimney which created a powerful draught in the firebox, known as steam-blast, a technique in which other designers had experimented.

On 28th February 1815, he registered a patent for an improved locomotive incorporating steam-blast, and was considered to be the first inventor to use this system efficiently with the full knowledge of its effect on power and speed. Stephenson still regarded the locomotive as a poor thing, crying out for its incredible potential to be exploited, and he was determined to do just that. Proper tools and skilled men in this unfamiliar field were sparse. Under his training, a works mechanic or a blacksmith did wonders within his limits. Lord Ravensworth, a Killingworth Colliery partner, had backed Stephenson financially, but people called his Lordship a fool for wasting his money.

Colliery owners, merchants and businessmen in County Durham, dissatisfied with transport between the coalfields and Darlington and on to Stockton-on-Tees, in 1810 considered building a canal. An alternative proposition was a railway with horses, but this was opposed by local canal owners for the competition could be catastrophic; landowners feared a railway would ruin their estates. However, a Quaker named Edward Pease (1767–1858) and his friends campaigned vigorously for a railway, securing an Act of Parliament in 1821 to build the Stockton to Darlington line. When Stephenson heard about it, he visited Pease to persuade him to consider locomotives for the new railway; several directors inspected Stephenson's Killingworth locomotives and were so convinced that they had the Act amended to authorise this power. By now, Stephenson had climbed out of his poverty and was a man of financial means; from 1820 he was part owner of Willow Bridge Colliery and had earnings from colliery tram-ways he had built; a new source of income had begun in 1819 when he started to build the Hetton Colliery Railway of eight miles, near Sunderland, which opened in 1822 using five Stephenson locomotives.

Pease and his partners appointed Stephenson as engineer of their projected railway, knowing that he was the best man for the job, and according to Samuel Smiles the salary was £300 a year. With the help of his son and hand-picked men, Stephenson spent three years surveying and building the railway. Opposition to the railway had been strong throughout; newspapers, canal and land owners had ranted against it as a dangerous monstrosity. Later, their chant was to change as benefits came to the north-east.

On 27th September 1825, the Stockton & Darlington Railway was officially opened by the directors. Stephenson drove his new *Locomotion No. 1*, heading an incredible train consisting of a coach for the directors, twelve waggons of coal and flour, and twenty-one carrying hundreds of people. Enormous cheering crowds assembled along the trackside. Among them were engineers and businessmen from Liverpool, Manchester and Birmingham.

Speeds of the inaugural train averaged about 5 miles an hour with occasional spurts of over 10. The single line with frequent crossing loops used a mixture of power: locomotives, horses, and stationary engines with hauling ropes. Though mainly a colliery line, people wanted to journey along it, and for some years a single horse pulled a simple passenger vehicle at walking pace. Through the Press, intelligence about the line soon reached transport-hungry Europe and America.

Stephenson's day of triumph had been marred only by the absence of his son, then twenty-two; the previous year, Robert had sailed to South America to supervise a mine engineering project in Colombia, a commission he had secured from the London agents, and stayed for three years. By an astonishing coincidence, in 1827 he met a dishevelled and dejected Trevithick at Cartagena returning home after his misadventures in Peru. During their time together by ship to New York – Trevithick had known Robert as an infant – they must have talked endlessly about steam locomotives and railways, Robert continuing home with revitalised enthusiasm.

In 1824, George Stephenson had opened a factory in Newcastle for building locomotives; he had used the £1000 awarded to him by local colliery interests for his safety-lamp invention, plus £500 from Edward Pease and £500 from his friend Thomas Richardson. The firm was called R. Stephenson & Co, father obviously ensuring son's participation, and it was to have tremendous significance soon for the projected line between Liverpool and Manchester.

By the time the Stockton & Darlington Railway was working, at least thirty steam locomotives had been built for work in England, and eighteen were then known to be in operation of which George Stephenson had built eleven since 1814:

4 Blenkinsop and Murray, Middleton Colliery near Leeds;
3 William Hedley, Wylam Colliery near Newcastle; *Puffing Billy* types;
4 George Stephenson, Killingworth Colliery near Newcastle;
5 George Stephenson, Hetton Colliery near Sunderland;
2 George Stephenson, Stockton & Darlington Railway.

What a fine list! – but the 'iron horse' was still a very primitive animal. Wheezing, leaking steam at every pore, it rattled its painful way along the rough tracks and often broke down altogether. Alive to its potential, Stephenson never wavered and his Newcastle factory gave birth to the locomotive as we know it.

A year before he had completed the Stockton & Darlington, he had heard about plans to build a railway, powered by horses or stationary engines with pulley ropes, between Liverpool and Manchester; this excited him enormously, for there might be a chance for his steam locomotives. With the promise offered by the Darlington line, he realised that a railway between Lancashire's two leading towns was a sensational opportunity for locomotive railways to prove themselves to the world. He visualised a network over England: indeed, steam from his locomotives would fly along rails across countries where mechanical power was still unknown. After building his first locomotives at Killingworth Colliery about ten years earlier, he had said to his friend Robert Summerside, "I will do something in coming time which will astonish all England!"

CHAPTER 2

The Battle for the Railway

Why was a railway so essential? Caught in the clamour of the Industrial Revolution that had been galvanised by coal and iron products, steam power and consequential canal developments, both Manchester and Liverpool were taking a growing share in the rapidly expanding markets of Britain and the world. Mechanisation in industry and the growth of overseas trade were soon to move faster in Lancashire than elsewhere in the kingdom. From here, goods – both raw materials and finished products – were being exchanged with all parts of the civilised world, and the port of Liverpool was entering a new phase in the shipping business.

Rum and sugar from the West Indies, Virginian tobacco, cotton and other commodities were arriving through Liverpool in ever-increasing quantities from America, whose thrusting emergence from colony status after her war of independence (1775–83) Britain had had to recognise. A major share of traffic with Ireland was also handled by the port, and Lancashire's growing resources and manufacturing potential were earning for the county a new rating in the nation's commercial and industrial life.

Salt from Cheshire, cotton goods and iron products, and business with the fast-growing areas in Staffordshire, combined to speed the growth of Liverpool, while Manchester and the surrounding towns were taking the lead in producing cotton goods. Because of the introduction of steam power to the looms and other machinery, and the rising demand by coal-fired steam packets at the port, greater demands for fuel were made from the coalfields of Lancashire, Yorkshire, Cheshire and Staffordshire. The county, and especially Liverpool, gained richly from these developments. The port also enjoyed, if that is the word, a lucrative trade in African slaves, until that was abolished in 1807.

Agriculture was bounding ahead, too, largely because of the incredible population explosion. Before the close of the century, the population of Liverpool had risen to 60,000 and by 1824 was 135,000. By early in the century, tonnages of British and foreign vessels entering and leaving the port had risen in recent years to over a million, requiring a massive expansion of the dock areas. Meantime, large numbers of people were flooding into Lancashire from Scotland, Wales and Ireland, mostly to seek work.

In Manchester and adjoining Salford, the population had risen during the new century from about 100,000 to 150,000 by 1824, by which time about 30,000 steam-powered looms were busy in the area. Based on several remarkable inventions by Arkwright, Hargreaves, Crompton and Cartwright late in the eighteenth century, spinning and loom machines rapidly replaced hand processes; and within a few decades the cotton industry had been revolutionised, lifting enormously the output per man. To the wide-eyed workers, power-operated machines were miraculous, except to those who lost fingers and limbs in the works. Nonetheless, it meant that thousands of men, women and children who had crowded the garrets and cellars weaving on hand looms were slowly but inexorably poverty-stricken. Yet operators in the factories found good work that was reasonably well paid at that time. Mechanisation increased massively the volume of output and reduced costs so that by the early 1800s, Lancashire was producing the world's cheapest clothing which quickly penetrated distant markets.

In Lancashire's two leading towns, life for the under-nourished masses was wretchedly squalid and their over-crowded earth-floor dwellings were "melancholy and disagreeable". In the absence of 'privies' in the poorest areas, the narrow, unpaved and deeply rutted streets became the common receptacles of mud, rubbish and filth. Drunkenness, immorality, child prostitution, cholera and other diseases, and a high infant mortality rate were accepted as the regular way of life. Health care was minimal, and when eyesight or hearing failed or their teeth dropped out, the poor souls had to grin and suffer. Men, women, and even children, worked twelve to sixteen hours a day in the harsh factories, the misery of their indigent lives relieved only by such popular sports as cock-fighting and bull-baiting.

From time to time, workhouses and hospitals were opened to house the sick, those crippled and maimed by the unfamiliar machinery, and the destitute: establishments often initiated by Quakers and others moved by Christian conscience to ease the burdens of their suffering fellows. William Wordsworth (1770–1850) perceived the privations of those turbulent times, as revealed in his memorable lines:

Beneath the hills, along the flowery vales,

> The generations are prepared; the pangs,
> The internal pants are ready; the dread strife
> Of poor humanity's afflicted will,
> Struggling in vain with ruthless destiny.

Following the defeat by the Duke of Wellington of the French Emperor at the end of the Revolutionary and Napoleonic Wars of 1793–1815, masses of men sought work; and among the upper classes, "Boney will get you!" was a sinister threat employed to bring their young charges to order long after the Emperor was dead.

This was the setting for the first railway of real historical significance. Growing populations, the fast-growing port of Liverpool and the factory revolution, revealed starkly the inadequacies of communications between the two great towns. It was mainly the surges of trade through Liverpool that hustled the Industrial Revolution into the heart of Lancashire. By 1812, America had become the principal source of cotton supply and the Liverpool cotton market grew. In the process, merchants and industrialists in the county were acquiring great wealth, hampered only by the lack of good transport. Lancashire roads were poor. The scene was that of a daily flow of hundreds of pack-horses, farm carts, lumbering horse-drawn waggons and stage coaches. Coach journeys between the two towns took four or five hours, including stops to change horses. Accidents on the roads were frequent. Waggons and stage coaches overturned, and in a hard winter were severely delayed.

From mid-eighteenth century, the new canals – themselves an intrinsic component of the Industrial Revolution – had offered an alternative. Networks built by the giant engineers of the Canal Age – Brindley, Telford and the Rennies – opened up Liverpool's comparatively remote harbour to the principal English manufacturers for miles around, elevating the port to the rank of a world distributive centre. First came the Mersey & Irwell Navigation Company which, from about 1750, monopolised much of the water traffic between the port and Manchester until the opening in 1791 of the Duke of Bridgewater's Canal which was later extended to link the two towns. Another serving the county was the Leeds & Liverpool Canal. Boats were powered by men, horses and sail.

Well into the new century, these fierce rivals handled much of the traffic on the route. But in common, they suffered severe handicaps. Heavy winds and storms, frozen surfaces in the winter, shallow water in the summer, and pilferage on the slow and circuitous routes through the quiet countryside all created problems. Setbacks or not, monopoly made the canal companies rich and powerful. Merchants were at their mercy in terms of services and charges. It is not surprising, therefore, that a band of disenchanted Liverpool merchants were driven to explore the possibilities of building a horse-drawn railway for general public use.

For comparison, a list of services and approximate distances between the two towns is given:

Turnpike roads	36 miles
Mersey and Irwell Canals	43 miles
Bridgewater Canal	46 miles
Leeds & Liverpool Canal	58 miles
Proposed railway	31 miles
As the crow flies	30 miles

Even before 1800, William Jessop, who built the Surrey Iron Railway opened in 1803, had proposed a waggon-way between Liverpool and Manchester and went so far as to approach Liverpool merchants and to survey a route; shortly after, Benjamin Outram made a similar proposition, but neither matured. Far grander ideas came from the avid quill of Thomas Gray, a native of Leeds who lived for a time in Brussels. In his *Observations on a General Iron Railway*, first published in 1820, his plan was for a network throughout Britain and proposed a "general iron railway" for the whole of Europe. He was already a supporter of locomotives and suggested that a trial should be made between Liverpool and Manchester, this "commercial part of England would thereby be better able to appreciate its many excellent properties and prove its efficacy". Jessop, Outram and particularly Gray campaigned doggedly for years, so that for at least a quarter of a century before the first practical steps were taken to build a railway, the idea itself was common knowledge among many who might be interested.

Next on the scene, but much more persistent, was William James (1771–1837) of London and Birmingham. As early as 1808, he had proposed, with remarkable foresight, a "General Rail-Road Company", needing a capital of one million pounds. It came to nought. Highly talented and articulate, James had built many colliery waggon-ways, owned collieries and as a land agent grew rich and influential, and people flocked to his London office. In 1821, he approached a Liverpool corn merchant named Joseph Sandars and proposed a railway to Manchester. Sandars agreed to pay him £300 to survey a route. In his researches, James had visited Stephenson, inspected his Killingworth Colliery waggon-ways and locomotives. Later he was to eulogise Stephenson as "the greatest genius of the age. . . . If he developed the full powers of that engine, his fame in the world would rank with that of Watt."

Sandars was sufficiently impressed to assemble a provisional committee of merchants in Liverpool to explore potential. A prominent Liverpool banker named John Moss was appointed chairman. While working on the survey, James wrote to Sandars, "The canal companies are alive to the danger. I have been the object of their persecution and hate; they would immolate me if they could; but if I can die the death of Samson, by pulling away the pillars, I am content to die with these Philistines." On the second survey, James was assisted by Robert Stephenson, then barely twenty; but busy elsewhere, his survey was incomplete.

In 1822, the provisional committee published their intention of petitioning Parliament for powers to build "an Iron Rail-Way" between Liverpool and Manchester. During the summer, it was widely reported, notably in the *Manchester Guardian* (now the *Guardian*, launched in 1821), the *Liverpool Mercury*, and *The Times* of London (opened in 1785).

James's delayed survey angered Sandars and his associates, for they missed the 1823 parliamentary session and valuable time was lost. The fact was that James had too many irons in his fires and he burnt himself out. He had personally lobbied in Parliament for the railway, was an ardent campaigner for steam locomotives and was the first to forecast a large passenger business between the two towns which others met with scepticism. For his work, he deserves a high place among the pioneers. Wealthy and talented though he was, in 1824 he ran into financial difficulties in London, which he claimed was a plot, and he was sent to prison. At the end of an incredible life, he was close to penury. Though friendly with Stephenson at first, he claimed later that Stephenson had stolen his thunder as the Father of Railways; so, too, did his daughter, Mrs E. M. S. Paine, in a biography of 1861. But let history speak for itself.

After the disappointment of James's delays, Sandars in 1824 published a lengthy pamphlet setting out the urgent need for a railway. He also led a working party on a visit to the north-east to inspect the Stockton & Darlington Railway which Stephenson was building. In the party were banker Lister Ellis, Manchester industrialist John Kennedy, and corn merchant Henry Booth of Liverpool; these men saw with their own eyes what Booth was later to describe as "the great theatre of practical operations upon a railway".

Fortified by assurances, they reported to the provisional committee in Liverpool which resolved to go ahead; the Liverpool & Manchester Railway Company was formally created and Charles Lawrence was appointed chairman. Urbane, kindly and gracious, Lawrence was then Mayor of Liverpool where he would have strong influence with the corporation; and as a highly reputed West India shipping merchant he commanded considerable respect. John Moss was one of the deputy chairmen; so too was Joseph Sandars who contributed unusual skill as a propagandist and had the support of his personal friend Egerton Smith, editor of the *Liverpool Mercury* which, with other newspapers, proved to be a valuable sounding board for all shades of opinion. Above all, he was a determined and persistent man, and a prime mover in the railway project.

Of the twenty-four members of the new company, twelve were from Liverpool and twelve from Manchester; all were wealthy and influential but in their battle for the railway were to face equally formidable opponents. Corn merchant Henry Booth quickly showed his ability as an organiser with a rare gift in writing; he had taken over from his father on the provisional committee and his colleagues, recognising his drive and energy, appointed him as the company secretary. He was thirty-eight.

An early decision of the company was that a capital of £300,000 would be required for their railway project.

All must have felt it was now a matter of life or death since the slow and wasteful conveyance by canal and road was rapidly strangling trade. It fell to Booth to compile the company's lengthy and detailed prospectus, dated 29th October 1824, which was widely circulated, the first major public announcement. A parliamentary agent was appointed ready for an assault on Parliament.

Earlier in the year, the company had sought an engineer to replace William James. From several possible candidates among Britain's most eminent engineers, Stephenson, then aged forty-three, was appointed to take charge of the entire project at the princely salary of £1,000 a year while labourers earned less than £1 a week. At this time his fine record embraced the construction of several colliery waggonways, nearly forty stationary steam engines and about sixteen steam locomotives. No other English engineer could match his unique talents.

In June 1824, he had taken up temporary residence in Liverpool to begin his survey, and on the 15th he wrote (with help) to his friend Michael Longridge, an engineer who had helped him to start the Newcastle factory, "We dined with Mr Sandars on Saturday. . . . He had three manservants waiting in the entrance hall to show us to the drawing room. There was a party to meet us, and kindly we were received. The dinner was very sumptious, and the wines costly. We had claret, hock, champagne, and madeira, and all in good plenty; but no-one took more than was proper. . . . We dined at seven and left at twelve o'clock. Sandars and Ellis are magnificent fellows, and are very kind; Mrs Sandars is a fine woman, and Mrs Ellis very elegant. . . .

"What changes one sees! – this day in the highest life, and the next in a cottage – one day turtle soup and champagne, and the next bread and milk, or anything one can catch. Liverpool is a splendid place. . . . The merchants are clever chaps, and perseverance is stamped upon every brow."

After four months of frustration in survey work, Stephenson confessed in a letter to Edward Pease, one of his original backers, "We have sad work with Lord Derby, Lord Sefton, and Bradshaw the great canal proprietor, whose grounds we go through with the projected railway. The ground is blockaded on every side to prevent us getting on with the survey. . . . The Liverpool Railway people are determined to force a survey through if possible. Lord Sefton says he will have a hundred men against us. The Company think those great men have no right to stop a survey. . . ."

Men threw stones. Fights frequently broke out. Stealthily, Stephenson and his team took levels at night by flame torch or moonlight. To mislead their Lordships' hired thugs, he sent his men some distance away to fire guns while he measured another length. Battle lines were now firmly marked. Opposition against the surveying took a new turn when the canal companies distributed leaflets to whip up public fear and hatred; they described the terrors of explosive steam locomotives (though no decision had been made yet that they would be used) which could set fire to nearby houses, farms and crops. Dirty tricks were matched by dirty tricks. For instance, a false document was circulated by the railway promoters among the tenants of Lord Sefton, purporting to grant his permission for the survey.

There were also costly and complex negotiations to purchase land for the line. Conscientiously, Stephenson avoided where possible the preserves of the nobility and landed gentry, and took care not to antagonise canal and turnpike owners. An additional problem with landowners was that many bridges and viaducts – sixty-three when finished – were needed, to cross over or under the projected line. After many fights with hired gangs, vigilante groups, gamekeepers, servants of the landed élite and every kind of opposition, Stephenson and his young assistants completed the survey in four months and the engineer presented it to the railway directors in October 1824, the month the railway prospectus was issued.

Meantime, the directors were working frantically to prepare a Parliamentary Bill and in December, Charles Lawrence, Joseph Sandars and John Moss journeyed by stage coach to London to lobby Members of Parliament. Two other directors travelled to Ireland to seek support from Irish M.P.s and to canvas goodwill among Irish merchants who should benefit by a railway.

John Gladstone M.P., owner of ships and overseas plantations, who had joined the railway committee, and had helped William Huskisson to win a parliamentary seat in Liverpool, called upon him for backing in the House. Huskisson was later appointed President of the Board of Trade and a member of the Cabinet; he proved to be an influential enthusiast for the project. Lord Liverpool himself was Prime Minister 1812–27; though during his long reign, he seemed to remain ambivalent in the hurly-burly of railway polemics.

To keep the issue alive, the directors stated their case in local and national newspapers and in magazines, and the opposition did likewise. Though in principle friendly, Egerton Smith of the *Liverpool Mercury* favoured a railway, but warned that if used "locomotives would vomit forth long and black trails of smoke" that would drift into private homes, and destroy private lawns and orchards. Yet another factor: jealous Manchester merchants and industrialists felt rather overwhelmed by the "Liverpool Party" and proved difficult; yet when the time came to open the subscription lists, much of the working capital came from Manchester itself, the town being fairly represented on the board of directors.

Anticipating stiff resistance to the line entering Liverpool, the directors presented a lengthy 'memorial' to the Mayor and Council, but their response was non-committal. Significantly, the directors had omitted any reference to carrying passengers.

To dilute the hyperbole of the opposition, the directors dispensed convincing counterpoint on a broad front: land values would rise, coal would be cheaper and more of it exported through Liverpool; farmers would find more markets for their produce with deterioration reduced; minerals of all kinds would be conveyed in much larger quantities, and work would be found for the unemployed poor. Goods could be carried at half the present costs and at four times the speed. An example of poor service was quoted which was typical of the exaggerations of both sides: merchandise from New York took longer from Liverpool to Manchester than the twenty-one days crossing the Atlantic. The railway would build many new warehouses in both towns. In short, the entire commerce and industry in Lancashire would be inspired by a great new impetus.

Now perhaps tasting blood, Sandars lambasted the canals; he claimed they were monopolistic and making huge profits, impervious to customers' complaints, giving inferior services and extracting insufferably high charges. He estimated that goods conveyed between Liverpool and Manchester taking a whole day, could be carried in three or four hours by a railway. In his published pamphlet, Sandars stated the quintessence of the case: "Permit me to point out that the only remedy the public has left, is to go before Parliament."

On 6th October 1824, Sandars had addressed a lengthy letter to Members of both Houses of Parliament. A slashing attack on the canal proprietors was followed by the assertion that the steam locomotive had now arrived; and if it was not quickly exploited, Britain would lose its world lead. Emperor Alexander I of Russia had obtained a model of an English locomotive and Russian agents had visited the north-east. There had also been exchanges of correspondence with and visits by many representatives from Europe and America where

English stationary steam engines had already made their mark.

On studying the company's prospectus of 29th October, *The Times* on 20th November crystallised the issue. "Canals superseded to a large extent the means of transport previously employed; if rail-roads are found better than canals, the latter must, in their turn, give way." Too long cocooned in the comfort of monopoly, canal owners began frenetically to cut their costs and mend their ways.

Fears of railways envenomed principal canal owners far beyond Lancashire. The Leeds & Liverpool, Grand Trunk, Birmingham and other canal companies issued leaflets calling upon "every canal and navigation in the Kingdom to oppose *in limine* the establishment of railways wherever contemplated".

In addition to lengthy reports, newspapers carried readers' letters, many under noms-de-plume, keeping the controversy alive throughout the land. Of all the fustian suggestions, the prize must go to 'Economist'; he proposed that the canals should be filled in and railroads built over them to take canal boats fitted with wheels and powered by wind and horses. But what would he do about the many canal locks?

Opponents of the locomotive foreshadowed inevitable calamities: stage innkeepers and owners of post-chaises and stage coaches would be bankrupted; hunters complained that fox coverts would be disturbed; cows would be prevented from grazing and hens from laying eggs, horses would become extinct, and frightened, pregnant ladies would miscarry. Poisoned air would kill the birds flying overhead and in a hot summer locomotive sparks would set alight trackside plantations, orchards and crops.

And so the public debate did rage. Clearly, the scene was now set for one of the most momentous parliamentary battles of the Industrial Revolution. Parliamentary agents were appointed by the railway company to prepare a Bill. Appropriate to the occasion, an extraordinary array of legal talent was commissioned by both sides, and the men from the north-west were soon to be groping through the labyrinthine procedures of Parliament. Among the witnesses to be called, both for the petitioners and the opposers, were engineers, merchants, bankers, landowners, tenants, canal owners, shippers and Members of Parliament. The canal lobby had "determined to wage war to the knife against all railways".

After necessary preliminaries, on Tuesday 8th February 1825, the petition for a Bill was presented to the House of Commons. Then followed weeks of committee meetings, each side briefing its own counsel. "Persons, papers and records" were summoned for witness. Intense controversy, sometimes restrained, sometimes heated, protracted the proceedings. Regular reports in the Press were perused avidly by the literate population of the land.

At the witness stand, scathing cross-examination by opposing counsel Mr Edward (later Baron) Alderson and Mr Harrison obfuscated the semi-literate Stephenson. His previous experience of parliamentary procedures had been in 1823 when the Bill for the Darlington line had cleared the hurdles comfortably. Now, he was trying hard to hold his ground. Questioners found his rich Northumbrian dialect difficult to understand, and one of them asked if he was a foreigner. Skilful probing exposed disturbing weaknesses. Under fire from Alderson, Stephenson's inadequate performance is revealed by extracts from the evidence:

"What is the width of the Irwell there?" (river in Manchester)

"I cannot say exactly at present."

"How many arches is your bridge to have?"

"It is not determined upon."

"How could you make an estimate for it, then?"

"I have given a sufficient sum for it."

Plans for the Irwell bridge then had to be withdrawn.

Ill at ease in these austere surroundings, Stephenson bungled other answers: "It may, I cannot speak of it," "I did but I cannot recollect," "It was a mistake." At one point, Harrison exploded heatedly, "It is ignorance almost inconceivable! It is perfect madness, in a person called upon to speak on a scientific subject, to propose such a plan." And the Hon. Edward Stanley, later Prime Minister, called upon the House to "prevent this mad and extravagant speculation". The honourable gentleman was probably more concerned about his family estates in Lancashire than the loss of money by investors.

Concerning the proposed route, Stephenson explained that he had merely set out the line for his other surveyors to follow. When asked, "Did you not survey the line of the road?" he answered lamely, "My assistant did." By now, Alderson had established that there were numerous errors in the levels of anything up to ten feet.

"What," he asked, "was the original base line on which all your levels are calculated as marked on the section?"

"Near the Vauxhall Road in Liverpool."

"Whereabouts?"

Thoroughly unhappy, Stephenson replied, "I think about a hundred and fifty yards from it, but I am not quite sure."

Pursued mercilessly by counsel, it seemed as though he had no real idea, or could not explain, how he had calculated the base line level of the entire route:

"Then it is possible you may be out at other parts?"

"It may be, but I do not think so."

"You do not believe you are out on your levels?"

"I have made my estimate from the levels which I believe are correct."

"Do you believe, aye or no, that your levels are correct?"

"I have heard it reported that they are not."

"Did you take the levels yourself?"

"They were taken for me."

"Other people have taken them for you and upon *their* estimate you have made *your* estimate?"

"Yes!"

Alderson's thunderous summary at one stage deepened the humiliation of the unhappy engineer: "This is the most absurd scheme that ever entered into the head of a man to conceive. . . . My learned friends almost endeavoured to stop my examination . . . but I had rather have the exhibition of Mr Stephenson in that box. I say he never had a plan. . . . I do not believe he is capable of making one. . . . He is either ignorant or something else which I will not mention. . . ."

Those hard-nosed canal navigation men must have been loving every minute of it. Of the Irwell Bridge estimates, Alderson warmed up, "I am astonished that any man standing in that box would make such a statement without shrinking into nothing. . . ." Then scornfully, "Is Mr Stephenson to be the person upon whose faith this committee is to pass this Bill involving property to the extent of £400,000 to £500,000 when he is so ignorant of this profession as to propose to build a bridge not sufficient to carry off the flood water of the river or to permit any of the vessels to pass which of necessity must pass under it, and leave his own Railroad liable to be several feet under water?"

On the subject of land, one committee counsel asked, "Do you suppose it a likely thing to obtain leave from any gentleman to survey his land, when he knows that your men had gone upon his land to take levels without his leave, and he himself found them going through the corn and through the gardens of his tenants, and trampling down the strawberry beds which they were cultivating for the Liverpool market?"

Naïvely, Stephenson replied, "I have found it sometimes very difficult to get through places of that kind!"

Francis Giles, a civil engineer who had built canals with John Rennie, vigorously opposed Stephenson's plans, especially the intention to float the line across five miles of a deep bog called Chat Moss. In the witness box on 25th May, Giles opined that if a train were ever to run across the Moss, it would sink out of sight. Even if, starting from the bottom of the Moss, a line could be built across it, the cost would exceed £200,000, but he was sure it was quite impossible. Sarcastically, counsel remarked, "My Learned Friend wishes to know what it would cost to lay it with diamonds. . . ."

"No engineer in his senses would go through Chat Moss," Alderson challenged. "Did you ever hear of such ignorance as this? How utterly and totally devoid he is of commonsense!"

Guided by counsel, Stephenson's friends such as Nicholas Wood, John Rastrick and William Huskisson M.P. did all they could to sustain the engineer. One supporter named Ferguson was noted by Thomas Creevey M.P. as "insane. He quite foamed at the mouth with rage. . . ." William Brougham, a counsel for the petitioners, had warned Stephenson to play down speed, otherwise he would "inevitably damn the whole thing, and he himself be regarded as a maniac fit only for Bedlam". Another adviser had suggested that the locomotive, too, should be played down.

For the entire railway, including locomotives, rolling stock, stations, depots and warehouses, Stephenson had estimated the total cost at £400,000, most of which had already been subscribed. Alderson probed every financial detail, and evoked the claim from Giles that it would be nearer £1,500,000.

Laughter embarrassed a cross-examiner when he asked a witness, "Suppose, now, one of these engines to be going along a railroad at the rate of nine or ten miles an hour, and that a cow were to stray upon the line and get in the way of the engine; would not that, think you, be a very awkward circumstance?"

"Yes, very awkward. For the cow!" In railway parlance, he was shunted.

Altogether, opposing counsel had had a field day and Stephenson often winced under the stinging attacks. Later, he recalled ruefully, "I began to wish for a hole to creep into!"

On 27th May 1825, after more than three months in thirty-seven working days in committee sessions, usually held from noon until four, Counsel Mr Adam, pleading for the railway and the steam locomotive to be given a fair trial, summed up: "All I ask you is, not to crush it in its infancy. Let not this country have the disgrace of putting a stop to that which, if cherished, may ultimately prove of the greatest advantage to our trade and commerce; and which, if we do not adopt it, will be adopted by our rivals." Presumably, he meant countries overseas.

On the last day, 31st May 1825, major clauses of the Bill were debated. In a tense atmosphere, the vote was taken. The saddened petitioners for the railway lost and the Bill was thrown out. Thomas Creevey M.P. had railed against the motion for half an hour. Elated, he wrote the next day to his step-daughter, Elizabeth Ord, "Well – this devil of a railway is strangled at last . . . we had a clear majority. . . . Sefton's ecstasies are beyond, and he is pleased to say it has been all my doing; so it's mighty well." Lord Derby and Lord Sefton had used all their influence to kill the Bill. In the culinary vernacular, the hapless engineer had been grilled and roasted, but totally underestimated.

Stephenson, of course, was shattered. His credibility as a witness and an engineer had been publicly destroyed and he knew he had failed his loyal supporters miserably. He had lost now because opposing counsel had unmasked serious technical errors in his calculations; some arose because Stephenson, hard pressed and out of his depth with paper work, had delegated too much important detail to his young assistants at a time when technical skills were still in embryo. Yet another blow, traumatic and distressing, struck the dejected engineer; young Hugh Steele had made some of the errors which weighed heavily on his mind, and he committed suicide in Stephenson's office in Newcastle. In all these setbacks, Stephenson, far from lachrymose, would have been glad of the solace and affection of his son Robert, who was still working in South America. But at least, he had the Darlington line to complete within the next four months, and this would occupy his talents. In his darkest hour, he could well have taken comfort from that illuminating epigram of Benjamin Franklin (1706–90), American scientist and philosopher: "The man who does things makes many mistakes, but he never makes the biggest mistake of all – doing nothing."

Now that the Bill was lost, the opposition was jubilant. But if they thought Stephenson was finished, they seriously underrated him. Many a man would never have recovered from such a deadly humiliation. Though Stephenson knew that he had bungled the entire parliamentary affair and had committed errors, he believed that counsel and opposition witnesses had talked much more nonsense than he, and he was convinced that he had been outwitted, and not proved fundamentally wrong, by clever lawyers. Contemporaries said that he erred by appointing and depending on inexperienced young men and paid them poorly. But bosses, being human, are reluctant to appoint assistants who might soon outshine them. Though he had his faults, Stephenson bore the mark of greatness by remaining utterly determined to establish the locomotive railway. That supreme self-confidence never deserted him. Though he had been made to look a fool, he was no man's fool, just not a man of tongues. Of such meagre literacy, it is astonishing that he had survived the ordeal at all.

But what did his masters think? To them, the defeat in Parliament had been costly in cash terms alone; but several of the railway's directors still had faith in him, as expressed in a letter from deputy chairman John Moss: "I regret the loss of the Rail Road Bill as much on your account as for the mortification we all feel. No-one can be more satisfied than I am that you deserved very different treatment than you met with from Mr Alderson. Your talents are of a very much more valuable nature than that of a witness in the House of Commons."

Admitting his "great grief", Stephenson replied confidently: "The

Darlington Railway will be opened out in a short time. I wish I could get Alderson to be alongside of me on that day and could run his hounds in a corner more than he could do an engineer in the witness box."

In the Liverpool railway office, the defeated directors licked their wounds. But certainly they would try again. Changes would be needed to meet the main objections, even if horses and stationary engines must be used, instead of locomotives.

On 17th June 1825, only a few weeks after the Bill had been thrown out, yet another blow for the dejected engineer: he was sacked. Loyal support from Joseph Sandars and Henry Booth failed to save the scapegoat; these were two of the few now who would listen and keep up his flagging spirits. Yet other railway promoters had confidence in Stephenson, for he received several offers, some of which he accepted. His replacement at Liverpool was now urgently needed, and the directors decided to approach George and John Rennie, famous sons of a famous father, noted for building bridges, canals and harbours. In masterly style at the meeting, John Rennie convinced the railway board that he could do the job and would also engage Charles Vignoles, aged thirty-two, who had undertaken surveys in America and was to carve a distinguished railway career.

Some of the directors wanted Stephenson to join the engineering team, but the Rennie Brothers were adamant; with such a reputation they wanted no truck with him. A board minute in June 1825 noted George Rennie's comments: "He would not object to Mr Jessop, Mr Telford or any member of the Society of Engineers being consulted, but would not be associated in any way with Rastrick or Stephenson." However, he would not object to Stephenson taking charge of the locomotive department.

In July, Vignoles surveyed the Stephenson route, and as instructed by the Rennies made changes to reduce opposition from canal and landowners. At the Manchester end, the line would finish at Salford just short of the River Irwell; at Liverpool, a tunnel would be needed to avoid the estates of Lord Sefton and Lord Derby. Supported by an estimate of £510,000 (Stephenson's had been £400,000), the revised survey was delivered to the directors and accepted on 12th August 1825.

While in Lancashire, George Rennie and Vignoles met Robert Bradshaw, superintendent of the Bridgewater Navigation Trust and a powerful leader in the canal lobby. A wealthy man with a stately home at Worsley near Manchester, he was a vituperative opponent of the railway. A biographer characterised this ruthless gentleman's policies as "profit extraction to the utmost limit, regardless of the feelings and interests of the users of the canal".

Bradshaw was invited by Rennie and Vignoles to buy shares in the projected railway: a stratagem more cunning than subtle. He countered that the Trust should become sole owners, the rejection of which left him livid and he threatened that the canal people would do everything possible to stop the railway passing a Bill. Secretly, Bradshaw's masters, some of whom disliked intensely his dictatorial methods, connived with the Marquis of Stafford for his (Stafford's) purchase of one thousand shares at £100 each which, ironically from a top canal personage, turned the financial corner for the railway company. This would entitle him to nominate three directors to the railway board. Nephew of the Duke of Bridgewater and principal trustee to the Bridgewater Trust Navigation, Stafford was heir to the Duke's fortune. His investment of £100,000, undertaken on the basis of if you can't beat them, join them, was almost a fifth of the estimated cost of the entire railway which, coupled with the appointment to the railway board of three directors from the canal world, undermined the influence of the combined opposing elements.

A renewed confidence attended the railway directors as they planned their second Bill and they set about seeking the finest counsel and the most convincing witnesses. Having missed the 1824 parliamentary session because of William James's procrastinations, and the 1825 session by the miserable performance of George Stephenson, four years had elapsed without a sod being turned. This time, they were determined to succeed. On 26th December 1825, they published a new prospectus. Part of the strategy was to avoid pressing for locomotives; they would have to be satisfied with parliamentary approval to build the railway itself, then decide later about the power; in any case, several directors did not favour locomotives.

There then followed the introduction of the Bill in the House and the procedures of the first, second and third readings in the Commons. Through their counsel, the promoters under cross-examination freely admitted their previous errors and confirmed specifically that everything possible would be done to meet the wishes of landowners and others. Full commercial values would be paid for all the land required. Objections by the canal lobby had been diluted by Stafford's investment in the railway which some opponents had denounced unfairly as blatant bribery; but for the railway it had been a master-stroke. Lord Sefton had made known his disapproval of the Marquis of Stafford for changing his attitude, and still opposed the railway.

Supporting the petitioners, General Gascoigne M.P. rejected the argument about possible accidents and maintained that inevitably, in any great engineering project, someone would get hurt. Turning to the objections of landowners, William Huskisson asserted that whatever improvements in communications were made, private property would be unavoidably invaded. Then he played a trump card: the railway company had already agreed that the maximum dividend on shares would be 10 per cent, but the canal companies were already paying more than 100 per cent. Under counsel's guidance, the petitioners' witnesses had demolished all opposition in the Commons by the third reading.

Stiff resistance still remained in the House of Lords; one member complained that the railway would run through his farms at a price the railway thought fit to pay. At the Upper House committees, Charles Vignoles and George Rennie disported themselves with aplomb and supreme self-confidence. Rennie assured members that horses could work the railway at an average speed of three miles an hour and still show a profit. At no time was he embarrassed for the want of a convincing answer; however, the petitioners had to accept reluctantly the stipulation that the line must end at Salford, near New Bailey Prison, on the edge of Manchester. On 1st May 1826, the Bill was passed in the House of Lords without a division and the Royal Assent granted on the 5th. In the event, success had finally plopped into the petitioners' hands like ripe fruit; they hardly had to shake the tree. It had been brought about largely by the public influence of the Rennies, by the railway company's willingness to compromise on several fundamental issues, and by the heavy investment in the railway company made by the wealthy and prestigious Marquis of Stafford.

Ever ready to record world events, *The Times* observed laconically, "The petitioners' faith in their project and their willingness to build in the face of such distress were to attract the admiration of all England and gave the Liverpool & Manchester Railway Company a reputation for courage and persistence."

One chronicler commented, "There was a world of difference in building a colliery railway from coalfields [such as the Stockton & Darlington line] and constructing a line to link the principal port of Liverpool with the great manufacturing centre of Manchester."

From the parliamentary journals of Luke Hansard and the welter of Press comment, the rest of Britain, Europe, Russia, America and Canada were soon to learn of this phenomenal Railway Act.

CHAPTER 3

Building the Railway

Jubilant was the mood of the directors now that they had at last cleared the hurdles in Parliament. But the problems which lay behind them were trivial compared with the dilemmas their incipient enterprise had in store. Anyway, there was a railway to be built and vast capital at stake. They knew that the eyes of the world were now upon them, for nothing could be private in building a public railway; they knew too that their enemies stood poised to strike.

Back from Westminster, the team shook the dust off their stage coach travel, and on 29th May 1826 shareholders assembled in Liverpool for a "General Meeting of Subscribers". From the working committee of twenty-seven, twelve directors were chosen, plus three nominated by the Marquis of Stafford, and their fees agreed. At their meeting the following day, the urbane Charles Lawrence (1782–1858) was elected chairman and John Moss deputy chairman. Moss, who had been with Sandars from the beginning, was an outstanding businessman, Liverpool's foremost banker, and a county Justice of the Peace. Dependable Henry Booth was appointed company secretary and treasurer, virtually the principal executive officer, at £500 a year.

Confidence was strong that there would be sufficient volume of business to earn a profit when the line was ready, running as it would through the rich and extensive coalfields of Lancashire, and linking the two great towns. Many passengers should be attracted from the four hundred who travelled daily by forty stage coaches and the few hundred journeying by canal. Realistic estimates of potential traffic had been compiled.

An immediate decision concerned a contract for the Rennies. At a board meeting, George Rennie proposed that he should take full charge, make six visits a year, and stipulated that resident engineers should be men of his choice, possibly the ageing Thomas Telford or

Josias Jessop. His conditions in total were unacceptable to the board and in a short time, the demanding Rennies were summarily dismissed. And how incensed these most eminent engineers were! Understandably. "After the passing of the Bill," John wrote afterwards, "my brother and myself prepared working drawings and estimates for carrying the work into effect, and we naturally expected to be appointed the executive engineers, after having with so much labour and anxiety carried the Bill through Parliament. The Executive Committee [the board] of the Railway behaved extremely ill to us."

Booth, Sandars and other directors still favoured Stephenson, who had completed the Darlington line the year before, and after talking it out, on 3rd July the board appointed him as principal engineer. He requested a salary of £800 a year, undertaking to be in attendance for at least nine months a year to allow him to cope with several other projects he had in hand. In the modern idiom, it was a case of, "Come back, George, all is forgiven!" After his recent parliamentary débâcle, his elation can be imagined; and he rolled up his sleeves and got on with the job.

First, he moved home to Liverpool, then made plans with the spirited Charles Vignoles, twelve years his junior, whom the board had appointed as an engineer. Together, they began to stake out the line, tramping over virgin hills and dales and seeking contractors for the major earthworks. During the autumn and winter, Vignoles endeavoured to establish equality with his master who regarded him as tainted by the Rennies. Their frequent clashes led Vignoles to resign on 2nd February 1827, after he had already written to a friend in January: "I also acknowledge having on many occasions differed with him . . . because it appeared to me he did not look on the concern with a liberal and expanded view, but with a microscopic eye, magnifying details, and pursuing a petty system of parsimony, very proper in a private colliery . . . but wholly inapplicable to this national work."

Some changes in the route set by the Rennies and Vignoles had to be made as experience dictated. Stephenson assembled a team of over twenty promising young acolytes, some from his home area in the north-east. He allocated them to specific sections, with responsibility for working with the contractors. To handle the enormous number of required drawings, he engaged Thomas Gooch from Newcastle, son of a small iron merchant. So meagre was knowledge in this strange new world that Stephenson had to train them. He sketched rough plans for bridges, level crossings, cuttings, embankments, machinery, turntables and track and Gooch translated them into working drawings.

Of the numerous navvies he hired, many were from the north-east;

others came from Lancashire and Ireland, to make a motley, quarrel-some workforce, though good at their jobs. In the absence of appro-priate tools and equipment, Stephenson had to design some of his own. He often chalked a rough outline on a piece of wood or the workshop floor. Reports, which he dictated to his assistants, flowed steadily between the engineer and the Liverpool office by post chaise, pony or by hand, on progress of the work. Such technical *accoutre-ments* as the typewriter and the telephone were still the dreams of vis-ionaries and we may wonder that the railway was built at all.

Within the simple management structure, individual directors were held responsible for specific major works to acquaint the full board with progress; clerks handled the paper work. Each of the resident engineers, when visiting Liverpool every fortnight to collect wages for their men, marked in colour a progress chart in the directors' room in Clayton Square.

Except in broad policy, finance, and subscribers' shareholdings, it was impossible, however, for the directors to take much weight from Stephenson's shoulders, for a line that was to be one of the largest engineering projects of the period. Marking out the line in detail occupied several months to January 1827; at the same time, the ground was cleared at several strategic points. Stephenson's aim, for obvious reasons, was to build a double track line as nearly straight and level as possible. This meant following the natural contours of the countryside, taking some guidance from rivers, canals and roads. Canal engineers built ingenious locks to compensate for rises and falls on the land; for the railway, some gradients were unavoidable, but were not to be too steep for a train's ascent or its safe braking. Neither must the general level of the line be too high or too low to reach con-veniently the towns at each end.

Bridges over and under the line, cuttings and embankments ensured a level route, spoil from cuttings being used to build embank-ments sometimes miles away. Hundreds of navvies in groups worked with horses, barrows, picks, shovels, windlasses and crude lifting gear. Temporary track was laid on sections to move waggons of material, and stationary steam engines aided men's muscles. Strata was varied: soil and sand, clay and rock. At some places, fields were bought or rented to take surplus spoil. Though local villagers and farmworkers were fascinated by all the activities, they kept their distance, for the navvies were rough, hard working, hard swearing, rowed with the foremen and often quarrelled to the point of violence. Minor accidents were frequent. Many of them slept rough near the site. In their spare hours, they invaded local inns, quaffed ale copi-ously and terrified the villagers. All worked long hours in summer and winter, sometimes into the night, and often up to the ankles in mud; and Stephenson and the resident engineers shared the load.

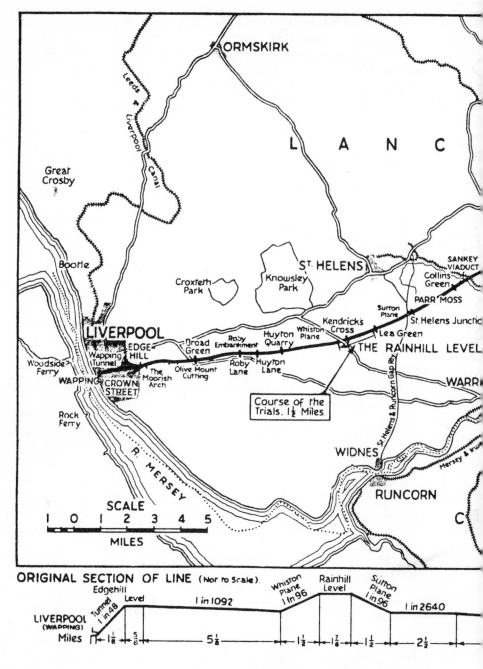

Liverpool & Manchester Railway 1830
(from C.F. Dendy Marshall, *Liverpool & Manchester Railway Centenary*, 1930)

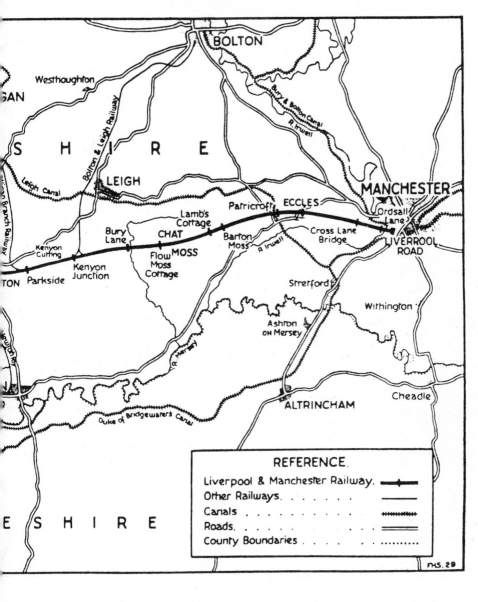

BOLTON

Westhoughton

GAN

S H I R E

Bury & Bolton Canal

R. Irwell

Leigh Canal

Bolton & Leigh Railway

LEIGH

Wigan Branch Railway

Parricroft

ECCLES

MANCHESTER

Ordsall Lane

Kenyon Cutting

Bury Lane

Lamb's Cottage

CHAT

Barton Moss

Cross Lane Bridge

LIVERPOOL ROAD

TON Parkside

Kenyon Junction

Flow Moss

MOSS

Moss Cottage

R. Irwell

Strerford

Withington

Ashton on Mersey

R. Mersey

Cheadle

ALTRINCHAM

Duke of Bridgewaters Canal

E S H I R E

REFERENCE.

Liverpool & Manchester Railway.

Other Railways. . . . . . .

Canals . . . .

Roads. . . . .

County Boundaries . . . . .

FKS. 29

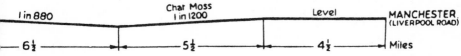

1 in 880

Chat Moss
1 in 1200

Level

MANCHESTER.
(LIVERPOOL ROAD)

— 6½ —   — 5½ —   — 4½ — Miles

As work continued, some property owners objected to trivial details concerning bridges and other works, and demanded lavish compensation. When bridges were built over canals, navigation was impeded. Reasonably, canal owners and boat operators sought payment for loss of business. Unreasonably, when opposition by landowners and farmers could not be staved off in any other way, the railway paid them bribes which some of them openly sought.

To purchase land and cope with the work in hand, the directors secured a second Act of Parliament on 12th April 1827 enabling the company to secure an Exchequer loan of £100,000. Landowners hostile to the railway pressed for exorbitant prices, but most of the land required was purchased at a reasonable rate. Some with land to sell in the open market mentioned in their advertisements the proximity of the coming railway.

To the north of the route approaching Manchester could be seen Worsley Hall, country seat of Robert Bradshaw, managing trustee of the Duke of Bridgewater's canal and estates. That eminent gentleman, who had battled so bitterly to block the Railway Bill, was shortly to witness the unwelcome sight and sound of Stephenson's handiwork.

For the track and all structures, Stephenson delegated three young and capable resident engineers to manage one section each: western including the Liverpool tunnel, Joseph Locke (1805–60); intermediate, William Allcard; eastern including the formidable Chat Moss, John Dixon. Locke's father was a close friend of Stephenson and Joseph later became one of the most famous of English civil engineers; Dixon had helped Stephenson survey the Darlington line and he and Allcard made railway careers. Superintendents under the resident engineers directed work at specific points.

Stephenson designed specifications for the rails, which were an improvement on the Darlington line. One outstanding problem had been that of the gauge, the inside distance between the two rails. The Rennies had planned it to be 5 feet 6 inches. But following Stephenson's recommendation, a Board minute of July 1826 had settled it: "Resolved that width of Waggon Way between the Rails be the same as on the Darlington Road, namely 4 feet 8 inches clear, inside the rails." Unknown then to the directors, but foreseen by the principal engineer, this gauge, adjusted to 4 feet 8½ inches, was to have general acceptance.

One decision of the directors concerning the track, for which Stephenson must bear some blame, was calamitous: only 4 feet 4½ inches space was allowed between the two pairs of rails; this meant that trains would pass each other dangerously close. Risk would arise from carriage doors bursting open or overhanging goods striking a passing train, especially on curves. It was more an error of inexperience than of judgement from which other railways were to benefit. A greater, safer distance would have increased total costs of construction.

Along the entire open track, the two most severe gradients were each one in ninety-six and between them, rising to and falling from, a level stretch of nearly two miles at a place called Rainhill. Some people, but not Stephenson, thought that these two gradients would be too much for locomotives and that stationary engines with hauling ropes would be needed. They were not. Most of the rest was no steeper than 1 in 880, virtually level, and free from speed-impeding curves.

The rails of wrought iron were rolled in fifteen-feet lengths (today's standard is sixty feet). Roughly every three feet, the rails sat in cast iron chairs which were plugged on to large stone blocks, or on to oak or larch sleepers which lay on the track bed, all to be boxed firmly in the ballast. Depending on the quality of the bed itself, which consisted of ballast and broken rock for good drainage on sand to a depth of about two feet, stone blocks were to be laid for eighteen miles and timber sleepers for thirteen. Strength and quality of the track to provide a firm load-bearing surface was judged to be adequate for the volume of traffic anticipated.

Among the suppliers of rails were Stephenson's old friend, Michael Longridge, a partner in the Stephenson works at Newcastle, and manufacturer at Bedlington Ironworks near Newcastle; and John Bradley & Co of Stourbridge in Worcestershire. The rails were conveyed to the sites by water and road.

Progress of the line was described in the *Liverpool Mercury* on 5th October. Complimenting the principal engineer on trying to build the "perfect railway in this great experiment," the editor added, "It is probably connected with changes in the country far greater than have hitherto been witnessed from any other recent development."

Wearing a tail coat, breeches and top boots, Stephenson walked every yard of the route many times, giving advice and urging the men at their tasks. He worked from dawn to dusk, stopping at nearby cottages for a snack. At home in candle-lit evenings, with his assistants he studied plans and drawings, discussed problems, dictated reports and arranged the following day's working programme. From time to time, he visited the directors' office in Liverpool for consultations, an essential chore he hated. No doubt conscious of his thick accent and blunt speech, he was often embarrassed in the austere presence of these men of wealth and education. Several major projects needed more time and money than some autocratic directors thought right, and they urged more economies and faster progress.

While building the railway, Stephenson was under pressure from other similar projects; but the one that concerned him most was the Stephenson locomotive factory in Newcastle, for it was neglected and losing money fast. What a relief and a delight it was when he learned that Robert was returning home from South America. And after three years, father and son were happily re-united on Liverpool Docks late in November 1827.

Robert's venture had been less profitable than expected, but at twenty-four, he was now a confident man of the world and found his father at forty-six fit and vigorous but white-haired and lined of face. Robert quickly took charge at Newcastle and soon had the business on its feet, and he shared other railway constructions with his father.

In the Liverpool office, Stephenson had many discussions about major works; one was the Roby embankment, not far out of Liverpool, three miles long and forty-five feet high, which required over half a million cubic yards of material. But the four which caused the directors the greatest anxiety were the line across the Chat Moss bog, the vast Sankey Viaduct, the deep Olive Mount Cutting on the edges of Liverpool, and tunnelling under the town itself. All were being built simultaneously.

Perhaps the most contentious was Chat Moss. Eminent engineers claimed it would be impossible to build a line of nearly five miles across it. Samuel Smiles described it as "an immense bog of about twelve square miles, a mass of spongy vegetable pulp . . . the result of the growth and decay of ages, one year's growth rising over another." In parts, it was twenty to thirty feet deep.

Under the direction of the thirty-year-old John Dixon, a gang of men laid timbers from which to unload filling material as a base for the track. It was in July 1826 when part-way across that Dixon slipped and quickly sank up to his knees. Terror-stricken, the more he struggled, the deeper he went. Labourers rushed to the rescue with more timbers and managed to drag him out, distraught and plastered in filth. Much persuasion was needed by his fellow-engineer, Joseph Locke, nine years his junior, before he would continue his work on the Chat Moss section.

Some of the labourers suffered the nightmare moment of falling in the filth. Back in 1822, William James, when making his second survey assisted by young Robert Stephenson, narrowly missed a horrible death, as recorded by a chronicler: "The Moss was very wet at the time. . . . Mr James was a heavy, thick-set man; and one day, when endeavouring to obtain a stand for his theodolite, he felt himself suddenly sinking. He immediately threw himself down, and rolled over and over until he reached the ground again."

Now, months of filling showed no signs of surfacing. Some directors, having taken further professional advice, considered it rather like weaving a rope of sand – impossible. Stephenson himself admitted that some of his own assistants felt wretched. But his encouraging message to the men was, "Persevere. Go on filling. It will soon begin to show!"

Time went on, but the filling still sank out of sight. Directors responsible began to get cold feet and a board meeting held on the site was in an ambivalent mood. But they were already committed to a heavy investment, and their only alternative was to buy more land and lengthen the route. In his memoirs, Stephenson was to recall shrewdly, "The directors were therefore compelled to allow me to go on, the ultimate success of which I never doubted."

Continuing the work, now using a brushwood base, hundreds of labourers and horses were employed. As each short section surfaced, a temporary track of rails was laid to take waggon loads further with filling. Along with the men, groups of boys earning a few coppers pushed the waggons. Sometimes, gangs worked through the night to the light of blazing fires and flaming hand torches.

By December 1827 a temporary railway track had been completed to transport waggons of men and materials. One man could push a waggon containing about eight navvies at a fast walking pace. In a show of strength, one bold fellow pushed a waggon the entire length in well under an hour. In January 1828, two men shouldered along a cleaned-out waggon carrying two important gentlemen and their brave ladies right across the Moss and back again and the passengers were "highly gratified by such a novel experience". After a few months, the filling material was standing firmly and before the year was out, the completed track on wooden sleepers had been laid. In Parliament, the most eminent engineers had sworn that it was impossible. Francis Giles had stated that it would cost over £200,000. Stephenson built it for about £27,000, and it turned out to be less than the average cost per mile for the entire railway.

During its construction, objectors had used Chat Moss as horror propaganda. Fearful for their calling, stage coach owners spread alarming rumours around Manchester, some seven miles distant; hundreds of men and young lads, horses and waggons, they said, had sunk in the bog and the works had been abandoned; Stephenson himself had been swallowed in the mire, to bring railways to an end for ever. But the track was firm, and in a short time the first train would cross it.

At Rainhill, an intriguing task for Stephenson was to build a skew bridge to carry the Liverpool-Warrington turnpike road at a sharp angle. He could see the shape in his mind's eye but was unable to commit it to paper. Samuel Smiles recorded that the engineer plucked a turnip from a nearby field and carved out the shape he desired. Booth described it as "of very curious and beautiful construction . . . each stone being cut to a particular angle to fit into a particular place". Somewhat extended, this fine skew bridge can still be seen near Rainhill station, nine miles from Liverpool.

Another challenging proposition for the principal engineer was how to straddle the deep Sankey Valley in which ran the Sankey Canal and brook, about half-way between Liverpool and Manchester. It was made necessary because permission to pass through nearby coalfields was refused. To make a level track an enormous viaduct was required, of a magnitude far beyond Stephenson's previous experience. During construction he lodged at a cottage nearby. Much negotiation with landowners was involved, numerous architectural drawings were made and close consultation held between the directors responsible, engineers and draughtsmen. Lengthy embankments were required at each end. Large numbers of navvies, masons, bricklayers, horses, wheelbarrows and machinery were assembled for the task. The viaduct consisted of nine arches, each of fifty feet. Massive piers were supported on some two hundred piles driven deep below the water beds, and the parapet coping rose about seventy feet above the valley, leaving room to spare for the highest sailing boats. Dressings and stone facings finished the mainly brick structure, to present an imposing simplicity of style.

Henry Booth watched the piling operations: "The heavy ram employed to impart the finishing strokes, hoisted up with double purchase and snail's pace to the summit of the Piling Engine, and then falling down like a thunderbolt on the head of the devoted timber, driving it perhaps a single half inch into the stratum below, is well calculated to put to the test the virtue of patience, while it illustrates the old adage of 'slow but sure'."

Contemporary writer James Scott Walker records that the viaduct cost £42,000 to build, against an estimate of just over £32,000. Remembering his slanderers, what a surging thrill of satisfaction Stephenson must have enjoyed as he watched the first train steaming proudly along on high. It was his finest piece of architectural masonry on the line, a model for others to come, and stands today as a monument to his native engineering genius.

Yet another Herculean task was tackled. To keep the railway reasonably level on the edges of Liverpool and to avoid wealthy landowners' property, an extensive cutting was carved out at Olive Mount. It ran for nearly two miles and at its deepest was over a hundred feet. Using a large team, nearly half a million tons, much of it solid rock, was dug or blasted out. Smiles calls it "the first extensive stone cutting executed on any railway", and Charles Vignoles commented, "It looked as if it had been dug out by giants."

As one of the early promoters of the line, Henry Booth recorded vividly his impressions after a test run, and can be forgiven for allowing his lyrical quill to scratch away in a mood of wonder: "At night, when the natural gloom of the place is further deepened, the scene from the bridges above will readily be imagined to be novel and striking. The light of the moon illuminating about half the depth, and casting a darker shade on the area below – the general silence interrupted at intervals by a noise like distant thunder – presently a train of carriages, led on by an Engine of fire and steam, with her lamps like two furnaces, throwing their light onward in a dazzling signal of their approach – with the strength and speed of a war-horse the Engine moves forward with its glorious cavalcade of merchandise from all countries and passengers of all nations. But the spectacle is transient as striking; in a moment the pageant is gone – the meteor passed; the flaring of the lamps is only seen in the distance, and the observer, looking down from the battlements above, perceives that all again is still and dark and solitary."

To reach the docks area at Wapping, a long tunnel had to be constructed. A short bore of 290 yards on a rising gradient would connect to the railway premises in Crown Street which was to be the principal station for railway carriages, and a depot for coal. Running between Edge Hill and Wapping, the main tunnel was to be just over a mile and a quarter long – 2250 yards.

Tunnel boring created little disturbance to the streets above, though some property owners had to be compensated for damage, real or supposed. One objector complained that it was wrong to "pierce the very bowels of the metropolis", and the Liverpool Corporation feared for the safety of their water supplies which might leak into the tunnel. Tunnels were not new, but this was the first major one to run under a busy town. Parliament had forbidden locomotives to run through the tunnels and stationary engines were built to haul trains through them by ropes fed over pulley wheels; vehicles were to be pulled up the gradients and allowed to run down them by gravity, control being ensured by brakesmen riding on them. The main engine to be installed at Edge Hill was ordered from the Stephenson Newcastle Works. It seems strange now, but a stationary engine remained in use in Liverpool practically to the end of the century.

John Rennie and Charles Vignoles had planned the route for the tunnel and by the time Stephenson took over its construction, Vignoles had been the sole resident engineer in Liverpool for the railway, and the sparks between him and his *bête noire* were still flying. Only months after the Railway Bill had been passed work began, and by October 1826 the first of several vertical shafts down from the streets had been excavated. Short on tunnelling experience, Stephenson had to depend on his assistants for accurate calculations to ensure that the seven or eight separate tunnel sections to be dug would hopefully meet in a straight line. Vignoles had erred in the preliminaries and confessed in a letter to a friend, "It is true there was an error in the survey of the tunnel made by me. . . ." Shortly after, he outlined plans for a tunnel under the River Mersey, a project which was to mature many years later.

Supervised by the contractors, hundreds of 'miners' wielded pick-axes, shovels, hammers and chisels by candle light. Blasting by explosives shifted stubborn rock. A narrow-gauge railway track was laid temporarily to move spoil in small waggons pushed by the men, either to the tunnel mouths or to be hauled up the shafts by mining machinery. Stephenson hired blacksmiths and wheelwrights from the Newcastle area to make special tools and equipment and to build the small waggons. Main excavations occupied a year and a half by which time Vignoles had departed. In an ambience of subsidence, poor lighting, moving waggons and flooding, accidents happened, most of them minor. For the final break-through, the usual warnings were sounded for a charge to be exploded. Several men neither heard nor acknowledged the alert and a superintendent and two men suffered severe burning. To make the tunnel safe, it was lined throughout by cement and brickwork. Young Joseph Locke, the section engineer in charge, by a happy combination of encouragement and example managed to keep reluctant and frightened men at their work. Understandably, they were terrified of being buried alive under a roof fall. Well trained under Stephenson, this extraordinarily handsome man was to distinguish himself as a builder of new railways at home and abroad.

Time and money had been wasted on the tunnel miscalculations which Stephenson failed to notice. He had sent Locke to survey another railway and it turned out that several vertical shafts were out of line and that the two pilot bores for the tunnel, if continued, would not at one point have met at all. Angry directors called back Joseph Locke over the master's head, to correct the errors. Stephenson, who never took kindly to criticism, emerged from this *contretemps* seriously embarrassed. It created an unpleasant breach between himself and his protégé which was to widen in later years as the two competed for new railway projects.

After all the dust had settled, on 7th June 1828 the tunnel was cleared throughout. Booth again: "On some occasions, the men refused to work . . . nor is this surprising, considering the nature of the operations: boring their way almost in the dark, with the water streaming around them, and uncertain whether the props and stays would bear the pressure from above till the arch-work should be completed . . . the light of a few candles . . . barely sufficient to show the dreariness of the place."

Dreariness was less evident when, in 1829, the tunnel walls were whitewashed; and, to be seen for the first time by thousands of folk, gas lamps were suspended at short intervals from the roof. Public approval of this attractive innovation was warm, and the directors believed that the lighting would temper the terror that some passengers might feel in plunging under the streets in an unlighted train. Potential panic was further dispelled during the summer of 1829 when for a while the tunnel was enjoyed as a popular subterranean promenade. On certain days, people could walk right through at 1s (5p) a time, an echoing band heightening the excitement of a novel and eerie adventure. On one day alone – 1st August – some three thousand people walked its length. Among them was William Huskisson, MP for Liverpool, who had worked so hard in the House for this railway.

He had a lame leg and an injured arm and was not especially prepossessing. He was no flamboyant speaker, but shrewd, and a member of the Cabinet. On this occasion in the tunnel, with a large throng before him, like any other Member of Parliament he could not resist giving voice. He described the wonders of the railway and said he envied George Stephenson for the "honour and the direction and completion of such an undertaking".

To win public support for the railway line, visitors were encouraged to see the "floating railway" across Chat Moss. After a test run with colleagues, Henry Booth wrote about the "embankments, riding above the tops of the trees and overlooking the surrounding country . . . presenting the traveller all the variety of mountain [sic] and ravine in pleasing succession, whilst in reality he is moving almost on a level plane".

Winning general approval was in the minds of the directors as they encouraged the engineers to design viaducts, bridges, tunnel entrances and other structures in attractive style. One of them was Foster's Moorish Arch which, with its two huge battlemented towers and decorated masonry, formed a grand and impressive entrance approaching the Liverpool terminus. As well as decorative, it had a functional purpose, for the archway served as a bridge across a deep, walled cutting to connect two engine houses.

Stephenson was more concerned with the functional nuts and bolts and found that he could shorten the entire route slightly by minor deviations; but these were not authorised in the original Act, and a third Act, passed on 26th March 1828, allowed the work to be done. This was the Act that authorised the gauge, previously approved by the directors, to be 4 feet 8 inches, which was standardised at 4 feet 8½ inches. It also allowed the railway to fine trespassers up to £2 and to keep the cash: two weeks' wages for a labourer.

Another amending Act passed on 14th May 1829 authorised the railway to serve as carriers. Originally, the idea was for the railway to own the track and to allow public carriers to provide their own rolling stock on payment of tolls. Deputy chairman John Moss had insisted that more profit would be earned by the railway to do the lot but additional capital would be needed and the Act enabled the company to raise an additional sum of £127,500; but public carriers would still be welcome.

Importantly, this Act also approved the extension of the line from Salford. Stephenson built an iron bridge with grand porticos across the River Irwell, and land was purchased to build a terminal with depots, yards and warehouses. True to form, the railway's old arch enemies, the Mersey & Irwell Canal, and the Bridgewater Navigation with Robert Bradshaw at the helm, threw in a few spanners; but with a bit of business give and take, opposition was suitably neutralised. The Act limited the iron-fenced lines in Manchester on which locomotives would run, for some people were afraid they might run amok on the streets like wild animals. Now that the railway could penetrate the sacred precincts of Manchester, its prestige and shares rose. The terminus was to be in Liverpool Road, and is now claimed to be the oldest passenger station in the world; it is thankfully preserved as a museum.

For Stephenson, the extension was an added responsibility. Though progress of the railway in the three years to 1829 had been satisfactory, he had endured a marathon of personal strain. His friend Samuel Smiles gives an insight: "Even his extraordinary powers of labour and endurance were taxed to the utmost . . . iron girders, siphons, fixed engines, and the machinery for working the tunnel at the Liverpool end, all had to be thought out by his own head, and reduced to definite plans under his own eyes. Besides all this, he had to design the working plant in anticipation of the opening of the railway. He must be prepared with waggons, trucks and carriages, himself superintending their manufacture. The permanent road, turntables, switches and crossings, – in short the entire structure and machinery of the line, from the turning of the first sod to the running of the first train of carriages on the railway – went on under his immediate supervision."

Led by chairman Charles Lawrence, the board early in 1828 had reviewed progress and were gratified by Stephenson's performance; and at a board meeting of 21st April 1828 it was decided to increase his salary to £1,500 a year. This was almost certainly higher than for any other engineer in Britain. Perhaps the directors were influenced by the amount of work he was doing for other embryonic railways, including projects at Bolton, Canterbury and North Wales. By the end of the year, the railway had spent £460,000 and the engineer was urged to "push on the works with increased vigour". One director named James Cropper, who opposed locomotives and favoured stationary engines with pulley ropes, in spring 1829 had pressed, "Now, George, thou must get on with the railway and have it finished without further delay. Thou must really have it ready for opening on the 1st January next."

The engineer protested, "It's impossible!"

"Impossible? I wish I could get Napoleon to thee. He would tell thee that there is no such word as 'impossible' in the vocabulary."

"Tush, Sir. . . . Give me men, money and materials, and I will do what Napoleon couldn't do – drive a railroad from Liverpool to Manchester over Chat Moss!"

In bad winter months, heavy rain had held up the work. Some cuttings looked more like canals than railways and the directors ordered the engineer to employ two sets of navvies on major projects and to work day and night. On top of this, a new setback made things worse; several hundred workers at the Liverpool end had been persuaded to emigrate to the fast-developing United States of America, as recorded in the *Manchester Guardian* on 22nd August 1829:

"Several large canals and railways are at present constructing there; and agents from the different companies have been some time in this country, offering high wages to workmen of various descriptions – excavators, masons, joiners, etc. – to engage in the completion of them."

Accidents, though not excessive, caused delays. Take 1829, for example: in March, one person was killed and another seriously injured from a landslide down a steep embankment. In September, a man was run over and killed while working on the line near Salford; and in November, the collapse of a temporary bridge killed one man and sent a score of others scuttling for safety.

Because major works were eating up money faster than expected, in 1828 the Board had sought to draw a further £10,000 against the loan of £100,000 authorised by the Government the previous year. Before approval, the Exchequer commissioned Thomas Telford, the first president of the Institution of Civil Engineers, to investigate and recommend. Stephenson, always prickly about criticism, was not amused. Telford's assistant, James Mills, who arrived to conduct the preliminary inspection of the railway, stated in one of his reports: "There does not appear to be a single contract existing on the whole line. Stevenson [sic] seems to be a contractor for the whole and to employ all the different people at such prices as he thinks proper to give them, the Company find all materials, not only rails and waggons but even wheelbarrows and plants etc. . . ."

Telford's eyebrows must have raised at Stephenson's primitive organisation for a civil engineering project of the first magnitude, a system fraught with abuse. Stephenson may have been obstinate, egotistical and professionally jealous; but his colleagues saw a man of high principles, though some businessmen exploited his talents and commercial naïveté to the full, especially through his railway building firm, George Stephenson & Son.

In January 1829, Stephenson conducted Telford and Mills along the entire route. The relationship between the two protagonists can only be surmised; the unlettered colliery worker from Northumberland and the eminent engineer with an esoteric interest in the literary arts who had published poems and was popular in high society. From this visit, the directors knew that the immediate future of their railway hung in the balance.

At age seventy-two and in failing health, Telford acknowledged that the inspection had been an exhausting ordeal. His report to the Exchequer contained several criticisms, including the choice of power and the lack of working capital; and the directors and the engineer, who could not afford to offend this most influential doyen, worked to put their house in order. Undertakings by the directors eventually satisfied him; he withdrew his disapproval and the Exchequer agreed to make the £10,000 loan. Telford wrote that his tour "upon a line of thirty miles in the present unfinished and complex state of the works was a tedious and laborious task".

These three phenomenal years – 1826–9 – in which Stephenson had employed about twenty different contractors, saw the railway nearing completion. Yet, one final battle had to be fought: not over practical or technical dilemmas, but against the obstruction, mistrust and prejudice of many public people and, worst of all, a vocal minority of the directors themselves – the battle for the steam locomotive. Whatever the board decided, it would influence powerfully the immediate future of this and of other pioneering railways waiting to stoke their boilers.

No doubts whatever remained in the mind of George Stephenson. He had been convinced for many years that the steam locomotive was capable of hauling a train of waggons or carriages safely, reliably and at a good speed along a firm track of iron rails; and he was determined not to be deflected from this philosophy.

To assess locomotives, in October 1828 Booth and two directors had visited the north-east and Stephenson's Darlington Railway which had been operating for three years. Henry Booth compiled their report: "The great theatre of practical operations on Railways was on the Stockton & Darlington line, and on all the Railways in the vicinity of Newcastle-on-Tyne. All the established modes of conveying carriages [meaning vehicles of all kinds] were there exemplified – Horses, Locomotives, and Fixed Engines." When the report was studied at a board meeting in Liverpool, opinion was still divided between stationary and travelling engines; the minutes confirmed, however, that "horses were out of the question".

Still uncertain, three months later the board commissioned engineers James Walker and John Rastrick to visit the north-east for further investigations. Their joint report on 9th March 1829, surprising to some directors, recommended a series of stationary engines with haulage ropes, at the same time noting the possibility of locomotives. While the debate continued, Walker wondered whether some form of competition for locomotives by different designers could be organised, to test their capabilities; and a director named Richard Harrison gave the idea his support.

Stephenson was angry that the directors should even consider stationary engines; after all, he had been building locomotives for fifteen years. Yet, he must have appreciated that they could not afford to make a wrong judgement on such a vital issue. On reflection, he must have looked forward to such a challenge with quiet confidence.

CHAPTER 4

The Rainhill Trials

As the construction of the railway was progressing, the twelve months of anxiety and ambivalence about the choice of power among the directors reached a head; and on 20th April 1829, the board passed a resolution to organise a public competition. This would prove whether locomotives were superior to stationary engines. The winner would be offered a prize of £500 (probably £10,000 to £20,000 today). Still smarting under the strictures of the great Thomas Telford, the directors intended to show the world that they meant business.

Though engineers John Rastrick and James Walker had recommended stationary engines, they left a loophole that there were grounds "for expecting improvements in the construction and work of locomotives". Robert Stephenson had written to an unknown correspondent, "We are preparing for a counter-report in favour of locomotives, which I believe still will ultimately get the day, but from present appearances nothing decisive can be said: rely on it, locomotives shall not be cowardly given up. I will fight for them until the last. They are worthy of a conflict."

He also consulted his old friend Timothy Hackworth (1786–1850), resident engineer of the Darlington Railway who had worked at the Stephenson factory. His reply was heartening: "I hear the Liverpool Company have concluded to use fixed engines. . . . Do not discompose yourself, my dear Sir; if you express your manly, firm, decided opinion, you have done your part as their adviser. And if it happens to be read some day in the newspapers – 'Whereas the Liverpool & Manchester Railway has been strangled by ropes', we shall not accuse you of guilt in being an accessory either before or after the fact."

Of stationary engines, Hackworth had earlier written that they "can never do for coaching; passengers cannot be accommodated. If endless ropes are used, there will be both danger and delay . . . a scene of endless confusion".

Robert's promised counter-report, written jointly with Joseph Locke, was entitled "Observations on the Comparative Merits of Locomotives and Fixed Engines as applied to Railways". Nearly twenty stationary steam engines, they contended, would be needed at intervals of a mile and a half, and all trains would have to be hauled by a system of ropes, pulleys and rollers which would make it impossible to construct connecting sidings or branch lines. About a hundred and fifty men would be needed to maintain the equipment and engines and to stoke them with fuel, and an accident would halt every train on the entire line.

When the report was completed, Stephenson senior, who probably mused that he had wet-nursed these two young pups, insisted on taking the credit. To assuage his demands, a suitable addition was made to the document: "Compiled from the reports of George Stephenson".

On reaching the boardroom, it really must have put the cat in the birdcage. The most distinguished engineers in England differed about the choice of power and it had to be settled one way or another.

For the Stephensons, the forthcoming trials could make or break them and lose the world lead which George Stephenson was so assiduously seeking; and the pioneering line itself, which was locking up enormous capital, lay at the crossroads.

No sooner had the board published its challenge than aspiring mechanics, crackpot eccentrics and misunderstood inventors of genius began to submit their own ideas, which must have offered comic relief to harassed directors. In Booth's own words: "Communications were received from all classes of persons, each recommending an improved power or an improved carriage; from professors of philosophy, down to the humblest mechanic, all were zealous in their proffers of assistance; England, America, and Continental Europe were alike tributory."

He quotes examples:

"Every element and almost every substance were brought into requisition, and made subservient to the great work. The friction of the carriages was to be reduced so low that a silk thread would draw them, and the power to be applied was so vast as to rend a cable asunder.

"Hydrogen gas and high-pressure steam – columns of water and columns of mercury – a hundred atmospheres and a perfect vacuum – machines working in a circle without fire or steam, generating power at one end of the process and giving it out at the other – carriages that conveyed, every one its own Railway – wheels within wheels, to multiply speed without diminishing power – with every complication of balancing and countervailing forces, to the *ne plus ultra* of perpetual motion. Every scheme which the restless ingenuity – or prolific imagination of man could devise was liberally offered to the Company; the difficulty was to choose and decide."

Though these obfuscating curiosities were welcome fun, less ephemeral men were to choose and decide. For instance, the directors drew up lengthy and stringent rules: "Stipulation and Conditions on which the Directors of the Liverpool & Manchester Railway offer a premium of £500 for the most improved Locomotive Engine".

Among the conditions were that locomotives must consume their own smoke as required by statute; two safety valves would be needed, one of which must be self-acting; engine and boiler must be mounted on springs.

Weight restrictions were defined: four wheels on a locomotive weighing under four-and-a-half tons, and six wheels for heavier weights, up to a maximum of six tons. Boiler pressure must not exceed 50 lb per square inch, the Company reserving the right to put any locomotive to an advance safety test of up to 150 lb; the boiler must be fitted with a mercurial steam pressure gauge. The wheels must fit a rail gauge of 4 feet 8½ inches and the cost of the locomotive must not exceed £550. Each locomotive would be required to haul three tons for each ton of its own weight, for a total of seventy miles at a minimum rate of ten miles an hour; this would entail over forty separate journeys on the trials section.

For the tests, which became famous as the "Rainhill Trials", a stretch of one-and-a-half miles was selected from a level length of nearly two miles, known as the Rainhill Level; at either end were two falling gradients of one in ninety-six: one at Whiston and the other at Sutton, and considered by many to be too steep for locomotives. Rainhill is nine miles from Liverpool.

Contenders from far and wide began to prepare. Principal engineer of the railway though he was, there was no guarantee that the Stephenson entry would be the winner; he had to compete with others on equal terms. If there were a better one, he would simply lose. No doubt he was sustained in the knowledge that he had built more steam locomotives than any other man alive. Naturally, his locomotive would be built in the Newcastle Works and he and Robert decided to model it on their *Lancashire Witch*, a much advanced machine ordered by the Liverpool & Manchester but transferred to the new Bolton & Leigh Railway the year before.

Confidently, the locomotive now to be built at Newcastle was known among the works men as 'The Premium Engine'. Instead of four coupled wheels as on the *Witch*, it had two driving wheels of 4 feet 8½ inches diameter – incidentally the same as the rail gauge – driven by two outside inclined cylinders of eight inches bore and seventeen stroke; and two carrier wheels of two feet diameter, to secure greater speed and freer running. The wheels were made of oak and were fitted with iron bosses and iron tyres. An ingenious mechanism fitted with slip eccentrics connected to the steam valves enabled the locomotive to run either forwards or in reverse.

But the most truly revolutionary idea was that instead of inserting in the boiler two large flues or tubes, a multi-tube boiler was devised. Hot gases from the firebox went through the tubes which were surrounded by water in the boiler, achieving a much larger area of heating surface. This would prevent the locomotive running out of steam and stalling. From the cylinders, the exhaust steam at each rhythmic pulse (the chuff-chuff chuff-chuff) was directed through the chimney, and in doing so drew the heat more fiercely from the firebox through the boiler tubes, known as steam-blast.

At the Newcastle factory, Robert Stephenson took complete charge of the design and construction of the Premium Engine. One of his most serious difficulties was to fix the twenty-five copper tubes of three inches diameter to the inside front and back plates of the boiler to make them watertight.

Other engineers had tried the multi-tube system. Marc Seguin, the great French railway engineer, fitted his experimental locomotive with a multi-tube boiler some months after the Rainhill Trials, probably the result of his earlier visit to north-east England to inspect the colliery railways. As early as 1784, James Watt had tried it, too, on his stationary engines. On 27th August, he had written to his partner, Matthew Boulton: "Perhaps some means may be hit upon to make the boiler cylindrical with a number of tubes passing through, like the organ-pipe condensers . . . but I fear this would be too subject to accidents." During the early 1820s, several inventors had experimented with multi-tube boilers but with little success. George Stephenson had been trying out the effect of small boiler tubes for some years and in 1828 he sent two locomotives so fitted, built in the Newcastle factory, to France for the projected Lyon & St Etienne Railway. In operation, the tubes proved unsatisfactory and were removed.

As soon as the Rainhill Trials had been announced, Henry Booth proposed to Robert Stephenson that a multi-tube boiler should be fitted on the Premium Engine and he became involved in the design; Booth also took on responsibility for having the firebox made in Liverpool for despatch to Newcastle for assembly. Booth was to write in later years, "I was in almost daily communication with Mr [Robert] Stephenson at the time; and I was not aware that he had any intention of competing for the prize till I communicated to him my scheme for a multi-tube boiler . . . and proposed to him that we should jointly construct an engine, and compete for the prize. Mr Stephenson . . . agreed to my proposal. . . ." This suggests that had not Booth invited

Robert to compete, the Stephensons would not have done so. Considering the large number of locomotives the two had already built, and their close involvement with the Liverpool & Manchester Railway, Booth's claim is difficult to understand. In the same letter, Booth says of the multi-tube boiler, ". . . I claim to be the inventor in England, and feel warranted in stating, without reservation, that until I named my plan to Mr Stephenson, with a view to compete for the prize at Rainhill, it had not been tried, and was not known in this country". This suggests he was unaware of earlier experiments with multi-tubes. But he was known as a warm-hearted man of integrity and his sincerity was not to be doubted. He certainly had an inventive turn of mind and later patented several pieces of railway equipment.

A world of difference lay between thinking about the multi-tube boiler and making the thing work. When the tubes were fitted in the Premium Engine and hydraulic pressures applied for testing, water squirted out at every joint with arrogant prodigality and flooded the factory floor.

In despair, Robert, never a bubbling optimist, wrote to his father in Liverpool that the whole thing was a complete failure. Back came the parental rubric from the man who always refused to be beaten, "Try again!" He offered practical suggestions to overcome the leakages, and eventually Robert constructed a watertight boiler which would stand the extreme internal pressure that might be required at the trials to test for safety.

Other mechanical problems were steadily overcome and in good time it was ready for the big day. In later years, Robert was to pay compliments to his father and to Booth. Nonetheless, it had been the well trained Robert and his team of mechanics at Newcastle who had patiently built the Premium Engine as a working locomotive; it was rated at 6¼ horse power.

At some stage in its new career, the Premium Engine was given an official name, *Rocket*, symbolising unexampled speed; and it is a pity that we are denied the story of how this inspired name became to be bestowed, lost as it now is in the mists of time.

The next stage was to try it on the track. In a lengthy screed, Robert wrote to Booth on 5th September 1829 and extracts are quoted: "I tried the engine on Killingworth railway . . . the fire burns admirably and abundance of steam is raised. . . . We started from Killingworth Pit, with five waggons, each weighing four tuns. Add to this the tender and forty men we proceeded up an ascent . . . at eight miles per hour after we had gained speed. . . . We went three miles on this railway, the rate of ascents and descents my father knows – on a level part laid with malleable iron rail, and we attained a speed of twelve miles per hour and without thinking that I deceived myself (I tried to avoid this), I believe the steam did not sink on this part. On the whole the Engine is capable of doing as much if not more than set forth in the stipulations. After a great deal of trouble and anxiety we have got the tubes perfectly tight. . . . On Friday next, the Engine will leave by way of Carlisle and will arrive in L'pool on Wednesday week." He gives the weight of the engine with water at 4¼ tons. In great joy, he wrote to his father to say that the locomotive would be "all right" for the trials. Perhaps he recalled how excited he had been as an eleven-year-old schoolboy to watch his father's *Blücher* make her maiden trip on that very line at Killingworth fifteen years before.

Back in Newcastle, the *Rocket* was partly dismantled for its journey to Liverpool and hoisted into horse-drawn waggons. On Saturday afternoon, 12th September 1829, the precious cargo lumbered all along the rough, tortuous roads for seventy or eighty miles from the east coast to Carlisle on the west. Two days later, it travelled in a lighter for the short trip to Bowness on the Solway Firth that divides England and Scotland, then by a Cumberland steamer for a journey of over a hundred miles round the coast to Liverpool. For Robert, the suspense was over as it arrived safely on 18th September; the parts were conveyed in horse-drawn waggons to Crown Street for assembly, where it was joined by its four-wheeled tender which had been built in Liverpool.

Meanwhile, other contenders had been making their machines. Timothy Hackworth, whom the Stephensons considered a possible, though not too serious, rival, was building his *Sans Pareil* (Without Equal) at his small Shildon factory near Darlington; John Ericsson, a Swedish inventor aged twenty-two, and his partner John Braithwaite, ten years older, were busy in London on their *Novelty*; and Timothy Burstall of Edinburgh was completing his *Perseverance*.

As an old friend of Hackworth, Robert Stephenson in the summer had kept an eye on the progress of *Sans Pareil* at Shildon, a piece of mild industrial espionage. Robert, too, had been spied upon, for he wrote to Booth that, "I was extremely mystified to find that he [Mr Burstall junior from Edinburgh] walked into the manufactory this morning and examined the engine with all the coolness imaginable before we discovered who he was. He has, however, scarcely time to take advantage of any hints he might catch during this transient visit. It would have been as well if he had not seen anything."

Braithwaite and Ericsson had named their locomotive after a London theatre and built it within two months; because there was no railway in London on which to make their tests, they were seriously handicapped.

Cycloped was another machine to enter: not so much a locomotive, more a walking horse. Within a framework on the vehicle, two horses (some old prints show only one), walked on an endless moving platform, treadmill fashion, which rotated the driving wheels to make a speed of walking pace. Its designer was Thomas Brandreth, friend of George Stephenson, a shareholder in the Liverpool & Manchester Railway and one of its early promoters. None of this did him much good, for his machine fell far short of the stipulations and was, of course, disqualified.

Wonders never cease when man's competitive penetralia is provoked. Witness, for example, the *Manumotive*, whose inventor Winans had the temerity to demonstrate his brainchild to the bemused spectators. It consisted of a simple carriage holding six passengers and was propelled by two strong men. According to the sparse contemporary reports, it moved "with no great velocity". But what an intriguing *divertissement*!

Only the four steam locomotives previously mentioned were acceptable for the trials, "out of a considerable number of engines constructed in different parts of the country," Smiles tells us, "many of which could not be completed by the day of Trial".

Trials of such momentous portent for this and other projected railways, required a strong team to monitor and time the operations. Three eminent engineers were appointed as judges – John Rastrick, Nicholas Wood and John Kennedy. To the chagrin of his old friend George Stephenson, Rastrick tended to favour stationary steam engines. Wood, some years younger than Stephenson, had worked with the master from *Blücher* days, knew Robert as a boy, and believed in the steam locomotive. Rastrick and Wood both became famous engineers. John Kennedy a Quaker of Manchester, once a poor boy in Scotland and friend of James Watt who had died in 1819, had made his fortune by inventing textile machinery and was now a wealthy Lancashire cotton spinner. A supporter of the locomotive, he had joined the railway promoters in 1822 and had more than a passing interest in the great trials to come.

On 31st August the directors passed another resolution: "That the place of trial for the Specimen Engines on the 1st October next be the level space between the two inclined planes at Rainhill for the two miles of level, and a single line down the plane to the Roby Embankment."

Some would-be contestants complained that they needed more time, so the directors put back the starting date to Tuesday the 6th and the trials in fact continued to the 14th, excluding Sunday and Monday 11th and 12th.

Estimates of the numbers of people there that first morning have ranged between 10,000 and 15,000. Smiles again: ". . . the ground at Rainhill presented a lively appearance, and there was excitement as if the St Leger were about to run. Many thousands of spectators looked on, amongst whom were some of the first engineers and mechanicians of the day. A stand was provided for the ladies; the 'beauty and fashion' of the neighbourhood were present, and the side of the railroad was lined with carriages of all descriptions." Scores of people watched from the parapet of the Rainhill Skew Bridge.

Among the crowds, two Americans identified themselves: Horatio Allen was chief engineer of the Delaware & Hudson Canal Company and his companion was E. L. Miller. Later, both were to promote the South Carolina Canal & Rail Road Company. They were among the many fortunate enough to attend this historic encounter, the first public contest between self-powered auto-motive machines the world had ever seen.

At the ends of the spectators' stand were hoisted huge flags which flapped noisily in the breeze. Nearby, a brass band blared raucously into the morning air to add pomp and circumstance for this exciting occasion. Large crowds meant good business for somebody, and the neighbouring innkeeper had never in his life dispensed such quantities of ale.

During the several days of the trials, people from hundreds of miles around flocked in. An uninformed stranger observing this race would have searched in vain for a parade of horses and jockeys; but if he had asked for a 'race card', he would have been handed a list of contenders:

No 1   Messrs Braithwaite and Ericsson of London, the *Novelty* Copper and Blue. Weight: 2 tons 15 cwt;

No 2   Mr Ackworth (sic) of Darlington, the *Sans Pareil* Green, Yellow and Black. Weight: 4 tons 8 cwt 2 qr;

No 3   Mr Robert Stephenson of Newcastle-upon-Tyne, the *Rocket* Yellow and Black, White Chimney. Weight: 4 tons 3 cwt;

No 4   Mr Brandreth of Liverpool, the *Cycloped*, Weight 3 tons, worked by a horse (this was disqualified);

No 5   Mr Burstall of Edinburgh, the *Perseverance* Red Wheels, Weight: 2 tons 17 cwt.

These four steam locomotives were the only ones in the world which could reach anywhere near the stringent conditions the railway directors had specified; and their inventors were poised on the brink of dazzling international fame and fortune to which the coveted prize would surely lead.

Of "The Battle for the Locomotive", the *Liverpool Mercury* predicted that it might "alter the whole system of our internal communications . . . substituting an agency whose ultimate effects can scarcely be anticipated." A trumpet call was sounded by Smiles; "The fate of railways in a great measure depended upon the issues of this appeal to the mechanical genius of England." But a sour note had been sounded by an eminent gentleman from Liverpool who declared that "only a parcel of charlatans would have drawn up such conditions". He maintained that it was impossible for a locomotive to travel at ten miles an hour, but if it was ever done, he would "undertake to eat a stewed engine wheel for breakfast." This eminent gentleman was later appointed to a safe position in the Government as an inspector of steam packets.

Ready for the trials, at either end of the section white posts had been erected at the line side as starting and finishing points; nearby, fuel and water supplies were available; there, too, were blacksmith's shops and other repair facilities for locomotives in trouble. The three judges did not take for granted the weights of the competing locomotives declared by their owners and a weighbridge was installed. The timekeepers (two judges) holding 'seconds watches' were stationed at each end of the section to record times taken over the course on each run; and between runs, the minutes lost by frenetic servicing. Also recorded were time and fuel consumed in raising a full head of steam from cold, and the amount of fuel and water used during the test runs. Detailed records were kept by the judges, making the total surveillance as watertight as the *Rocket*'s boiler tubes.

What was George Stephenson's mood as the tension mounted? Smiles notes, "He had fought the battle for it until now almost single-handed. Engrossed by his daily labours and anxieties, and harassed by difficulties and discouragements which would have crushed the spirit of a less resolute man, he had held firmly to his purpose. . . . The hostility which he experienced from some of the directors opposed to the steam locomotive was the circumstance that caused him the greatest grief of all; for where he had looked for encouragement, he found only carping and opposition. But his pluck never failed him."

And so the great Rainhill Trials went into session. Characteristically, the *Rocket* was ready first, but because it was listed third in the sequence, it had to wait; however, the judges allowed it out to make test runs. Early on the first day, the *Novelty*, a "pretty machine", showed her paces before an admiring crowd. Running on four wheels, it had a roomy, railed platform, an upright boiler in the front and a tall, thin chimney just behind it. In a striking blue livery and with cylinders clad in highly polished copper, her simple lines made a brave showing. Judge Nicholas Wood described the boiler as little more than a glorified domestic copper. George Stephenson was not worried, for it was an adaptation of a vehicle to run on roads, and not really suited to pull heavy waggons on rails. George is alleged to have remarked to a doubter in his broad Doric, "Eh, mon, we needna fear yon thing, hers got nae goots!"

Yet an enraptured reporter of the *Mechanics Magazine* was to write of the *Novelty*, "The great lightness of this engine, its compactness, and its beautiful workmanship, excited universal admiration; a senti-

Charles Sylvester (holding quill), a distinguished engineer who recommended locomotives for the L & M in 1824, with pioneer promoter Joseph Sandars (centre) and George Stephenson.

From a painting of a Stephenson family group, with George, seated, and his son Robert on the right.

ANNO SEPTIMO

GEORGII IV. REGIS.

****

Cap. xlix.

An Act for making and maintaining a Railway or Tramroad from the Town of *Liverpool* to the Town of *Manchester*, with certain Branches therefrom, all in the County of *Lancaster*.

[5th *May* 1826.]

WHEREAS the making and maintaining of a Railway or Railways, or Tramroad or Tramroads, together with the Two several Branches therefrom herein-after mentioned, with proper Works and Conveniences adjoining thereto or connected therewith, for the Passage of Waggons and other Carriages, from or near the Town of *Liverpool* in the County of *Lancaster*, in and through the several Parishes or Places herein-after mentioned, to the Township of *Salford* within the Parish of *Manchester*, and adjoining to the Town of *Manchester* in the same County, will be of great Advantage to the Inhabitants of the said County, Towns, and Places, by opening a cheap and expeditious Communication between the Two large trading Towns of *Liverpool* and *Manchester*; and by affording an additional Mode of Transit for Merchandize and other Articles and Matters between these Places, and also to and from the neighbouring Country, will be of great public Utility: And whereas the King's most Excellent Majesty, in right of His Duchy of *Lancaster*, is entitled to certain Lands in the Township of *Salford* within

[*Local.*]   16 B   the

The front page of the Railway Act of 5th May 1826, the date on which the battle for the railway was won.

George Stephenson's only son, Robert, who took over from his father, became a millionaire and worked himself to death.

Below left: William James, one of the earliest pioneers to plan a railway route between Liverpool and Manchester – but he had irons in too many fires.

Below right: Henry Booth, friend of the Stephensons and foremost among the founders of the Liverpool & Manchester Railway.

What remains of the original *Rocket*, built by Robert Stephenson at Newcastle-upon-Tyne, can be seen in the Science Museum, London. With this tiny engine, now the most famous in the world, George won at the Rainhill Trials in 1829 – and changed history.

The losers, from *left to right*: pioneer Timothy Hackworth, whose *Sans Pareil* met near-disaster in the Rainhill Trials of 1829; Ericsson (*centre*) and his partner, Braithwaite, put on a great show at the Trials with their *Novelty*, marred only by an explosion or two!

The other contenders at Rainhill –

Timothy Hackworth's *Sans Pareil*, whose leaking boiler and terrifyingly fierce chimney-blast nearly broke his heart – but it survived to do useful work.

Novelty, by Braithwaite and Ericsson of London, achieved high speeds and delighted the watching crowds; one reporter confessed that "It actually made one giddy to look at it". But it lacked the stamina of *Rocket*.

Perseverance, by Burstall of Edinburgh, managed five or six miles an hour, despite various faults, and John Dixon described it as "all covered with copper like a new tea-urn".

How serious Brandreth was in entering his horse-powered *Cycloped* for the Trials is a mystery: it provided light relief to the massive crowds but was inevitably disqualified by the judges.

Two of the three judges at the Rainhill Trials: Nicholas Wood (*above left*), an apprenticed engineer from a middle-class background who in his late teens worked with George Stephenson; John Rastrick (*above right*), who was later to build locomotives for America.

Below: The notice board at Rainhill station today.

8 Octr 1829 — Had on Board at Starting 8..3..2.. of Coke & 300 Gallons of Water
(Thursday)

Lighted the Fire — 9..37..0 } 0..57..0 Time of Getting up the Steam
Steam up — 10..34..0 }
Started — 10..36..50 } 0..2..50 Time taken up before Starting

First Experiment

Table of the Time Occupied each Trip & the Time of going 30 Miles at full Speed
and 5 Miles in starting and stopping.

Observations	Nº of Trips	Time in getting up the Speed & the Time at Westof	L.N.R.'s time taken when the Engine pass the Post Nº 1 to Nº1	Time in coming up from Post Nº1 to Nº1	Time in going down taken when the Engine pass Post Nº2 to Nº2	N.W.'s time taken when the Engine pass Post Nº2 to Nº2	Time in Stopping & getting up the Speed & the time	Observations
Started 10..36..50		0..1..25	10..38..15		0..7..43	10..45..58		
Stopped to Oil.	1	0..3..42	10..54..55	0..6..43		10..49..12	0..2..14	
	2	0..2..25	10..58..37		0..7..8	11..5..45	0..4..35	Greased the Pistons.
			11..16..42	0..8..22		11..10..20		
	3	0..2..55	11..21..10		0..7..52	11..29..2	0..2..45	
			11..39..50	0..8..3		11..31..47		
	4		11..42..45		0..6..7	11..48..54	0..2..20	
			11..58..15	0..7..3		11..51..12		
		0..2..27	0..0..42		0..6..31	0..7..13		
	5	0..2..5	0..15..45	0..6..5		0..9..40	0..2..27	
			0..17..50		0..5..55	0..23..45		
Stopped to take in 6 Buckets of Water equal to 19 Im. Gals.	6	0..4..5	0..35..20	0..8..42		0..26..38	0..2..53	
			0..39..25		0..5..55	0..45..20		
	7	0..2..24	0..55..30	0..7..35		0..47..55	0..2..35	
			0..57..54		0..5..40	1..3..34		
	8	0..3..25	1..13..45	0..6..57		1..6..40	0..3..14	Took in 16 Im Gallts of Water
			1..17..10		0..5..18	1..22..28		
	9	0..2..15	1..33..35	0..7..5		1..26..30	0..4..2	
			1..35..50		0..4..12	1..40..2	0..2..1	
Stopped 1..48..38 again Starting at noon 1..28..	10	0..1..23	1..47..15	0..5..12		1..42..3		8 In of Water left in Cask at End of this Experiment
Total Time } 3..11..48		0..28..34	Time in going 30 Miles calculated 2..14..8	1..11..47	1..2..21	Time in going 30 Miles 0..48..15	0..29..6	

Rastrick wisely preserved the notebook which he compiled during the Rainhill
Trials. This page shows the *Rocket's* performance on 8th October 1829.

ment speedily changed to perfect wonder, by its truly marvellous performance. . . . Almost at once, it darted off at the amazing velocity of twenty miles an hour, and it actually did one mile in the incredibly short space of one minute and fifty-three seconds!' One wonders how closely his figures tallied with those of the judges. Elsewhere, it was reported "to have gone at the rate of twenty-four to twenty-eight miles an hour", running alone without a load.

A supporting view appeared in the *Liverpool Mercury* on 9th October; "It seemed, indeed, to fly, presenting one of the most sublime spectacles of human ingenuity and human daring the world has ever beheld. It actually made one giddy to look at it, and it filled thousands with lively fears for the safety of the individuals who were on it, and who seemed not to run along the earth, but to fly, as it were on the 'wings of the wind'. It was a most sublime sight, indeed, which the individuals who beheld it will not soon forget." Since those days, the human eye has adapted itself to the most incredible speeds.

On the morning of the 10th, an advertisement appeared to say that the *Novelty* would perform more work than "any other engine on the ground". Yet, hauling a load of only seven tons, it ran into trouble, pride before a fall – a sudden explosion, a belch of smoke, flame and sparks from her nether regions, halted her triumphal progress. Charles Vignoles, one of her supporters, as well as Ericsson and Braithwaite, suffered a nasty shock. It appears that severe steam pressure burst the leather bellows used for forcing the draught through the furnace. Exit one locomotive.

Timothy Hackworth was soon on the scene. His *Sans Pareil* with four coupled wheels was little different from the earlier Stephenson locomotives which he knew so intimately. But lacking facilities for heavy work at his small factory, he had had to farm out some components, the boiler to Bedlington Ironworks and the cylinders to the Stephensons in Newcastle. This put him at some disadvantage.

When his turn came, he was hot and disgruntled to find that the boiler was leaking and he begged for more time. Heavy odds were against him. First, he had failed to fit his machine with springs as specified and the boiler was faulty. When a judge told him that his locomotive was overweight, he was really angry and complained that the weighing machine must be inaccurate, not the most winning line from a player to a referee. Anyway, out he went on the line for a run. In no time, the steam-blast was found too fierce and the chimney spurted out showers of burning coke cinders which scared nearby onlookers, and the records showed that coke consumption was consequently far too high. During the trials, officials did all they could to help Hackworth, an able engineer aged 43 who was later to build an impressive career, as did his son. But this was just not Timothy's day. The directors could place no confidence in a locomotive of such poor quality for their new line and *Sans Pareil* had to be withdrawn from the competition. Exit another locomotive.

Timothy Burstall's *Perseverance* persevered into trouble even before it reached Rainhill for, on the way there from Liverpool, the road waggon conveying the machine overturned with dire results; this was a risk all the contestants took. When repaired it managed to run on the track for a short distance at five or six miles an hour, but it was still faulty. After watching the performances of the other locomotives, an unhappy Burstall and his friends withdrew. Exit the third locomotive.

Now it was the turn of the *Rocket*, the nineteenth locomotive the Stephensons had built in their Newcastle factory. Before the official tests, it had paraded in short preliminary canters but was not very popular with the spectators; it seemed to have too many external working parts; and though it emitted little smoke and sibilant steam, it was noisy and from its tall white chimney it scattered a profusion of red hot cinders from which onlookers shrank, and which confirmed previous fears of track-side fires.

In these unofficial displays, the canny Stephensons made no attempt to haul heavy loads, holding their fire for the big moments. However, on one such run, the locomotive hauled a carriage containing about thirty people; and according to Smiles, George Stephenson "ran them along the line at the rate of from twenty-four to thirty miles an hour, much to their gratification and amazement." He was hoping also for the gratification of those directors who supported the locomotive, including Charles Lawrence, Joseph Sandars and his partner Henry Booth. But he was much aware that director James Cropper was dead against him.

The judges ordered the *Rocket* to be out at eight o'clock the next morning, and on 8th October the machine was ready for the trials in accordance with the directors' stipulations. Huge crowds of spectators were already gathering. An anxious moment faced Robert as his locomotive went on the weighing machine; the judges found it to be two cwt heavier than the weight he had declared, but fortunately it was well under the maximum allowed in the conditions. From cold, steam was raised to 50 lb per square inch in just under an hour. Two waggons loaded with stone were hitched to the locomotive to make a total load, which included the fuel tender, of nearly thirteen tons. To record running and terminal times, John Rastrick took up his position at the Liverpool end of the trials section, and Nicholas Wood at the Manchester end. John Kennedy, the third judge, took little part in the proceedings.

Shooting under the Rainhill Skew Bridge, on that first run the distance of a mile and a half was covered in six and a quarter minutes, a speed that was maintained on several other runs there and back. In the absence of positive confirmation, it can be assumed that in the locomotive team with George and Robert were George's younger brother Robert, and young Robert M'Cree, all rather confusing. M'Cree's father had been killed in an accident at Killingworth Colliery in 1812 and George Stephenson had been appointed in his place as enginewright, a turning point in George's career. Whatever the shared duties at the trials, George Stephenson was the driver and M'Cree the fireman.

On the tenth eastward run, the distance was covered in 4 minutes and 12 seconds. Precious seconds were saved at the end of each run as the Stephensons, in 'pitwork fashion', bucketed gallons of water into the water butt on the tender, oiled moving parts and greased the cylinders. On the return runs, the locomotive pushed the waggons, for there were no means of shunting the locomotive to the front, and these journeys were taken with more caution. Back and forth they ran and things were going well. One can fairly feel the excitement of George Stephenson as he approached the western post for the last time, with success in sight. He would be keeping an eye on the long mercurial steam pressure gauge beside the chimney, note that it was holding steady at the 50-lb mark, then give the *Rocket* full regulator. His long battle for the locomotive was almost won. He would show the sceptics, those superior gentry from London who now watched from the grandstand with their fine ladies. What new power he now commanded! Flying a stream of steam from the tall white chimney, the *Rocket* thundered past the grandstand and away to the eastward post. Nicholas Wood must have looked at his watch and noted – 3 minutes and 44 seconds, equal to a speed of twenty-nine miles an hour, a dramatic and historical performance which put all the other contenders in the shade.

Shouts and cheers and clapping from the crowds must have been music to his ears and he would feel that the struggle had been worth the effort. As the *Rocket* proudly chuffed along towards the grandstand, James Cropper, the director who had bullied Stephenson to get on with the railway construction and had campaigned for stationary engines, commented, "Now has George Stephenson delivered himself."

What a dazzling spectacle it all was for the peasantry and gentry alike who never before had seen anything faster than a horse. At nearly thirty miles an hour, the risk for the Stephensons was incalculable. A fractured rail or a broken wheel, a jammed piston or even a boiler explosion, all of which happened frequently, could well have ended in disaster and death. What iron men they were! The conditions of the trials demanded a speed of ten miles an hour in a total of seventy miles of running; the *Rocket* had averaged fourteen with occasional spurts much faster. For the Stephensons it was a triumph;

with consummate ease, they had more than fulfilled the conditions, and convincingly clinched their case.

During the trials period, the judges did all they could to help both Hackworth and Braithwaite and Ericsson. In a further run for the *Novelty*, the joints on the feed pump piping to the boiler failed, "the water flying in all directions". *Sans Pareil* made a few more runs despite boiler faults, then suddenly, in full view of the grandstand, Hackworth's darling disappeared in a great cloud of steam; the fusible plug, which is the final safety device against a boiler explosion, melted because the water level had fallen too low. For a locomotive man, a blown fusible plug is just about the most humiliating experience. Alas for poor Timothy, his beloved locomotive had to be pushed by a crowd of willing hands to the blacksmith's shop at the end of the course.

Of the four contenders in the great Rainhill Trials, three were virtual failures, while the *Rocket* covered herself with glory. Her victory, far from marginal, was masterly, and the Stephenson contingent could be forgiven if they quaffed more than their usual quantity of the local brew.

Would it not be titillating to the intellect to speculate on the historical significance of the *Rocket* being absent from the trials? Those directors who favoured stationary engines with ropes and pulleys would have had their way and the development of locomotive railways throughout the world might well have been delayed for several more vital years. One anxiety for the directors had been – could a locomotive haul a train of loaded waggons up the two heavy gradients, each a mile and a half long on either side of the Rainhill Level? Henry Booth tells us, "The *Rocket* frequently ascended the Whiston inclined plane, with a carriage holding twenty to thirty passengers, at a speed of fifteen to eighteen miles an hour; and the ease and regularity with which this was effected produced a general and confident impression. . . ." Onlookers were "dazzled and gratified with the spectacle . . . moving up the plane at a speed hitherto not attained by the swiftest means".

Booth again: these trials "constituted a new epoch in the progress of mechanical science, as relating to locomotives. The most sanguine advocates of travelling engines had not anticipated a speed of more than ten to twelve miles an hour. It was altogether a new spectacle to behold a carriage crowded with a company, attached to a self-moving machine, and whirled along at the speed of thirty miles per hour." With a stake in the winner, he was entitled to be lyrical.

Though George Stephenson had been inarticulate in Parliament, he could now forget about the clever-clever Mr Alderson, the opposing counsel, for he had articulated in the way he knew best – a practical and convincing demonstration. Bearing in mind his long experience and the infinite devotion with which his son Robert and the Newcastle mechanics had built the winning locomotive, the *Rocket* shot to its unrivalled success largely because of the efficiency of its two outstanding features – steam-blast and the multi-tube boiler, two principles that still remain in steam.

Voluminous reports were produced by the judges; copies of John Rastrick's time records can still be seen in the Science Museum in London. Of the *Rocket* the judges wrote: "We wish to call the particular attention of the Directors to the remarkably short time in which the last Eastward trip of one and a half mile was performed . . . as demonstrating in a very eminent degree the practicability of attaining a very high velocity even with a load of considerable weight attached to the engine."

For Rastrick, formerly advocating fixed engines, the trials presented a salutary lesson; but he was sufficiently wise to make good use of it, and at age 49 he was well on the way to a distinguished engineering career.

On a special occasion, the directors awarded the cash prize of £500 jointly to the Stephensons and Henry Booth, and the company became the new owners of the *Rocket*; its success had driven from the intellectual battlefield all unreasonable opposition.

It is fortunate that today, after a century and a half of railways, such a rich variety of eye-witness accounts of the Rainhill Trials, and indeed about the entire railway project, has survived, evidence that the contemporary personages realised fully that they were living in the presence of history. An irresistible account comes from the pen of young John Dixon, who had come so close to death in the filthy mire at Chat Moss, a scribe of numerous letters and reports dictated by the master, and who was in the thick of things. It is written to his brother in Darlington:

"Dear James,
We have finished the grand experiment on the Engines and G. S. or R. S. has come off triumphant and of course will take hold of the £500 so liberally offered by the Company: none of the others being able to come near them. The *Rocket* is by far the best Engine I have seen for Blood and Bone united. . . .

"Timothy [Hackworth] has been very sadly out of temper ever since he came, for he has been grobbing on day and night and nothing our men did for him was right, we could not please him with the Tender or anything; he openly accused all G.S.'s people of conspiring to hinder him of which I do believe them innocent, however he got many trials but never got half of his 70 miles done without stopping. He burns double the quantity of coke that the *Rocket* does and mumbles and roars and rolls about like an empty

Beer Butt on a rough Pavement and moreover weighs above his
4½ tons consequently should have had six wheels and as for
being on Springs I must confess I cannot find them out. . . . She
is very ugly and the Boiler runs out very much, he had to feed her
with more Meal and Malt Sprouts than would fatten a pig. . . ."

Hackworth and his team made no secret of their dissatisfaction.
Various unjustifiable excuses were advanced and the weighbridge
which he complained about was proved to be accurate. Some of his
supporters sourly hinted that as both the railway company's principal
engineer and its treasurer were involved with the *Rocket*, only one
result could be expected. Analysis of the trials, the probity of the
three judges and the need for the directors to find the best locomotive
for the work, prove the innuendos unfounded.

After describing the faults of the *Novelty*, Dixon pictures the
machine, "all covered with Copper, like a new Tea Urn all which
tended to give her a very Parlour like appearance. . . . Burstall upset
his [*Perseverance*] in bringing from L'pool to Rainhill and spent a
week in pretending to Remedy the injuries whereas he altered and
amended some part every day. . . ." He teases about Burstall's locomotive travelling at a "full six miles an hour creaking away like an old
Wickerwork pair of Panniers on a cantering Cuddy Ass. Vox Populi
was in favour of London [*Novelty*] from appearances but we showed
them the way to do it for Messrs Rastrig [*sic*] & Walker in their report
as to Fixed and permt. Engines stated that the whole power of the
Loco. Engines would be absorbed in taking their own bodies up the
Rainhill Incline' of 1 in 96 consequently they could take no load.

"Now the first thing old George did was to bring a Coach with
about twenty people up at a gallop and every day since has run up and
down to let them see what they could do up such an ascent and has
taken forty folks up at twenty miles an hour."

This was only the beginning of an illustrious life awaiting the
Rocket. For some years it was to work on the Liverpool & Manchester
Railway where it had its mechanical troubles. Before parting with it,
the directors, appreciating its importance, had "a good drawing made
of it". In 1837, it was sold to James Thompson of Carlisle and it
worked for three years at Kirkhouse Colliery. It also did service on
the Midgeholme Railway where, according to Smiles, it travelled four
miles reaching over fifty miles an hour.

Thousands of visitors were to see it in 1851 at the Great Exhibition
of Britain's industrial might at Crystal Palace in London. Before
display, it was overhauled in the Stephenson Works at Newcastle.

Probably more models, both scale and full size, have been made of
the *Rocket* than of any other locomotive and it is safely enshrined as
the most celebrated steam locomotive in history. The original, which

was sent to South Kensington in 1862, and now somewhat sad and naked, has been seen by countless millions of people from all over the world, resting proudly in the Science Museum in London. Nearby is Timothy Hackworth's *Sans Pareil*, both tiny locomotives overshadowed, but not upstaged, by the Great Western Railway's giant *Caerphilly Castle* adorned in its sparkling green livery of 1923, and itself, through Daniel Gooch and his GWR successors, virtually a direct descendant from the *Rocket* family.

Success at the Rainhill Trials brought some happy features. Though the company's share prices hardly rocketed, they rose quickly by about 10 per cent. And within a month, the Stephensons received an order from the directors for four more locomotives which were later named *Meteor, Comet, Dart*, and *Arrow*. Delivery was required – just imagine it! – within three months. Life was simpler then. Three were delivered on time in January 1830 and Dart a month later.

Father and son were made. Foes became friends, as one chronicler expresses it: "Very different now was the tone of those directors who had distinguished themselves by the persistency of their opposition to George Stephenson's plans. Coolness gave way to eulogy, and hostility to unbounded offers of friendship."

Only ten days after the trials ended, the first known published illustration of the *Rocket* appeared in the *Mechanics Magazine*; five weeks later another appeared, about which it was said that some trivial inaccuracies had been corrected. Both were probably drawn by Charles Vignoles who executed a number of drawings of the Liverpool & Manchester Railway.

Other publications waxed eloquent in their prognostications about the locomotive puffing away into the Industrial Revolution; few perhaps realised then how it would monopolise the stage in the world's transport systems for well over a century, but all appreciated its immediate impact. One of them, the *Scotsman* published in Edinburgh and currently flourishing in the Thomson Organisation, said, "The experiments at Liverpool have established principles which will give a greater impulse to civilisation than it has ever received from any single cause since the Press first opened the gates of knowledge to the human species at large." That the superiority of the steam locomotive over every other form of inland transport had at last been demonstrated beyond doubt was generally accepted. A new beginning was in sight, and newspaper reporters closeted in their paper-strewn dens lit by candles, oil or even gas, were keeping their goose quills poised for the next dramatic episode in the railway saga.

CHAPTER 5

Completing and Testing the Railway

At last, the great controversy about the merits of the steam locomotive had been settled for a long time to come and a whole new world of feverish activity burst forth. Now that the company's shares were rising, other railway promoters up and down Britain began to prepare for their Parliamentary Bills. Stephenson was urged by his masters to complete the railway with all speed, with the hope that the line could be ready for its public opening in July 1830. Meanwhile, plenty of troubles were brewing in the pot. One good locomotive would be of little use if the railway was to run many trains every day, carrying goods and passengers, and the four new locomotives being built in the Newcastle Works must be ready in good time. They were to be in the style of the *Rocket* but improved in design and heavier at nearly six tons for more speed and power. This order was to be the first of many more from different parts of Britain and overseas, and it brought the Newcastle factory in Forth Street alive with hammers and chisels, screwdrivers and hoisting equipment, and the employment of more labourers and mechanics. Both the Stephensons realised that this was the turning point in their promising careers.

Yet in the immediate future they faced more threats. James Cropper, Stephenson's *bête noire*, the man he had routed on the choice of power, still showed bitter enmity to father and son, and lost no opportunity to bring them down a peg or two. As a director, he seemed to allow his personal vendetta to colour his judgement. For example, he encouraged Sir Goldsworthy Gurney, a carriage builder, to build locomotives for the Liverpool & Manchester. Negotiations went on, but nothing materialised. Cropper had also championed Braithwaite & Ericsson and had later persuaded the board to order two of their locomotives in the *Novelty* design. What a shocking aberration of judgement this proved, for they failed abjectly and cost far more than the Stephenson locomotives.

How difficult it is now to analyse Cropper's motives and how puzzling to understand another anti-Stephenson tactic. On the grounds that advice about the whole enterprise should be sought from an independent civil engineer, Cropper was the instigator of the board's far from unanimous decision to engage William Chapman of Durham to examine and report on the state of the works. Certainly Chapman was an engineer of standing and an associate of John Buddle, known on the Tyne as the 'King of the Coal Trade'. As early as 1812, Chapman had experimented with steam locomotives and had come up with the brilliant idea of mounting his machine on two separate bogies, each with four wheels, to spread the axle loadings and to reduce damage to primitive track; this was the parent of articulated locomotives which later became standard practice. Though Chapman's locomotives were not successful, he remains on the record as a pioneer.

Booth, Sandars and other directors must have known how furious Stephenson would be at the very thought of being supervised – by anybody! Interference he would not brook. All were soon to know, for he committed his contentions to paper in a rarely published letter penned by an assistant; extracts reveal his uncompromising character and are typical of his stormy passage. He acknowledged that he had not objected to Chapman's appointment because he understood from the board that it involved only reporting progress, but without interference. "Whatever might be my private opinions of the utility of this officer . . ." his intentions had "extended to things which I trust you will consider strictly within my department." He claimed that Chapman had sacked a man simply because he could not answer him satisfactorily, questions which the man might not understand anyway. "I cannot help but feel some reluctance to bringing Engine-men with their families from the North, who alone are capable of managing this class of engine . . . if they are to be interfered with by an individual unacquainted with the nature of the work."

He criticised Chapman also for directing one of his assistants concerning the Newton embankment which Stephenson had only recently visited. "It is direct interference with my duty and by a person entirely ignorant of Engineering; nor can he be acquainted, when he views a piece of work on the line, what plans I intend adopting, why I am doing it, or what I intend to do afterwards."

Stephenson referred to the damage Chapman had already inflicted on him by trying to talk the Bolton & Leigh Railway out of using his *Lancashire Witch* and that this had resulted in the promoters treating him in a "most unpleasant manner. I endeavoured by repeated journeys to Bolton to convince him that he was wrong, without success. Experience I hope by this time has accomplished what I then failed in my argument." He was certainly right on this point.

Warming up, he refers to the doubts and suspicions that had been thrown at him in the building of the Liverpool & Manchester Railway. "I have been accused of jealousy . . . instead of jealousy operating, I confidently state that I have been only influenced by a disinterested zeal for the complete success of your work and a laudable desire to support and establish my own credit."

Then the crunch questions: "May I now ask if I have supported your interests or not? Has Mr Brandreth's carriage answered? [the horse *Cycloped*] Was not Walker & Rastrick's report wrong? [recommending stationary engines] Has the *Novelty* answered your expectations? Have not the *Lancashire Witch* and the *Rocket* performed more than I stated? These facts make me bold, but they also stimulate me to still further improvement. But I cannot believe that you will permit me to be thwarted in my proceedings by individuals who neither understand the work nor feel the interest which attaches me to this railway. Allow me therefore to ask if you intend Mr C. to continue on the works." Exit Mr Chapman. What happened in the boardroom on receiving this powerful missive is not recorded; but among his fellows, director and substantial shareholder, James Cropper, ought to have blushed. Stephenson, of course, remained in the saddle.

Throughout the world of English engineering, strong jealousy and antagonism assailed the Northumbrian engineer; in the eyes of the sophisticated who had earned justifiable engineering reputations – canals, bridges, roads, ports, harbours – in fact, the best civil engineers in the world in these thrusting days of the Industrial Revolution, here was a project of such vast potential that the man rising to the top could not fail to emerge as a figure of great wealth and prestige. Yet, in charge, they saw a mere colliery worker, uneducated, stubborn, coarse of speech, crude of dress, ignorant of polite society and a laughing stock in Parliament, who stood squarely in their way. No wonder that jealousy drove them to criticism and ridicule. Stephenson's manners provoked aggravation and animosity. Fundamentally, he was a simple man, honourable, and a law unto his native self. Reading his letter concerning Chapman, no-one could fail to admire his dogged and spirited courage and his unshakable determination. One burden he continued to bear was the vacillation of the directors as they lent an anxious ear to this adviser or that, Henry Booth, Joseph Sandars and a few others excepted.

Stephenson hated boardroom rows; he just wanted to get on with the job. His faithful assistant Thomas Gooch noted that his master, normally cheerful and kind-hearted, grew increasingly irritable and impatient, the fun only occasionally shining through. Starting early in the morning, he would take leave of his wife Elizabeth at their home in Upper Parliament Street in Liverpool, get astride his pony Bobby, and tour the line. In the evening, tired and mud-spattered, he would be in the company's office in Clayton Square with Gooch to study drawings, make rough sketches and review progress. Gooch lodged with the Stephensons and after supper in candle light there was more paper work to tackle. Sometimes they would be joined by the sectional engineers Locke, Dixon and others. These young men were to learn directly from the doyen himself, and acquire valuable knowledge for their future careers. Did they suspect how privileged they were? Many observers questioned whether Stephenson, lacking in formal training and struggling along with a band of 'young amateurs' who learnt as they went on, could have possibly coped with such a range of formidable engineering works; no civil engineer in Britain had ever attempted a construction of such magnitude. Mistakes were frequent: some serious, others mere peccadilloes; the marvel is that the railway was ever built at all. Meanwhile, day by day, sweating, swearing navvies and contractors could see the end of their labours; and when problems arose, that huge white-haired figure was at hand to decide and encourage.

At a late stage, mile and quarter-mile posts were erected, useful markers for drivers to estimate their speeds, for identifying proximate locations for engineering works, and as a basis of charges and for administration. Mile posts on all lines can still be spotted by a quick eye, even from a fast Inter-City train. Bridges were numbered consecutively.

As the line neared completion, more visitors travelled to see the main installations, which the Company encouraged. The *Liverpool Mercury* had noted in 1829: "This noble undertaking will always be an object of interest and curiosity, as well as a striking monument to the skill and enterprise of the projectors and proprietors."

Various locomotives made trial runs on completed sections of the permanent way, including the Stephenson *Lancashire Witch* and the *Rocket*, largely to locate and rectify mechanical and track faults. At the same time, drivers and other railway servants became familiar with moving trains, and the public slowly acclimatised to the railway in general, with the hopes that their fancied fears would be allayed.

Exactly ten days after the Rainhill Trials had ended, Robert Stephenson drove the *Rocket* hauling loads of twenty tons at speeds of up to twenty miles an hour, well within its capabilities. In a number of varying tests five days later, a load of forty tons was pulled, maintaining fourteen miles an hour and managing well the two steep gradients.

Parties of passengers were occasionally carried along short completed sections. On 14th November 1829, Thomas Creevey MP, that precocious parliamentarian and sycophant of Lord Sefton, who had ranted so bitterly in the House about the "Steam locomotive monster", took a ride. In a special coach behind the *Rocket*, he was joined by Lady Wilton and other friends. This prolific writer and diarist, that very day while the smell of the locomotive and the rattle of the coach were fresh in his memory, fired off a crepitation to his stepdaughter, Miss Elizabeth Ord, his enthusiasm tempered by terror: "Today we have had a *lark* of a very high order. I had the satisfaction, for I can't call it a *pleasure*, of taking a trip of five miles in it, and we did it in just a quarter of an hour – that is, twenty miles an hour. As accuracy upon this subject was my great object, I held my watch in my hand at starting, and all the time; and as it has a second hand, I know I could not be deceived. . . . But observe, during these five miles, the machine was occasionally made to put out or *go it*; and then we went at the rate of twenty-three miles an hour, and just with the same ease as to motion or absence of friction as the other reduced pace.

"But the quickest motion is to me *frightful*; it is really like flying, and it is impossible to divest yourself of the notion of instant death to all upon the least accident happening. It gave me a headache which has not left me yet. Sefton is convinced that some damnable thing must come of it; but he and I seem more struck with such apprehension than others. . . ." Unknown then to Creevey, the *Rocket* itself was doomed soon to be a killer.

He continued in a complaining vein that sparks spewed from the locomotive and burned one's cheek, another's gown and another's silk pelisse (long garment). He was glad to have made the trip, but was sure that this first was to be also his last.

Several trips, challenging to Stephenson, took place during December 1829. With the support of James Cropper and others, the dainty *Novelty* tried her paces. On the 16th, by which time Braithwaite and Ericsson had overhauled the machine, it ran light (alone) on the Rainhill section to average twenty-two miles an hour, and a week later hauled thirty-one tons at about twelve miles an hour: a fair performance but not matching the winner.

Question marks still lurked around Chat Moss. The directors were anxious to dispel the horrifying public fear that a train of passengers might sink out of sight in the deep bog. Stephenson harboured no such fears, and on 28th December, the *Rocket*, pulling several carriages conveying about forty passengers, crossed the Moss in seventeen minutes to average seventeen miles an hour. On the return journey, the train reached the amazing speed of thirty miles an hour on this 'floating railway'. Some passengers found the ride smoother than on firm ground.

John Moss, deputy chairman of the company, took a special interest in the trial trips and on 14th December 1829 he wrote to William Huskisson MP, commenting that their success "has so opened the eyes of the canal people, the landowners and public that almost everyone is desirous to get in a rail-road." A tiny shadow of the yet distant madness in new railway schemes was presaged.

Trial runs were regularly reported in the newspapers. One writer, perhaps a little over-excited, guaranteed that water in a wine glass placed on the tailboard of a train would not spill and that passengers would be able to read and write while travelling "as readily as in their arm-chairs at home". A Dr Chalmers published his assurance that even at speeds of thirty-five miles an hour there would be no cause for alarm, or even inconvenience, and that the eyes would not be disturbed while viewing the passing scenery. Such glowing reports could not have made happy reading for the seething Robert Bradshaw and other canal leaders of his ilk.

By early June 1830, the sections of the railway were all connected to make a long-awaited through line between Liverpool and Manchester. Some structures were still being finished and various directors journeyed along the route, stopping to inspect major works.

A full dress journey was made on 14th June, ending just short of Manchester. A train of coaches carrying directors and "about thirty other gentlemen" and seven waggons of stone made a load of thirty-nine tons; heading the train was Stephenson's new locomotive the *Arrow* with the master himself at the controls.

In Manchester, the party visited the home of a friend and there and then a resolution was passed: "That the directors cannot allow this opportunity to pass, without expressing their strong sense of the great skill and unwearied energy displayed by their engineer, Mr George Stephenson, which have so far brought this great national work to a successful termination, and which promises to be followed by results so beneficial to the country at large, and to the proprietors of this concern." What more could a man ask of his bosses?

Excluding stops for fuel and oiling, the journey had taken about two hours. A rather elated Stephenson was determined to show his paces on the return run to Edge Hill, Liverpool, with only two carriages. Across Chat Moss, the little train reached twenty-seven miles an hour, covering the complete journey in running time of just over an hour and a half plus service stops of twelve minutes. What a great day it had been for the Northumbrian pit-man and what an inventory of incredible work he and his team of 'young amateurs' had accomplished in just four years.

Twelve days later, King George IV died, casting a shadow of mourning over the élite of England; he was succeeded by King William IV, the Prime Minister being that great national hero, the Duke of Wellington, who had brought such glory to the country by defeating the French Emperor Napoleon at the Battle of Waterloo in 1815.

Such was the confidence of the railway directors that they fixed the official opening day for the new line for Wednesday, 15th September. In preparation – they wanted no failures – a full rehearsal was held on 21st August in which three trains ran from Liverpool to Manchester and back; they were pulled by three Stephenson locomotives – *Rocket, Arrow* and *Phoenix*. Over a hundred ladies and gentlemen were much impressed by the novel performance and crowds of on-lookers gathered at the terminals. Among the guest passengers were several noble earls, Members of Parliament and promoters of railways planned for the Sheffield and Birmingham areas. Similar trial services were run on 28th August and 4th September, by which time the directors and engineers felt fully confident for the opening day.

There had to be the first lady to travel on the footplate of a Stephenson locomotive, and the distinction fell to a bright young light from English drama, not quite twenty-one, who happened to be playing at a Liverpool theatre. Fanny Kemble (1809–93), *diva* of Shakespearian readings, was distinguished in other ways; a niece of Mrs Sarah Siddons, she became one of the most prominent actresses of the nineteenth century in England, Europe and America. In later years, she married a wealthy American named Butler, and while in Georgia in the Deep South she must have met obduracy from one side and encomium from the other by campaigning relentlessly for the emancipation of slaves, which Abraham Lincoln finally announced in 1863.

During a long and colourful life, Fanny's facile and prolific pen filled several volumes of reminiscences. In 1829, she had made her debut as Juliet at Covent Garden in London, and while on tour with her actor father to Dublin, Birmingham, Manchester and Liverpool in 1830 she was introduced to the directors of the railway. A lady of strong Christian convictions, with much sympathy for the suffering poor, she often visited factories; and in Liverpool her admiration was reserved for the workmen and engineers who had "created this marvel of transportation".

On 26th August 1830, the day after her exciting ride, she wrote vividly from Liverpool to a friend about her fifteen-mile run to Sankey Viaduct, part-way on the locomotive with George Stephenson. In an astonishingly detailed and accurate description of his new locomotive *Northumbrian*, she reveals a remarkable conception of the mechanics of a machine as novel to the contemporary layman as the first moon rocket was in recent times. Fanny, capable horsewoman and experienced traveller by stage coach and private carriage, punctuates her flowery prose with equestrian metaphor and simile.

"My dear H.," she begins, "A common sheet of paper is enough for love, but a foolscap extra can alone contain a railroad and my ecstasies. . . . We were introduced to the little engine which was to drag us along the rails. She (for they make these curious little fire-horses all mares) consisted of a boiler, a stove, a small platform, a bench, and behind the bench a barrel containing enough water to prevent her being thirsty for fifteen miles. She goes on two wheels, which are her feet, and are moved by bright steel legs called pistons; these are propelled by steam, and in proportion as more steam is applied to the upper extremities (the hip-joints, I suppose) of these pistons, the faster they move the wheels; and when it is desirable to diminish the speed, the steam, which unless suffered to escape would burst the boiler, evaporates through a safety valve into the air.

"The reins, bit, and bridle of this wonderful beast – a small steel handle, which applies or withdraws the steam from its legs or pistons, so that a child might manage it. The coals [it was coke] which are its oats, were under the bench. . . . There is a chimney to the stove, but as they burn coke there is none of the dreadful black smoke which accompanies the progress of a steam-vessel." She also describes the glass pressure-gauge.

"This snorting little animal, which I felt rather inclined to pat, was then harnessed to our carriage, and Mr Stephenson having taken me on the bench of the engine with him, we started at about ten miles an hour. . . .

"You can't imagine how strange it seemed to be journeying on thus, without any visible cause of progress other than the magical machine, with its flying white breath and rhythmical, unvarying pace, between these rocky walls [Olive Mount Cutting], which are already clothed with moss and ferns and grasses; and when I reflected that these great masses of stone had been cut asunder to allow our passage thus far below the surface of the earth, I felt as if no fairy tale was ever half so wonderful as what I saw.

"Bridges were thrown from side to side across the top of these cliffs, and the people looking down upon us from them seemed like pigmies standing in the sky. . . . We then came to a moss or swamp, of considerable extent, on which no human foot could tread without sinking, and yet it bore the road which bore us. This had been the great stumbling block in the minds of the committee of the House of Commons; but Mr Stephenson has succeeded in overcoming it . . . we passed over it at the rate of five and twenty miles an hour, and saw the stagnant swamp water trembling on the surface of the soil on either side of us. At the Sankey Viaduct, Stephenson made me alight and led me down to the bottom of this ravine, over which, in order to keep his road level, he has thrown a magnificent viaduct of nine arches . . . through which we saw the whole of this beautiful little valley. It was lovely and wonderful beyond all words. . . ."

Down in the valley, the powerfully built, white-haired engineer, in his long black tailcoat, must have been bewitched by the candid admiration of the beautiful, slim and brown-haired young actress, he must have felt years younger, a welcome change from the bitter criticism and hostility he had suffered from his opponents.

And so they returned to the *Northumbrian* and its carriage. His elation no doubt prompted him to speed up on the return journey, for it produced from Fanny one of the most delightful descriptions in contemporary literature of the sheer exhilaration of a pace through space "greater than man had ever known before".

"The engine," she continues, "was set off at its utmost speed, 35 miles an hour, swifter than a bird flies. . . . You cannot conceive what the sensation of cutting the air was; the motion is as smooth as possible, too. I could either have read or written – as it was, I stood up, and with bonnet off 'drank the air before me'. . . . When I closed my eyes this sensation of flying was quite delightful and strange beyond description; yet, strange as it was, I had a perfect sense of security, and not the slightest fear . . . this brave little she-dragon flew on. . . ."

She turns her attention to the man of the moment:

"Now for a word or two about the master of all these marvels, with whom I am most horribly in love. He is a man of from fifty to fifty-five [he was forty-nine]; his face is fine, though careworn, and bears an expression of deep thoughtfulness; his mode of explaining his ideas is peculiar and very original, striking, and forcible; and although his accent indicates strongly his north-country birth, his language has not the slightest touch of vulgarity or coarseness. He has certainly turned my head."

Fanny leaves us with an enigma by omitting to say who, if anyone, accompanied or chaperoned her on this notable peregrination.

". . . The railroad will be opened upon the fifteenth of next month. The Duke of Wellington [Prime Minister] is coming down to be present on the occasion, and, I suppose, what with the thousands of spectators and the novelty of the spectacle, there will never have been a scene of more striking interest. . . . The Directors have kindly offered us three places for the opening, which is a great favour, for people are bidding almost anything for a place. . . ."

In full, Fanny's letter is nearly three times longer than the above extracts. But this was not all; other perceptive reporting appears in her 1830 diaries: "All that wonderful history, as much more interesting than a romance as truth is stranger than fiction . . . I heard from his own lips . . . the fascination of that story told by himself . . . and I listened to him with eyes brimful of tears of sympathy and enthusiasm . . . how the 'Parliament Men' had badgered and baffled him with their book-knowledge, and how when at last they thought they had smothered the irrepressible prophesy of his genius in the quaking depths of Chat Moss, he had exclaimed, 'Did ye ever see a boat float on water? I will make my road float upon Chat Moss!' . . . and so the railroad was made, and I took this memorable ride by the side of its maker, and would not have exchanged the honour and pleasure of it for one of the shares in the speculation." One share at par was valued at £100, perhaps £4000 to £6000 today.

CHAPTER 6

The Opening Day

On Wednesday 15th September 1830, as the sky had begun to forget the night and to welcome the new dawn, massive crowds were lining the route and overbridge parapets at strategic points of vantage. This was the official opening day of the new Liverpool & Manchester Railway. Reporters from newspapers and magazines, and other chroniclers, were taking up their positions to record for posterity their own vivid impressions; today, they would find news far more dramatic than expected.

During the final weeks, invitations had been despatched and most accepted. Among them were the Prime Minister (the Duke of Wellington), William Huskisson MP who was President of the Board of Trade and a Cabinet Minister since 1823, Sir Robert Peel the Secretary of State who was to become Prime Minister, and the Borough Reeves (magistrates) of Salford and Manchester. Some brought their wives, one being Mrs Elizabeth Huskisson. Special guests included sanguine shareholders and other Members of Parliament. True to her word, Fanny Kemble was there with her apprehensive mother. Among the religious leaders invited was the Bishop of Lichfield, to start a long line of railway enthusiasts from among the clergy. Present also were foreign diplomats, including Prince Esterhazy, the Austrian Ambassador, all no doubt briefed to report back to their governments. One chronicler reported that the names of the famous were bellowed out by a Liverpool town crier.

Not surprisingly, distinguished engineers joined the entourage – John Rastrick, Nicholas Wood, George Rennie, Charles Vignoles and others. How much of a strain the presence of such eminent personages – only to be matched by a royal occasion – played upon the two pivotal characters, George and Robert Stephenson, can be only conjectured. Surely, among the scrutinous eyes were those of railway opponents who, even at this late stage, might hope for calamity, though not the calamity that was to come.

No public gathering of such magnitude could escape the attentions of enterprising traders, poised to cash in on the act. "Sitting Apartments and Bedrooms" had for days been advertised, with a service of "wines and spirits of the choicest quality". For two days, Manchester and Liverpool had been flooded with people, and by the previous evening many found it impossible to locate somewhere to eat or sleep. Fanny Kemble, with her mother, Lady Wilton and their friends had arrived in Liverpool the night before the official opening and records, "The throng of strangers gathered there for the same purpose made it impossible to obtain a night's lodging for love or money; and glad and thankful we were to put up with a tiny garrett by our old friend, Mr Radley, of the Adelphi [hotel], which many would give twice what we paid to obtain."

One report said, "Liverpool was never so full of strangers. . . . All the inns in the town were crowded to overflowing, and [private] carriages stood in the streets at night, for want of room in the stable yards. . . . Never was there such an assemblage of rank, wealth, beauty, and fashion in this neighbourhood." Grandstands had been erected in Liverpool, Manchester, and in the wilds of Sankey Viaduct, where "abundant refreshments" were offered; near another grandstand by the Sutton incline, services included "wines and spirits, and cold collation".

For the poorer classes of Liverpool in those finger to forelock days, there was the dazzling spectacle of splendid horses and ornate carriages bringing top-hatted gentlemen and their lavishly dressed ladies to their drab town. Setting the scene, the *Albion* described the event which "attracted the greatest number of men of eminence in the political and scientific world that ever assembled together in this town. . . . Precisely at ten o'clock, the Duke of Wellington drove up to the station in the Marquis of Salisbury's carriage, drawn by four horses. . . ."

In the railway yard at Edge Hill just beyond the new railway tunnel, eight trains were assembled, carrying colours to match passengers' special tickets and the flags on the locomotives which would pull them. By half past nine, the eight steaming and panting locomotives, all of them Stephensons', were allocated to their trains and took up positions.

Never before or since has a railway line been worked by such a distinguished array of locomotive drivers, every name now enshrined in history.

Locomotive	Flag	Driver
Northumbrian	lilac	George Stephenson
Phoenix	green	Robert Stephenson (George's son, aged 27)
North Star	yellow	Robert Stephenson (George's younger brother)
Rocket	light blue	Joseph Locke (aged 25)
Comet	deep red	William Allcard
Arrow	pink	Frederick Swanwick
Meteor	brown	Antony Harding
Dart	purple	Thomas L. Gooch

In this truly family assembly, the five named last were all George's young acolytes serving in various capacities, and now rarin' to go. Naturally the principal engineer should be the star driver for the Duke of Wellington's special train of three carriages. The two locomotives ordered months ago at the behest of James Cropper from Braithwaite and Ericsson of *Novelty* fame, failed to arrive, otherwise many more passengers could have been carried. Unlike some of his fellow directors, Cropper evinced no joy from the news.

One eyewitness reported that thirty-two carriages of every conceivable style were available, "decorated with silken streamers and all the paraphernalia of a joyousness and delight". They had a capacity of well over seven hundred people. Naturally, no carriage was permitted to upstage that of Wellington. Of this ornate vehicle, a contemporary account tells us:

"This carriage was truly magnificent; its appearance was imposing, and its workmanship was perfect and tasteful; superb Grecian scrolls and balustrades, richly gilt, supported a handrail running round the carriage, while ascending from it were gilded pillars, maintaining a canopy of 24 feet long, so contrived as to be lowered at pleasure; the drapery was of rich crimson cloth, and the whole was surmounted by the Ducal coronet; the interior had an ottoman seat, and the floor was 32 feet long by 8 feet wide, running upon eight large iron wheels." It was described by the *Morning Post* (which was absorbed in the *Daily Telegraph* in 1937) as "one of the largest and one of the most splendid ever built".

Assembly, greetings and other preliminaries ticked the minutes away. Wellington made a brief opening speech, and in his response, Charles Lawrence, chairman of the Railway Company, said: "In time to come, this day would be remembered for the spiritual as well as the physical union which was affected between the sister towns of Liverpool and Manchester."

As Wellington had entered the railway yard, he was greeted by clapping and cheering and one of the military bands present struck up, "See the conquering hero comes!" He and his private guests climbed into the ducal carriage. To signal the splendid cavalcade away, at twenty minutes to eleven a cannon was fired. Then, to the horror of the onlookers, a piece of wadding from the explosive round struck a labourer in the face and the poor fellow lost an eye. Sad though the incident was, the railway show must go on, leaving the injured man in the care of his comforters.

So that Wellington's carriage and occupants might be seen from the other trains, his train departed on the southerly line and the rest on the northerly; by running trains on the two parallel lines in the same direction at the same time, the organisers, lacking operating experience, created an additional accident risk. However, by the use of both lines in this way, George Stephenson was able to stop Wellington's train for viewing special attractions on the route without delaying those trains on the other line.

Headed by *Northumbrian,* Stephenson's train consisted of three carriages; the first contained a military band, the second the Duke of Wellington and his personal guests, and the third the railway directors and friends. The other trains consisted of three, four and five carriages. Stephenson notched up another 'first', as driver for the first British Prime Minister to travel on a public railway.

On the journey of about seventeen miles to Parkside, speeds ranged up to about twenty-five miles an hour; the Prime Minister was clearly impressed by first one piece of engineering and then another, especially the Sankey Viaduct, for he was heard to exclaim, "Stupendous!" and "Magnificent!" Boats and banks of the Sankey were alive with upturned faces.

Along the route, large crowds cheered the cavalcade and gazed agog at the most spectacular sight that had ever met their rural eyes. Fanny Kemble, who was travelling in a carriage next to the Duke's, wrote: "Enormous masses of densely packed people lined the road, shouting and waving hats and handkerchiefs as we flew by them. What with the sight and sound of these cheering multitudes and the tremendous velocity with which we were borne past them, my spirits rose to the true champagne height, and I never enjoyed anything so much as the first hour of our progress.

"I had been unluckily separated from my mother . . . but [by] an exchange of seats which she was enabled to make, she rejoined me when I was at the height of my ecstasy, which was considerably damped by finding that she was frightened to death, and intent upon nothing but devising means of escaping from a situation which appeared to her to threaten with instant annihilation of herself and all her travelling companions."

A lengthy eye-witness account, published soon after the official opening day, comes from the pen of James Scott Walker (1793–1850), who was to live through the Railway Mania and to survive George Stephenson by two years. Writer, traveller, pen-friend of Sir Walter Scott and personally acquainted with the two Stephensons, he had been entranced to watch at close quarters the railway being built, a privilege he cherished.

"The passenger," he writes, "having seated himself in one of the Rail-way coaches, chaises, cars, barouches, or 'indescribables', will be whirled away. . . ." He will "recover, with a glow of animation which will inspire him with confidence to prosecute the journey he has commenced. . . . He may be puzzled by the puissance of the fire and steam, of the present application Euclid never dreamt in his philosophy . . . his machine, and many others are yoked to a charger snorting steam and fire . . . the passengers all being seated, the engineer opens the valves, the hissing of the steam is suppressed. The engine moves, and is heard as if to pant, not from exhaustion, but impatience of restraint, the blazing cinders falling behind it, and the train of carriages are dragged along with a sudden and agreeable velocity, becoming, as it were, the tail of a comet.

"The spectators are soon left behind, the Turkish archway is passed, and the first view is obtained of the extent of the open Railway." He describes the railway as "the greatest national triumph of the age . . . which for speed, elegance, and economy is altogether novel and astonishing".

Assuming a pontifical stance appropriate to the studious historian, he sounds a prophetic note: "Never has the dominion of mind more fully exhibited its sovereignty over the world of matter than in this instance, and the commotion furnishes an example of successful enterprise which will not only give rise to similar undertakings in other parts of the country, but, it is not visionary to assume, may beneficially influence the future destinies of mankind throughout the civilised world." Few prophets live to see the day; happily for James Scott Walker, he was one of the few.

His feelings were not exactly shared by the Duke of Wellington clattering and chuffing along on this opening day. Though he had lent his Prime Ministerial presence at the ceremony, his reservations were that the new line might supplement, but not supplant, the canal system. He could not believe that sensible people would risk being whirled along at the terrifying speed of twenty miles an hour, except as an occasional novelty. Appropriate enough, perhaps, in Lancashire, but he saw no real future for railways elsewhere in the realm. Although in later years the Duke was to be won over, his characteristic antipathy to railways was once expressed publicly: "They encourage the lower classes to travel about," a splendidly Wellingtonian pronouncement! His fears of the railway were soon to be shockingly confirmed.

As arranged in advance, after about one hour's run all trains stopped just over half way along the route at Parkside to take fuel and water and to oil and grease the machinery; and strict verbal and written instructions had been given to all passengers not on any account to leave their carriages.

While Stephenson on the *Northumbrian* halted the Duke's train at Parkside, trains on the adjacent parallel line passed slowly along in review by the Duke and his party. When the other line was temporarily clear, William Huskisson MP and several friends disobeyed orders and foolishly alighted from the Duke's carriage to stretch their cramped limbs, then stood between the two lines. He talked with his friend William Holmes MP who had helped him to get the Railway Bill through Parliament. Also chatting with them were Lord Wilton, Count Batthyany and Count Matuscewitz.

Recently, relations between Huskisson and the Prime Minister had been strained and the moment seemed propitious for patching things up. As the Duke leaned from his carriage door, Huskisson, still standing between the two lines, approached him to shake hands and chat.

At that very moment, loud shouting through a speaking-trumpet warned that the *Rocket* was approaching, "Get in! Get in!" Seeing the imminent danger, Wellington called out, "Huskisson, for God's sake get to your place!"

People scrambled madly in all directions, some with great presence of mind pressing themselves against the side of the carriage. In the panic, Huskisson, hampered by a gammy leg and a damaged arm, was now flurried and confused. He struggled desperately to climb back into the Duke's carriage, missed his footing and fell back on the track in the path of the oncoming *Rocket*.

What a frightful moment for young Joseph Locke aboard the footplate, probably with Robert M'Cree, on a day that should have been the highlight of his career. He must have helped feverishly and hopelessly with the primitive brakes, contending with the momentum of the unbraked carriages. His train failed to stop in time and the locomotive and carriages ran over Huskisson's leg, fracturing the thigh and lower limb "in a most dreadful manner". As frantic helpers hurried towards the badly bleeding man, his first words, according to the *Gentleman's Magazine* a few weeks later, were, "I have met my death. God forgive me!"

In the coach behind the Duke's, Fanny Kemble did not actually see the accident, but later made notes of the eye-witness account from her friend Lady Wilton who was only a few yards away: "Lord Wilton saved his [own] life only by rushing behind the Duke's coach. Lady Wilton said she distinctly heard the crushing of the bone . . . and poor Mrs Huskisson's shriek. . . . Lord Wilton was the first to raise the poor sufferer, and calling on his surgical skill, which is considerable, he tied up the severed artery, and for a time, at least, prevented death by loss of blood."

Notably cool in a crisis, George Stephenson quickly took command of the horrendous situation. Now, he was impelled not by the admiring eyes of a pretty young actress but by the groans of an elderly dying man. Lord Wilton, Holmes and Mr Parkes a solicitor from Birmingham helped the failing patient into one of the carriages, presumably the leading one of the three, which had conveyed the military band. Stephenson then climbed on to the footplate of the *Northumbrian,* and with one carriage including Wilton and two doctors comforting the victim, raced off towards Eccles, four miles short of Manchester. Smiles records that it reached thirty-six miles an hour: "This incredible speed burst upon the world with the effect of a new and unlooked-for phenomenon", a speed which, a few years ago, would have been ridiculed as lunatic.

On arrival at Eccles soon after one o'clock, friends carried the injured man to the Rev. Blackburne's vicarage and placed him on a couch. Physicians arrived from Manchester and upon consultation they decided amputation was out of the question.

During the late afternoon, Huskisson, in great pain, was rapidly sinking, and the vicar read from the Bible and administered the Holy Sacrament. Huskisson managed to dictate a codicil to his will which was witnessed by three earls at his side. Part of it read, "The country has had the best of me. I trust that it will do justice to my public character. I regret not the few years which might have remained to me, except for those dear ones whom I leave behind." Lately, he had been in failing health and during the evening he died. He had had his sixtieth birthday on 11th March. There were no children.

While Stephenson had been racing off to Eccles, the scene at Parkside was chaotic and confused; Wellington, Sir Robert Peel and a few others preferred that the unhappy procession should return directly to Liverpool and call it a day. Civic dignitaries from Manchester and several directors, anxious not to offend the Prime Minister, nevertheless pleaded that the journey should be continued and the ceremonies in Manchester completed, despite the accident they deeply deplored. Many people still lined the route ahead and the great concourse of frustrated spectators in Manchester might "exaggerate the mischief". The directors thought that "a false panic today might seriously affect the future of railway travelling and the value of the Company's property". Mr Sharpe, the Manchester Borough Reeve, was afraid that the impatient throngs in Manchester would be greatly disappointed, and in the light of recent troubles with the working population, violence and riots could easily flare up.

After lengthy discussion on the track side and a modicum of composure had returned, Wellington and Peel were persuaded. The procession would continue on its course, but the buglers attached to each train should remain silent, the military band must return to Liverpool and passengers were requested not to respond to the cheers of the crowds.

That all was not sweetness and light approaching Manchester was noted by the *Morning Post,* for there was "frequently hooting from the workmen who are opposed to this great national improvement, and on more than one occasion stones were hurled at the carriages when passing them . . . the populace having taken determined possession of many parts of the railway, and in some evinced a bold and daring anxiety to tear it up. . . ." Stephenson was to recall how he and his son were worried by belligerent groups on the track ahead of them. Again, the *Morning Post,* as the trains reached Manchester station: "The garrison was under arms and at various points within sight of the railway, picquets of cavalry were placed. Without this display of military force there would certainly have been a breach of the peace."

By the time the gloom-ridden procession had rumbled over the iron bridge, adorned by massive Doric columns, to cross the River Irwell into Manchester station, it was around three o'clock. The impressive little train was greeted by a military regiment and an inflamed mob which authority tried to control. Wisely, Wellington remained in the safety of his carriage, for the angry mob was now poised precariously on the brink of violence. Predominating were two opposing factions; those against Wellington wore tricolour cockades and hailed his carriage with hoots and abuse; those for him cheered wildly. Lucky ones shook hands with the great man which he accepted graciously; and, according to one doubtful record, he kissed a few babies, that vote-catching ordeal still borne stoically by parliamentary candidates.

Observing that the dark September clouds had turned to rain, Fanny Kemble confirms the mood: "The vast concourse of people who had assembled to witness the triumphant arrival of the successful travellers was of the lowest order of mechanics and artisans, among whom great distress and a dangerous spirit of discontent with the Government at that time prevailed. Groans and hisses greeted the carriage, full of influential personages, in which the Duke of Wellington sat.

"High above the grim and grimy crowd of scowling faces a loom had been erected, at which sat a tattered, starved-looking weaver, evidently set there as a *representative man,* to protest against this triumph of machinery, and the gain and glory which the wealthy Liverpool and Manchester men were likely to derive from it. The contrast between our departure from Liverpool and our arrival in Manchester was one of the most striking things I have ever witnessed."

In what proportions the hostility was directed at the railway or at Wellington's Government's policies is difficult to assess; but no doubt remains that among the suffering masses in Manchester at that time, and indeed elsewhere in Britain, his Government was far from popular, and Wellington himself was known to be resolutely opposed to any measures of social reform. In Manchester, he witnessed the groundswell among the populace. His association with a railway riddled with controversy and now the tragic death of one of his most popular cabinet ministers could not have helped. In fact, two months later he was to resign the premiership and was not to entrust himself to another railway journey for thirteen years.

In Manchester, for about an hour the formidable Duke had endured the harassing tribulation and towards half past four he and his humiliated party, chastened by tragedy, trundled off in their two carriages behind Stephenson's *Northumbrian*.

After that? He would be a bold chronicler indeed to recount with confidence the complex movements of locomotives and carriages on the way home from Manchester; they involved the assemblage in some sort of order, to allow for taking water and fuel, and servicing, and shunting trains on to the proper line.

Several locomotives were coupled together to haul a long train of carriages instead of running too many separate short trains which, in the absence of any formal signalling system, would have been fraught with danger, especially after dark. The long train left Manchester towards half past five in pouring rain. On restarting at Eccles, some couplings broke and had to be replaced by ropes. From Parkside, the *Comet* locomotive was sent cautiously ahead as a look-out pilot, a man on the footplate holding aloft a flaming tar-rope as a warning signal. Along the Rainhill level, the pilot locomotive ran over a wheelbarrow which had been placed, probably maliciously, on the rails, but without mishap.

Some distance behind the pilot, coupled locomotives, probably three, were unable to pull the long train up the Sutton gradient towards the Rainhill level and the men were made to get out and walk in the rain for about a mile and a half.

Hours late, the first train did not reach Liverpool until about seven o'clock, but on the way home, according to the *Gentleman's Magazine*, ". . . the Duke of Wellington quitted the rail-road about three miles before the cortège reached Liverpool, and posted off to the Marquis' seat at Childwell. The splendid corporation dinner which had been prepared at Liverpool was suspended. . . ."

Not until after ten o'clock did all the other trains reach Liverpool. Weary and travel-stained, the passengers must have been heartened by the cheering from a small crowd who had waited patiently at Edge Hill. The locomotives had ended their journey and the carriages were hooked up to the ropes of the fixed engines to be eased gently through the tunnel to Wapping. This was the last scene in the day's dramatic events and it would have taken maybe an hour for the last tired passengers to totter from their carriage as they looked forward to a good night's rest. But what a contrast! The procession that had so bravely set off that fine morning in style, state and splendour, had straggled back home in disarray and drenching rain. This was a story the intrepid travellers would retell to their children and grandchildren for the rest of their lives.

After the débâcle came the inquests, both private and public. Huskisson's death evoked much venom from the I-told-you-so brigade. In the *Edinburgh Review,* Lord Brougham wrote, "The folly of seven hundred people going at fifteen miles an hour in six [there were many more] carriages exceeds belief. But they have paid a dear price." A modern equivalent of the tragedy would have entailed the death of a cabinet minister in the presence of the Prime Minister at the first public showing of *Concorde*. One outcome was certain: the fatality dramatically alerted the Government as well as the public at large to the potential dangers inherent in the new railways.

A more philosophical note was sounded by the *Albion* newspaper; ". . . it has pleased Almighty God to remove Mr Huskisson from the troubles and the anxieties of this vain and transitory world, and, though his death has been sudden and violent, it is our humble duty to acquiesce in the mysterious dispensations of a supreme governing intelligence." The event was described as "the awful catastrophe which has snatched away Mr Huskisson . . . from an affectionate and admiring country".

A lengthy report was carried in the *Morning Post,* much of which was devoted to the fatality and to the hostile reception in Manchester. The reporter opens with a flourish of rhetoric: "Who shall tell what the events of a day may bring?" and estimates that "between the towns of Liverpool and Manchester, there could be not less than one million spectators". He concludes; "Thus was opened this great national undertaking, which is to shorten distances and facilitate communication in a manner which a few years back it had not entered into the mind of man even to conceive." Fanny Kemble's diary noted that "the papers are full of nothing else".

The very presence at the accident of so many eminent personages severely tarnished the bright image of this railway and others to come; and newspapers, which seem to thrive better on bad news than good, disseminated the tragic story around the civilised world.

Nearer home, what of the master himself? Stephenson's emotions can only have been in conflict; not only had his new railway killed the man who had campaigned so persistently for the railway in its darkest hours, but his beloved *Rocket* had been the engine of death.

In later years, at Parkside an impressive memorial to the victim was erected. In the centre is a plaque on which the incident is described at length but the locomotive is not named. "This tablet – A tribute of personal respect and affection has been placed here to mark the spot," it begins, ending, "In the midst of life we are in death." A statue was erected in the cathedral at Chichester, a town he had represented in Parliament for ten years as a young man. Another, clad in classical robes, stands prominently on an imposing mausoleum on a site near the new Anglican cathedral in Liverpool, the city in which he is buried and which he had served so well as a Member of Parliament. All three stand in silent witness.

Yet, was the *Rocket* really the killer? Most of the evidence says that it was. But that repository of revered authority, the *Dictionary of National Biography,* without question names the *Dart,* which was certainly near by at the time; so does the *Gentleman's Magazine* dated September 1830. Even a single reference to another locomotive niggles the questioning historical researcher, and invokes the wild hypothesis that mischievous enemies of the railway and of Stephenson himself might have circulated an ugly rumour. However, many newspapers of the day, and numerous historians, among them Dr Samuel Smiles, personal friend and biographer of both the Stephensons, unequivocally name the *Rocket*. A note in the diary of Charles Vignoles, who attended the opening ceremony, reads, "Here Mr Huskisson was killed by the *Rocket* engine passing over him."

From this eventful day, many lessons were to be learnt by the Liverpool & Manchester and all new railways. The full significance of the great conquest achieved for science and civilisation was yet to be perceived. Reflecting on the recent past, culminating with the distressing fatality, the Stephensons and the directors had been subjected to the most probing and gruelling tests, but the sheer *force majeur* of the entire enterprise had won through. So ended this memorable day in the world's history. The Age of Railways had really begun and the trains would run tomorrow.

CHAPTER 7

The Railway Makes a Start

Accidents, Carriages, Locomotives, Waggons

At last, the railway that had been the distant dream of so many dedicated men was now a reality and rarin' to go. If the directors and engineers had endured six years of accumulating troubles in its creation, these were quickly forgotten, overshadowed as they would be by a whole new series of enigmas increasing with the years. A long period of empiricism bringing surprises, shocking accidents and unexpected developments, lay in store. Today, now, there was a live new railway to be managed and yesterday's pall of Huskisson's death to be shaken off.

On Thursday 16th September, the day after the official opening, a special excursion train, departing at midday and hauled by *Northumbrian*, ran from Liverpool to Manchester and back, each journey, including stops for servicing, taking about one hour and fifty minutes. Of about one hundred and thirty passengers, most were members of the Society of Friends – many Quakers were in business in the north-west – attending their quarterly meeting. Fare for the round trip was 14s. (70p), almost a labourer's wages for a week. Three tons of luggage was aboard. Excited and curious sightseers crowded the terminals.

From the next day, regular services began, three trains leaving each terminal daily, at 7 am, 12 noon and 4 pm. Though each train had room for over a hundred passengers, a total of only about two hundred and fifty were carried throughout the day; but the numbers increased daily, especially from the 22nd, when second class carriages were introduced at a through single fare of 4s (20p). During the eight days to 25th September, 6,014 people had travelled; and on one day, the 30th, according to *The Times* of 6th October, 550 had journeyed from Manchester. Some days earlier, this influential newspaper had dispensed opinion as well as fact: "For my own part, when I have the choice of travelling by the steam or by the horse-coach, I shall certainly select the former, not merely because the journey is performed more rapidly, but also because it is performed more easily, equably, steadily, and comfortably."

Sheer novelty was beginning to build up the numbers, and many busy merchants were tempted to desert road for rail. Stage-coaches were taking about four-and-a-half hours for a fatiguing ride between Liverpool and Manchester; so as to compete, road operators reduced their fares to 10s. (50p) inside and 5s. (25p) outside. Within two weeks, the railway directors were able to announce additional regular trains. From mid-October, extra trains were run daily, except on Sundays, as excursions from both Manchester and Liverpool, at 5s. a head to view Stephenson's engineering masterpiece, the Sankey Viaduct. Sunday trains were frowned on by church leaders and a minor battle resulted in good old English compromise: the railway agreed not to run trains that would interfere with divine service.

As the year ended, passengers flocked to the stations in such numbers that the railway was running out of locomotives and the Stephensons were urged to get on with their building programme. The directors were poised to begin services for goods and minerals which had been delayed partly by passenger demand; and so to make a start, goods waggons were attached to some coach trains.

Few had expected that so many passengers would be attracted to the railway so soon; and by the end of the year, stage-coach operators, worried about going out of business, had withdrawn fourteen of the twenty-six coaches serving the route. This evoked from the *Manchester Courier* the comment that, "the coach operators could see only a bleak future." Liberal numbers of stage-coach travellers from London, Scotland and other distant places, began to complete their journeys on the new railway.

Studied carefully by other railway promoters up and down Britain, the railway by the end of the year had earned a profit of nearly £14,000 which allowed shareholders a modest dividend of £2 per £100 share, the Railway Act restricting the maximum to 10 per cent a year. The next figures which appeared, accounting for the first five months of 1831, showed a profit of over £30,000 and the dividend was lifted to £4 10s.

On the roads of Britain, for a century or so the strident warning and greeting blare of the bugle had been traditional for stage-coach travellers, and it seemed natural that the trumpet should sound as railway carriages departed from the station; and as first-class carriages were virtually stage-coach bodies mounted on wheeled underframes, the familiar note was reassuring. Samuel Smiles records that the trains were "played out of the terminal stations by a lively tune performed by a trumpeter at the end of the platform", a practice, he says, that continued for some years at the Liverpool station and for much longer at Manchester. At both stations, porters were employed to carry luggage for first-class passengers who could travel on horse-omnibuses to and from the town centres without extra charge. All porters were strictly forbidden by the company to accept gratuities.

New business came to hotels, inns and eating houses near the terminals, and owners' advertisements tempted travellers with "well-aired beds", "old wines" and "home-brewed ale"; new premises for such services soon began to proliferate. For passengers arriving early in the day from Manchester, a good breakfast was offered at the small Adelphi Hotel in Liverpool. Built in 1826, it was rebuilt and extended over the years, and was to be purchased by the Midland Railway company in 1892. It is still owned by British Rail.

Local taverns near the few busier intermediate stopping places – hardly yet proper stations – began to serve alcoholic drinks to passengers during their few minutes' wait. Train delays often arose and the directors ordered that the drink practice must cease. Shortly afterwards, a traveller spotted a "local serving wench" at the Patricroft stopping place walking alongside a train with a large tray containing glasses and the forbidden liquors and cigars which she sold surreptitiously to first-class passengers.

Not yet used to railway operations, both travellers and railway servants suffered frequent accidents which prompted the directors to issue on 1st March 1831 their first comprehensive set of rules, regulations and orders; these were to be adopted and modified by other new railways as a permanent component in their operating administration.

In time, this railway and others were to build up a plethora of byelaws; one of the first on the Liverpool & Manchester Railway read, "No smoking will be allowed in any of the First Class Carriages, even with the general consent of the Passengers present, as the annoyance would be experienced in a still greater degree by those who may occupy the same coach on the succeeding journey." What happened in inferior classes of carriage mattered little, since some were literally open waggons. At that time, long before cigarettes had become popular, cigars and pipes were the mode among the gentry, while labourers enjoyed their tobacco as a chew and a spit.

Quite soon after the trains had got into their stride, a feature of railway administration made its controversial début with a tiny department that was to expand indefinitely to keep the railways on their toes: passengers' complaints. This must have been the first public relations function in railway history. Directors were already conscious of their public image and to show an open mind they instituted at the Liverpool and Manchester stations a Passengers' Diary. Travellers were invited to record for the Company "complaints on account of incivility on the part of the Company's servants, or with reference to the charge for luggage, or the loss of any parcel or package or the delay in forwarding the same." Only the élite could read and write, so it was hard luck on the rest. In severe winters, frequent complaints were made when ice and snow delayed the trains.

Inevitably, accidents were endemic among people in an unfamiliar environment of noisy, moving vehicles, and they earned their share of newspaper reports. Mishaps with locomotives, carriages and waggons brought injury and sometimes death, often because of inexperience and faulty equipment. On one train, a broken carriage wheel derailed three vehicles; on another, a passenger jumped while the train was still moving and his crushed arm had to be amputated; and when a locomotive was running in reverse, an underpart of the leading tender broke, threw a man on to the rails and the locomotive ran over his body, fatally.

Accidents also shattered the Stephenson family. Four months after the railway had opened, George Stephenson's new life was just beginning, but it was the end of life for his younger brother John who was fatally injured in the Newcastle Works; so too was his sister's husband John Liddell and George supported both their families. Steam had been the cause of blinding his father in 1805 in a boiler-house mishap.

In 1831, Edward Bury (1794–1858) persuaded the railway to test his locomotive *Liverpool* whose driving wheels were six feet in diameter. Though George Stephenson was against it, mainly because he considered the wheels dangerously large and possibly from professional jealousy, he consented unwillingly but undertook to make a full report to the board. In the trials, the locomotive overturned, killing both the driver and his fireman. On 30th July, the *Manchester Guardian* blamed the directors or their servants, adding, "They ought to exercise the power vested in them by their Act, of preventing any engine from running on the line which, in the opinion of their engineer, is at all unsafe. . . ." The large wheels seem to have been the culprit. Stephenson's report prompted the directors to restrict driving wheels to five feet. But Bury, still young, was not to be defeated and the locomotive-building world was yet to hear of his remarkable accomplishments. He had been building primitive locomotives since he was about twenty, and had planned to enter a machine in the Rainhill Trials but was months too late.

Some years after this mishap, Stephenson's *Patentee*, while overloaded hauling thirty-one waggons, exploded its outer casing, killing the driver and fireman. On another occasion, when a train was being unloaded at a station, a passenger named John Lees stood up in an open carriage to enjoy the scenery; suddenly, the train started with a fierce thrust by the locomotive and Lees was thrown on to the line and

The opening-day of the Liverpool and Manchester Railway, 15th September 1830, showing the Moorish Arch at Edge Hill, Liverpool, and the Prime Minister the Duke of Wellington's coach on the left, as seen by a contemporary artist.

Another drawing of Wellington's train on the opening-day, undoubtedly by a different artist!

Stephenson's locomotive *Northumbrian* which hauled the Duke of Wellington's train on the official opening-day.

Soon after the railway was opened, cartoonists and satirists used their arts to rebuke and ridicule lax railway managements. This one, dated 1831, features the *Northumbrian*.

Above left: The distinguished engineer Thomas Telford, who inspected for the Government the work in progress as Stephenson was building the railway. A rather arrogant George was not too pleased.

Above right: John Rennie, who, with his brother George, almost secured the commission from Stephenson to build this famous line.

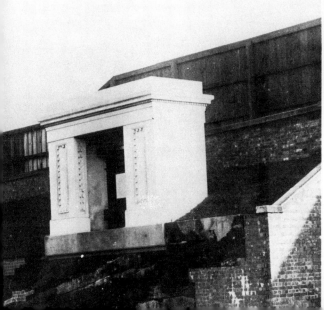

Above: The Rt Hon. William Huskisson MP, who became the first railway casualty.

Left: The Memorial at Parkside on the railway commemorating the spot where Huskisson was run down. The inscription ends, "In the midst of life we are in death".

Bury's drawing of the station and yard at Wapping, near Queen's Dock, Liverpool. Omnibus passengers would enter the railway carriages which were hauled by rope through the tunnel to Edge Hill, where they were joined by a locomotive.

Wapping Tunnel: note the new-fangled gas-lighting.

The new grand entrance of 1836 to Lime Street Station and an early example of opulent railway architecture, from an Ackermann print. In 1871 the famous North-Western Hotel (now offices) was added.

The interior of the new station at Lime Street showing the entrance to the tunnel; and the other end of the tunnel at Edge Hill, where locomotives were hooked to the trains.

The Adelphi Hotel in Liverpool, long associated with the railway, opened in 1826. Its owner accommodated Fanny Kemble, the famous young actress, who stayed there the night before the railway was opened in 1830. The hotel is now owned by British Rail.

Even this was more comfortable than swaying on the top of a stage-coach on a rough road! Here, a train is seen crossing the bridge over the Duke of Bridgwater's Canal near Patricroft, a few miles from Manchester. Note the policeman (signalman) on the right.

A spectacular section of Olive Mount Cutting, near Liverpool, which Stephenson and his men had to cut to reach the town.

Two of Stephenson's famous viaducts, both still in use. *Above:* Newton Viaduct over a turnpike road and a brook. *Below:* The Sankey Viaduct about midway on the route crossing the Sankey Canal, on which is seen a sailing-boat. (Taken from a colour-view by Bury of 1831).

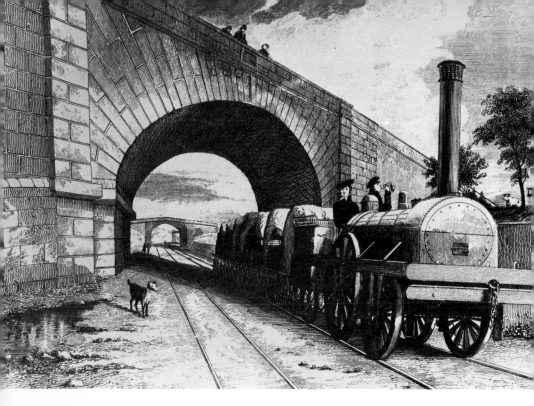

Stephenson's famous Skew Bridge, the awkward shape of which, a contemporary writer said, he carved from a turnip plucked in a nearby field. The cows seem more interested in the driver's bugle-call.

The Skew Bridge as it is today, at the end of Rainhill Station platform.

he was killed by the next carriage. Elsewhere, several workmen rather foolishly left a plank across the track to sit down and have some food; along came the locomotive *Phoenix* which struck the plank, threw its fireman Thomas Wright on to the line and the locomotive killed him outright. A horrible accident that was all too frequent, even in the twentieth century, happened to Joseph Bates, a fireman on the *Mercury*; as he was disconnecting the chain which coupled the locomotive to a waggon, his head was crushed between the vehicles.

New causes of mishap continually came to light, challenging the ingenuity of directors and engineers alike in staving them off. A main cause was speed, which reached levels that people had never witnessed before. Drivers often misjudged braking distances and ran into terminus stop-blocks. Fog was always a nightmare. In a thick fog in 1832, a train standing in Rainhill station was ploughed into from the rear by another, killing several people. Venturesome boys, not recognising the danger, often wandered along the track to be injured or killed; hooligans and drunks flung timbers and other materials across the rails causing derailments, and the Board offered rewards for the conviction of culprits. Youthful stone-throwing at passing trains was a common menace.

In Olive Mount Cutting near Liverpool, a man, probably drunk or just showing off, walked along the rail, tight-rope fashion, and was struck from the rear by a train. Many a drunk met injury or death on the track, and one man in his cups fell to his demise from a second-class carriage at Bury Lane. One day in 1833, three passengers walked up and down the line impatiently while their train was held up; clouds of steam and smoke hid them from view and a locomotive approaching on the other line ended their lives.

Wrongly positioned points at St Helens Junction caused two locomotives to collide and to be seriously damaged, killing an engineman and crushing the foot of a mechanic. Indeed, several accidents arose from the same cause and the men responsible were instantly dismissed from the service. A tired policeman (signalman) dozed off to sleep while the points were in the wrong position; several waggons were consequently derailed and for his sins the company fined him £3. A guard fell asleep as his train ran through the tunnel at Liverpool; luckily there was no damage or injury, but he was taken to court and the reeve (magistrate) sent him to prison for two months' hard labour. But it was easy enough for a man who worked twelve to sixteen hours a day to doze off at a crucial moment. Lancashire ale in those days must have been strong stuff, for many enginemen, guards and other railway servants were frequently to be found drunk on duty, alcohol no doubt offering some solace in their lives of real hardship. Dismissals failed to deter many others from the demon drink and in board minutes for December 1832, the directors noted their perplexity.

Today, sadly, drunken driving, not on the railways but on the roads, still perplexes modern society. But drunk or sober, it was surprising how many passengers, usually the younger men, insisted on jumping from a train before it had stopped; and others who alighted from a train on the wrong side and fell to injury or death from a train on the adjacent line, a risk reduced by the board's instructions that offside carriage doors must be locked.

Regrettably, it has to be said that the accidents described here are but a representative few of many. Though great wonders were being achieved, considerable risks remained. Within a few years of Huskisson's tragic death, much blood had been spilt on this pioneering line, devastating the victims' dear ones and alarming the management. Meanwhile, men of driving vision battled doggedly forward in this great new urgent revolution, whose simple but compelling objective was to move, more cheaply and efficiently, people and goods from one place to another. This continuous and relentless pursuit has motivated man throughout the centuries and civilisations.

Certainly, the directors and engineers did everything humanly possible to make their railway safe, and in 1831 a register was opened to record all personal accidents for analysis and action; the stringent safety regulations formulated were, in time, backed by Statute. The company had every motivation to avoid accidents, for they cost money and time and damaged the railway's reputation. Newspapers constantly kept the railway on its toes with criticisms and suggestions. In *The Times* dated 31st October 1840, letters from readers demanded stricter action, and some papers accused railway employees of "trifling with the lives of the public". Accidents were regularly featured in bizarre and gruesome cartoons in newspapers and magazines. In support of the railway, a reader wrote to a newspaper claiming that "for one accident which would happen by this mode of conveyance, fifty would be by coach".

Safety, it was realised, was largely a matter of educating railway servants and the public about the new dangers now being met.

On the credit side, how delighted the directors were to announce in November 1830, that the new railway was to be entrusted to carry Post Office mails. This was indeed national prestige, soured only by the incessant wrangling disputes about the services and charges. Other government business came from the conveyance of military troops and their baggage. According to the contract, women "belonging to the regiment" were allowed to travel free of charge, providing that there were no more than ten women to every hundred men.

Quite soon, the excursion business by non-scheduled trains was increasing the revenues. Groups hired carriages or full trains for special parties. Typical was a group of Sunday-school teachers who hired, at £20 a time, second-class Blue Coaches for a return trip from Liverpool to Manchester. Special trains were run during Whit-week, other public holidays and for public exhibitions. Parties of racegoers frequently travelled to the course at Newton. Such were the beginnings of the railway excursion business, so brilliantly exploited from 1841 by the young Thomas Cook (1808–92) of the Midlands and eventually developed into a world-wide travel enterprise.

In the hope of attracting more business, in May 1831 the directors offered the use of the railway to private carriers on payment of tolls. Stage-coach proprietors and common carriers wishing to use this facility were required to provide their own carriages and waggons fitted for railway use and, if they wished, their own locomotives. To the surprise of the Board, there were few takers. The facility had been allowed for by Parliament to curtail unfair railway competition, but because it failed to materialise, it left the railway, as owners of lock, stock and barrel, in a happy and powerful position.

What of the carriages themselves? James Scott Walker takes up his quill: "The most elegant and costly contain three apartments, and resemble the body of a coach and two chaises, one at each end, the whole joined together. Another resembles an oblong square of church pews, panelled at each end, and the rail which supports the back so contrived that it may be turned over, so that passengers may face either way, and the machine [carriage] does not require to be turned. Besides these, there is a variety of others, of various grades of elegance, taste, fancy or convenience. . . ."

On some first-class trains, a guard or brakesman, carrying a bugle, sat perched high on the front of the leading carriage and another on the last one, stage-coach fashion. Stage-coach men had to contend only with the extremes of weather; but in addition, the railway guards after a two-hour journey must have arrived at the destination begrimed somewhat from the smoke, steam and hot ashes spurting from the locomotive.

For carriage design, the directors were in a world of experiment and leaned on traditional builders of stage and private coaches; the early first-class railway carriages thus had a familiar and publicly-acceptable look, rather as we see imitation log embers in modern electric fires, and other commercial gimmickry. Though mounted on springs and strong frames, riding was rough. On starting, accelerating, braking and stopping, carriages tended to jolt and to see-saw in a sickening motion: unpleasant movements aggravated by the closeness of the two wheel-axles which were about seven feet apart. The fastidious well-to-do made loud their complaints.

Carriages were linked by chains or other couplings which, when the vehicles were close together, hung down in the slack; on starting and stopping, a driver needed to be skilful, otherwise the carriages banged noisily and fiercely together, frightening travellers or throwing them across the interior. To some extent, the nuisance was relieved around 1832 by introducing a spring arrangement in the couplings, and padded buffers fitted to the ends of carriages to take the impact. So that passengers might brace themselves against a jolt, someone suggested that "a bell should be rung, or the guard should sound his horn, a moment or two before the train is set in motion". But despite the jolting, it was travel far superior to stage-coach journeys. On some carriages, Stephenson self-acting brakes were fitted; they were not very efficient and were replaced by the hand-operated variety.

Travel was smoother after Henry Booth's patented screw couplings were gradually fitted. An outstanding invention at the time, they held the carriages closely together, buffer to buffer, preventing the vehicles banging into each other. The Liverpool & Manchester was the first railway to use screw couplings and they were soon adopted by other new railways, of a type that remained in use for about forty years. One historian recorded that Abel Turton, who was later to become station master at Parkside, recollected that at the official opening of the railway he met Booth, and suggested to him the idea of a screw coupling.

What about lighting? After sundown, travellers were seated uneasily in the noisy darkness, unless they took their own tallow candles or oil lanterns, until 1834 when one oil lamp was provided in one compartment of each first-class carriage. Elegant button upholstery offered a modicum of comfort and the three seats on either side of the compartment were separated by arm rests. Carriage exteriors were painted in bright colours and scroll designs. Like their fellows on the highway which they so closely resembled, the "most elegant coaches" were named, among the first being *Experience, Times, Traveller,* and *Victor.* Also in the idiom of stage-coaches, railway carriages were fitted with rails around the roof edges to prevent passengers' luggage falling off. Some early first-class carriages were open at the sides and hot ashes from the locomotive chimney burnt holes in the passengers' clothes and scorched their skin.

To accommodate servants travelling with their masters or families, an adjacent compartment was allocated to them in a first-class carriage, but at the second-class fare.

Second-class carriages were less salubrious, as befitted the 'lower orders'; some were little better than open waggons with benches seating four abreast. Spartan travellers had to brave the elements, from scorching sun to driving rain and snow as well as the hot rubbish chucked out of the locomotive. The directors decided that this just could not go on, and from 1834 had the waggons roofed over, but still open at the sides and without artificial light. From their exterior painting, they were known as the 'Blue Coaches', which was perhaps less of a social slight than 'second class'. By about 1840, side windows closed them in completely.

Though many coach bodies were purchased from private builders, the Liverpool & Manchester began to build more of their own. During the 1830s, the directors invited other railway promoters to visit their stations, warehouses, workshops and locomotive sheds. Several projected railways, among them the Grand Junction, Manchester & Leeds, and London & Greenwich modelled their carriages on the Liverpool style.

One of the greatest contributions the pioneering line made was in the steam locomotive itself, the entire *raison d'être*. For only seven months, the Stephenson locomotives ruled the roost. Starting with the *Rocket*, by that time they had supplied eighteen machines. Some engineers who had trained with the famous pair had gone off to build their own or help other manufacturers then entering the field. Fenton, Murray broke the Stephenson spell in May 1831 when they supplied the *Vulcan*. Other independent builders began to supply locomotives. Four more Stephenson locomotives went into service late in 1831, three in 1832, one in 1833 and *Patentee*, the very last, in 1834, making a total of twenty-seven from the Stephenson stable. Technical improvements were made and sizes increased. Eyes always on the stars, the Stephensons searched the heavens for astral names; among them were *Meteor, Comet, North Star, Planet, Mercury, Mars, Jupiter, Saturn, Sun* and *Venus*. Other builders' names seemed a little tame after such a galaxy.

During the first year or so, the directors stipulated that new locomotives should not exceed eight tons, nearly twice the weight of the *Rocket*; but *Goliath* and *Samson*, with four coupled driving wheels, were already in service and weighed about ten tons. Stephenson's *Planet*, delivered in 1830, running alone on a test completed the throughout journey in one hour; and to average 30 miles an hour, at some points it must have reached 40.

From the beginning, Stephenson locomotives were the best in the business; but even they had their troubles; in the first few years, three were returned for attention because of cracked axles and wheels and the railway sent bills for the work. Apart from minor setbacks, Stephenson locomotives launched the railway on the road to success, and in ordering machines from other builders, the directors stipulated that they should follow the Stephenson pattern. Once, when a competitor bid for a locomotive for the projected Manchester & Leeds Railway, old George challenged, "Hang one of his to one of mine, back to back. Then let them go at it, and whichever walks away with the other, *that's the engine!*"

Father and son had no need to worry, for orders to build locomotives and railways on the Liverpool & Manchester pattern were coming in from Britain, Europe and America faster than they could possibly cope. Over the years, costs of locomotives rose from around £400 to £1400 and were increasingly larger and more powerful, using higher boiler-pressures. Stephenson locomotives ranged from about £500 to £800, but the larger *Samson* and *Goliath* were £1000 apiece. Because George was the railway engineer and Robert the locomotive builder, competitors accused the directors of running a monopoly, and in 1831 the *Mechanics Magazine* indicted the *Manchester Guardian*, champion of the Stephensons, for publishing lies to discredit other locomotive builders; but in this now fiercely competitive business in which big money was to be made, the directors applied price and quality as their criteria and reminded people that the Rainhill Trials had been wide open to any contestant. They proved their impartiality by purchasing machines from a dozen different firms mainly in and around Lancashire and after 1833 called for a guarantee of twelve months.

Thomas Gray of Nottingham, who had been advocating a railway between Liverpool and Manchester since 1820, campaigned for Blenkinsop and Murray's system of a toothed wheel on a toothed rail, rack-and-pinion fashion, and had urged the Liverpool & Manchester to adopt this. In 1834 he was still peddling the idea in the *Mechanics Magazine* and added, "As the original projector of the system, you may be sure that I am particularly anxious about the success of my darling scheme. . . ."

A comparison of locomotives from various makers was made by John Herapath (1790–1868) who, as joint owner, began the monthly *Railway Magazine* in 1836, direct antecedent of popular railway journals still greatly loved. A man to see for himself, he travelled for eighty-six miles to and fro on the Liverpool & Manchester line in 1839 behind various machines, some of which, he said, rolled about more than they ought. But the one he found the most superior for riding qualities was the *Arrow* (presumably the 2-2-2 Mather, Dixon's of 1837 and not Stephenson's *Arrow* of 1830) and he writes: "This engine, whatever the speed, sticks closely to the road, and yet passes over its faults with as much tenderness as a parent over the failings of its offspring."

All locomotives were fitted with steps to reach the 'footplate' (driving platform), but on some, including the Stephenson *Samson*, the steps were fashioned in the style of stirrups, for the driver to mount his 'iron horse'.

Simplicity is the hallmark of locomotive power; steam under pressure enters a cylinder to push the piston inside it back and forth; the piston rod is hinged, similar to a cyclist's knee joint, to a connect-

ing rod which then converts the movement into a rotary action on the
driving wheels. Four or more driving wheels coupled together plus
small carrier wheels provided greater hauling power. Better fuel and
refinements of the equipment led to better and more reliable performance. At the Newcastle Works, successive locomotives were
improved. On the *Northumbrian*, the firebox was integrated into the
boiler for better heating, the first example of what was settled as
standard practice; and on the *Planet*, the two cylinders were horizontal instead of inclined and were placed inside the frontal smokebox
instead of outside as on previous machines.

Delight was expressed by the directors at these improvements. But
they were not so delighted with the rocking motion of locomotives
generally because of the damage to the primitive track, and adjust-
ments were made to eccentrics on the driving axles and the gearing
and valve arrangements to bring smoother running.

Purchase by the Liverpool & Manchester of *Patentee*, the last to be
supplied by Stephenson, is recorded in board minutes:

28th April 1834	" . . . letter from R. Stephenson & Co. offering their 6 wheeled engine for £1050."
19th May 1834	"Offered R. Stephenson & Co. £1000 for the engine . . ."
7th July 1834	"Read letter from R. Stephenson & Co. accepting above offer . . ."

Patentee was then Stephenson's best locomotive, the six wheels
distributing the weight evenly. It was fitted with a radical piece of
equipment, a steam-operated brake; but its practice failed to measure
up to its theory and it had to be replaced by a traditional handbrake to
press shoes against the wheels. But it was not long before the steam
brake was improved and adopted widely as standard practice. Half a
century later, the *Engineer* journal in March 1883 was to comment
that the *Patentee* with its 2-2-2 wheel arrangement had ever since
been established as the prototype of express train locomotives in
Britain and other countries. In 1930, Dendy Marshall, Cambridge
scholar and locomotive historian, was to name this locomotive as "a
striking landmark in progress." Oddly, its significance does not seem
to have been noted in Liverpool & Manchester Board minutes.

Based on accumulated experience, the directors in 1836 drew up
detailed "Specifications for a Locomotive Engine" for all their suppliers. They were always sharp of eye for their "Grand British Experimental Railway". From 1832, most small repairs could be done in the
company's own workshops, some going to outside contractors when
the workload was heavy. Economies were constantly sought; some
saving was made when John Dixon substituted brass boiler tubes for
copper. According to records of the early 1830s, locomotives were

already averaging some 20,000 miles a year; this could be achieved easily by two double trips a day on six days a week for seven months.

For some years, it had been the ambition of the directors to build locomotives in their own workshops, for much talent as well as that of the busy Stephensons was emerging. Building began in 1841. From then on, throughout its brief independence and one year afterwards, the company built thirty-seven locomotives under the command of John Dewrance, the first of a long line of distinguished locomotive superintendents. Every machine except *Atlas* bore the name of a bird, from *Albatross* and *Cuckoo* to *Owzell* and *Woodlark*. They were known as the 'bird class'. Most weighed around fifteen tons, well over three times that of the *Rocket*. More than half had the same wheel arrangement as the Stephenson *Patentee* 2-2-2; others were 2-4-0 and 0-4-2. Besides Stephenson, eleven other builders supplied various small numbers of locomotives, to make a total of 105 throughout the life of the company. Other names chosen represented animal speed and power – *Lion, Panther, Elephant, Mastodon*, and for good measure, *Thunderer* and *Lightning*. The quixotic romanticism of these rumbustious pioneers is quite enchanting.

Cylinder bore and piston-rod stroke had increased from 8 inches by 17 inches on the *Rocket* to 13 inches by 20 inches on some of the locomotives built by the railway company. Early experimental locomotives were fitted with one cylinder, to be followed soon by a second. In the present century, three and four cylinders became common, Stephenson and Howe having registered a patent for a three-cylinder design as early as 1846.

At some stage, an American engineer named Whyte devised a simple description (Whyte notation) of wheel arrangements for steam locomotives to indicate the number of wheels, powered and carrier wheels separately. In 2-2-2, for example, the number of powered wheels is shown by the centre figure, and front and rear carrier wheels on either side (if there are any); 0-6-0 indicates six coupled power wheels and no carrier wheels.

We have noted that in planning the railway, the promoters based their preliminary calculations almost entirely on the conveyance of goods – coal and other minerals, cotton, timber and miscellaneous merchandise; in the event, the revenues remained substantially behind those from passengers. Goods trains did not begin running until some weeks after the line was opened. For these services, a fleet of waggons from various suppliers was building up.

Unlike the locomotive, the goods waggon had a long history on colliery tramways and on the roads, and it was a question of adapting vehicles for the railway. Most of them were little more than heavy timber boxes mounted on wheels without springs, some with sides of up to five feet high. A few specially designed waggons were built for specific purposes: for example, long flat ones for timber. It was a period of expediency. Privately owned coal waggons were allowed to use the line providing they met safety requirements and tolls were paid.

Sometimes, merchandise in open waggons caught fire from locomotive sparks or was damaged by rain and snow, against which large canvas sheets were introduced.

Surprising to some modern railway operators, two innovations appeared in the 1830s which, in more sophisticated form, remain in extensive use today; for use at the Manchester terminal, some waggons were designed with bottom-floor doors for gravity unloading; and in Liverpool, two containers of coal could be hoisted from a flat railway waggon and transferred to a horse-drawn cart for local delivery, presaging British Rail's high-speed freightliner trains carrying containers, which can start and complete their journeys by road.

To cope with cattle and other livestock mainly from Ireland, pig waggons were built with vertical rails to about four feet; sheep waggons had slatted sides to a similar height. One of the first livestock consignments was in May 1831 when forty-nine pigs imported from Ireland were conveyed from Liverpool to Manchester at 1s. 6d. (7½p) per head; soon afterwards, sheep and cattle came on the scene, the charge for sheep being half that for pigs. Cover sheets were thrown over these open waggons in bad weather. Grunting pigs, lowing cattle and baa-ing sheep along the railway soon made their sounds and smells as familiar as those of snorting locomotives. As a highly perishable commodity, waggons of livestock were frequently attached to passenger trains, to the entertainment of travelling town dwellers and familiar companionship for country folk. Livestock was never really big railway business, but added usefully to revenues.

During long journeys, animals had to be fed and watered on the way, otherwise claims might be made by the owners. Many a time in railway life, distressed cows with bulging udders needed to be relieved, and local railway servants surreptitiously secured a supply of fresh milk for their families, as well as rich manure for their vegetable patches.

Pig travel could hardly be thought of as luxurious, but the new type of waggon was described by the *Liverpool Times* as "a vehicle constructed for the accommodation of the latter respectable class of quadrupeds, which certainly is a much handsomer and more commodious vehicle than those in which His Majesty's liege subjects were accustomed to travel fifty years ago."

Horses to be slaughtered for the meal table travelled in open cattle waggons, and in 1833 two special horse boxes were constructed for race horses and other equestrian nobility. Each had slits for ventilation, swinging shutters, well-padded inside walls, a foodbin, and a side door that could be let down to form a loading ramp.

At some intermediate stations, cattle docks had been erected to serve local farmers; and in Liverpool cattle market, a clerk was appointed to canvass for cattle traffic: probably the first railway salesman. In Manchester, a goods agent was appointed to call on merchants to tout for their business.

During the construction of the railway, a large number of ballast and spoil waggons had been in use; some were retained to convey maintenance men, their tools and equipment, but a large surplus remained. Henry Booth, the company's treasurer, was authorised to sell a hundred large and three hundred small ballast waggons to the Dublin & Kingstown Railway, a short precincts line opened in December 1834, the first in Ireland.

Services for goods really showed their paces when the first commercial train of significance ran from Liverpool to Manchester on 1st December 1830, hauled by the Stephenson *Planet*. The journey, including three stops for servicing, was completed in just under three hours. Among its mixed bag of merchandise were sacks of malt and oatmeal, two hundred barrels of flour, one hundred and thirty-five bags and bales of cotton from America, plus fifteen passengers, to make a load of about eighty tons. On some stretches of line, the train reached fifteen miles an hour, much faster than by either road or canal, and a good load to boot.

By the end of December, goods hauled totalled 1,432 tons and in the following spring had risen to some 5,000 tons a month. It was common practice to attach to passenger trains waggons of goods and livestock; these 'mixed trains' continued, especially in sparse areas of Britain, until well into the twentieth century. No time-tables were made for goods trains which ran as required. Some ran through the night. Within a few years, ten to fifteen goods trains were running on most days and the company's locomotives hauled trains of privately owned colliery waggons.

Goods trains ran intermittently between passenger trains which they frequently delayed, and the directors soon heard about it from irate first-class personages journeying to conduct important business. Therefore, the board issued instructions that no goods train should leave Edge Hill goods depot less than fifteen minutes before a passenger train was due to leave the Liverpool terminal; and on the route, any goods train immediately ahead of a passenger train must be shunted over points out of the way as soon as possible. A board minute dated 29th August 1832 made it clear that any engineman failing to do so would be promptly sacked. In one of the company's regulations, such trains were called 'goods and luggage' and for a century they were known far and wide among the public as luggage trains.

Railway servants along the line were instructed to keep a sharp look-out for overhanging loads, for goods falling off waggons, or anything untoward, and to signal the train to stop. In 1833, three waggons of cotton from America were set ablaze by locomotive sparks while crossing the bleak Chat Moss; and in the following year, an extensive fire erupted on a goods train but not spotted until it was well alight. Such disasters prompted the directors to order a brakesman to travel on the last vehicle, a most uncomfortable ride. At some distant time, there would be a goods brakevan furnished with bench seat, locker, and a coal stove for the guard or brakesman to heat food and drink in his billy-cans.

From time to time, some notable goods train journeys were made which brought no joy to the die-hard critics. On 26th February 1831, the *Manchester Guardian* reported how *Samson*, living valiantly up to its classic name, pulled a huge load of "107 tons 5 cwt at 20 mph" from Liverpool to Manchester. "We imagine that the performance yesterday will, at any rate, put an end to the system of petty detraction which has been so long and so incessantly levelled at Mr Stephenson and his engine, by a little knot of pseudo-mechanics. . . ."

In the first full year of 1831, over forty-thousand tons of merchandise was carried, a volume that had increased five-fold by 1835; in the same period, coal carrying rose from 11,000 tons to 116,000. And for the next ten years, the railway held its own but had to contend with falls and rises caused by general trade conditions. As carriers of goods, the railway promoters had proved their point magnificently.

CHAPTER 8

Down the Line

Signalling, Stations, Structures

As a complete entity to serve the needs of travellers, traders and industrialists, the railway company had to devise some kind of signalling system; to establish main stations and a number of intermediate stopping places; and to erect locomotive sheds, workshops, warehouses and other premises at strategic points. For these necessities, much of the structural work had been started and major ones completed even before the railway had officially opened.

Apart from simple shelters against the elements, there were no structures of note for the primitive methods used for signalling the trains. Policemen, as the signalling men were then termed, stood at intervals of a mile or so along the whole route, usually at intermediate stations, giving hand signals and displaying coloured flags and lanterns to indicate to drivers whether to slow down, stop or proceed. Even in fine weather, the driver's view of signals was hampered by smoke and steam.

In a rather hit and miss affair, to reduce the chances of a train colliding into the rear of the one ahead, a time interval, usually about half an hour, was allowed between trains departing from the terminals or main intermediate stations. Poor drivers! In good visibility it was safe enough; but in storms, fog, snow and during darkness, they were steaming along almost blind, putting their faith and their lives in the hands of the policemen with their lanterns, flaming tarred rope and fire braziers sometimes hoisted high on a pole by rope and pulley. Policemen using hand signals were also stationed at the hand-operated points which guided a train from one line to another, or on to a branch line or siding, and at level crossings. Railway policemen were soon to become known as 'peelers', 'roberts' and 'bobbies' after Sir Robert Peel who had formed the Metropolitan Police Force in 1829. Intriguingly, even today railway signalmen are known among their mates as 'bobbies'.

It was impossible for the policemen to communicate with each other, and in little or no visibility it was equally impossible for a policeman to be sure, when giving a signal to proceed, that the line ahead was really clear and safe, apart from knowing that the previous train had been gone some time. With such primitive safeguards, depending so much upon the man on the spot, hopefully sober and awake, nervous ladies must have suffered unbearable anxiety until the journey's end was safely reached.

Policemen were carefully instructed in their unfamiliar duties. In normal visibility, arms outstretched indicated to the locomotive driver that the line was clear; arms at the sides meant that something was wrong and that the driver must approach cautiously and enquire. When passengers were waiting to be picked up at an intermediate station, the policeman in daylight would hoist a red flag, and at night swing a lantern. On the last carriage of passenger trains, two oil lamps – tail lamps – were fitted to display blue while the train was standing and red when moving.

After about a year of operation, the directors proclaimed proudly – if prematurely – that their railway was the safest mode of transport. They realised that speed was still a prime danger, and though trains were now capable of travelling at more than thirty miles an hour, a maximum of twenty was imposed, much to the relief of agitated passengers. George Stephenson had recommended that first-class trains should complete the journey in two hours, and second-class trains in half an hour longer. These timings were speeded up by half an hour after track improvements.

In December 1832, a driver named Simon Fenwick who revelled in a burst of speed, driving the Fenton Murray locomotive *Vulcan*, completed the journey in sixty-eight minutes, which means that on some stretches he exceeded 30 miles an hour. When he was called to face the music, smiles must have creased the faces of the interviewing directors as he offered the lame excuse that a strong wind was behind him. Nevertheless, disobedient speeding drivers were warned that they would be fined or sacked.

Reduced speeds were required along high embankments, at public and private level crossings of which there were many, and also when the rails were wet which impeded braking. Long and heavy goods trains were allowed extra running times. In 1833, the directors compiled a set of operating instructions for issue to its servants, incorporating the dire warning that any failure "would incur the serious displeasure of the directors", the kind of railway management threat that has long lost its industrial relations bite.

At a later stage, hand bells were supplied for the use of level crossing gatemen and policemen when trains approached. As well as warning the public using the crossings, the bells were supposed to alert drivers; but whether they could be heard above the thunderous rhythm of the locomotive is doubtful. Earlier, the *Manchester Guardian*, ever ready with gratuitous and often helpful advice, suggested that a free-swinging bell should be mounted on locomotives as a warning in foggy weather. The writer argued that a free swinger would not depend on the will of the driver. He had a point.

Gates at thirteen public level crossings were normally open for the trains, and closed against the railway when road vehicles had to cross; but at a few crossings which carried heavy road traffic, the gates were normally open to the road, and were closed in good time for a train to pass. Unknown at the time, the rapidly increasing road traffic in years to come was to turn railway level crossings into veritable death traps and to involve legal and financial wrangles with local authorities, especially when bridges instead were proposed.

Gatemen who opened and closed the crossing gates usually worked for fifteen hours a day at about £1 a week, a night watchman covering the remaining nine hours. After a while, small huts were erected along the lonely countryside to protect the men from the extremes of weather. In old records, gatemen are sometimes called policemen, for the work had similarities.

It was about 1833 that the next modest developments in signalling began and flag poles were erected which took the fatigue out of continuous signalling by hand. Some fixed signal posts were put up to hold revolving boards and lamps; they were the harbingers of substantial fixed signal posts which eventually became standard practice on all railways. During the early 1830s, board minutes frequently expressed the dissatisfaction of directors with the signalling methods and equipment and they continuously sought improvements; and in the late 1830s, signals for day and night use were installed at intervals along the line.

Standard hand signals were formulated. A white light held steadily indicated all clear, waved from side to side meant caution, and up and down meant stop. A blue flag displayed told the driver of a second-class train that it should stop for passengers or luggage, and a black flag warned that the line ahead was under repair. One hand signal, still in use, was that any flag or lantern violently waved signalled danger, and the driver must stop his train. A train at speed needed a considerable braking distance before being halted, otherwise vehicles might become derailed, goods jolted off waggons, or passengers flung violently from their seats.

On night journeys, locomotives carried a large lighted lantern with powerful lenses as a head lamp. Locomotives frequently travelled tender first and a swivel lamp was fitted to tenders which could be turned to show a white light for reverse running.

Steam-operated whistles were fitted to locomotives; and in 1840, the company devised a simple whistle code for various situations such as when approaching a level crossing or station, or if the driver needed the assistance of the rear guard's brakes. Nowadays, one occasionally hears a diesel train siren, at the hand of a matey driver, sounding those first few familiar notes, "On Ilka Moor baht 'at!"

For extra safety, red bull's-eye reflectors were carried on the last vehicle of both passenger and goods trains; these could be picked up by the head lamp of a following locomotive if it were getting too close. Fixing the bull's eye was the responsibility of the guard or brakesman of the train. Safety was improved at level crossings when lamps were fitted on the gates, lighted from dusk to dawn, and a spare kept for emergency.

Crude and primitive though the signalling methods were, they were still the best so far formulated; and taking account of the number of trains using the line, the directors believed that serious accidents were comparatively few. The newness of the enterprise promoted caution at all levels.

As time went on, better signalling and track encouraged the company in 1837 to increase train speeds and during the summer the through journey time for fast passenger trains was down to an hour and a quarter. Now that locomotives were larger and more powerful, higher speeds were possible, but prudence prevailed.

Stray trespassers were often injured and sometimes killed by passing trains, and in 1840 the Board of Trade stepped in to warn the company that it would be held responsible. Consequently public warning notices were displayed and new instructions issued to railway workers.

About this period, the many other railways being built or opened sought the guidance of the Liverpool & Manchester about signalling methods. Late in 1840, a conference was held in Birmingham to discuss accident prevention and railway safety generally. Among the railways represented were the Grand Junction, London & Birmingham, Birmingham & Gloucester, Manchester & Leeds, Birmingham & Derby Junction, Chester & Birkenhead, Newcastle & Carlisle, London & Croydon and Great Western. The Liverpool & Manchester had been invited to send to these and other leading railways copies of their own signalling and operating regulations which might have general application. It was to be the *avant-coureur* of regular signalling conferences for all Britain and eventually embracing railways overseas.

At the second conference on 19th January 1841, also in Birmingham, chairman Charles Lawrence and treasurer Henry Booth had a warm reception and were immensely gratified to find that their regulations, printed copies of which were handed round, were accepted, without major changes apart from local ones, by the other railways.

However, lacking the experience of the Liverpool & Manchester men, other railway managers ran into their own accident troubles, which prompted in May 1841 the formation of a Parliamentary Committee to enquire into regulations for the safe working of all railways. These events were fully reported in the local and national Press, including *The Times*.

True to loyal form, on 6th February 1841, the *Manchester Guardian* had reported, "During the same year [1840] 1,052,000 passengers were conveyed upon the Liverpool and Manchester Railway with but one accident – and that one was the case of a passenger who recklessly jumped out of a second-class train, whilst at full speed, to save himself a few miles' walk." Despite that report, there had, of course, been many other accidents of varying seriousness. After studying the L & M regulations, that same newspaper had suggested on 2nd January 1841 that red should be the colour of flags and lantern lights to denote danger. Though red is of the highest physical frequency and the strongest colour in the spectrum, it seems not to have been adopted immediately by the L & M as its danger warning, but was soon to be accepted as such by all railways.

After the five-mile Warrington & Newton Railway had been connected at Warrington with the Grand Junction Railway opened from Birmingham in 1837, Newton was soon to be used as the junction for trains from the south, turning east for Manchester and west for Liverpool, and vice versa. It grew into a busy junction and an accident black spot, a nightmare for rural policemen coping with the tricky signalling. To enable policemen to identify Warrington-bound trains and to set the points off the L & M line, these trains carried on the front a diamond sign serving as a simple route indicator. Reporting on 24th December 1841, *The Times* commented on the dangerous complexity in which two curves connected with the Grand Junction, and served two branch lines, one to a colliery and the other to a chemical works.

A novel signalling device was fitted in the Liverpool tunnel in which signals in code about train departures for Edge Hill were sent by air pressure through a tube laid inside – an early example of direct communication between one signalling point and another. From those days, various kinds of air speaking-tubes came into use, and the phrase "You're wanted on the blower" can still be heard on railway premises to call a colleague to the telephone.

Meanwhile, along came a new invention that was to revolutionise railway signalling throughout the world, the electric telegraph. The system required electric signalling instruments, the impulses from which would be transmitted in code through wires erected on a series of telegraph poles along the trackside. They would be operated in conjunction with the policemen, or signalmen, displaying the signals.

Credit for this pioneering railway invention is attributed to the partners Professor Wheatstone and William Cooke. It would be an expensive installation needing sheds (signal boxes) to house the equipment, but much less costly than accidents. After experimenting in Heidelberg, Cooke was in England in 1836 to improve his instruments, and the following year the Liverpool & Manchester engaged him to conduct trials in the Liverpool tunnel, the most vulnerable section of the line. Almost certainly, the L & M was the first railway to anticipate electric telegraph signalling, yet another ten years elapsed before it was installed on the line.

All the other substantial railways steadily adopted the system. Bell codes of electric telegraph instruments may still be heard at the track side in old-type signal-boxes with their traditional red and yellow semaphore arm signals, a few of which, incredibly, are still oil lit. Most of these ancient edifices have made way for modern power signal-boxes equipped with electronic circuits, diodes, computers, automatic train describers, automatic colour-light signals and points, the one power installation controlling an entire section commonly of sixty to eighty miles, and maintaining high standards of safety, speed and punctuality.

Reasonably substantial passenger stations for the purpose had been built as terminals in Liverpool and Manchester, about which more anon; but the first intermediate stations were little more than halts. In a time-table of February 1831, sixteen intermediate stopping places were named: Wavertree Lane, Broad Green, Roby Gate, Huyton Gate, Kendrick Cross Gate, Top of Sutton Incline, Bottom of Sutton Incline, Collins Green, Viaduct, Newton Bridge, Parkside, Kenyon Junction, Bury Lane and Reids Farm, Patricroft, Eccles, Cross Lane Bridge. "Gate" stopping places were usually located where turnpike and other roads crossed the line on the level. Names were changed from time to time, some were closed and new ones opened to meet demand. In the absence of raised platforms, passengers had to climb in and out of carriages on the steps. After the Warrington & Newton Railway of nearly five miles was opened in 1831, Viaduct was renamed Warrington Junction, giving to the stranger no clue of its locality.

Around 1840, shelters as 'waiting places' were erected, platforms built, and tickets and time-tables printed to give official recognition to the wayside stations; station names were further consolidated by railway time-tables published by George Bradshaw which began in 1839.

Those primitive wayside stations may have been idyllic in summer, but were dreary outposts in winter.

In a Select Committee enquiry in Parliament in 1841, Henry Booth gave evidence about time-tables. "We have twenty stopping places," he explained, "and power to make more if the directors like, and it should be found convenient to the public; we do not stop at all places, but we do stop sometimes at six or eight on half the line, and we have scarcely any stoppages on the other half, but if we are to be limited to a time-table, we must be stopping at every one of the twenty stations."

Was a record kept of actual departure times from each intermediate station? "No," Booth answered, "it is hardly desirable with the number of stations on our line. The man merely has to open and shut the gate; the train stops, takes up the passengers, and goes on." All rather charmingly casual.

Though departure times from the terminal stations were published, the directors not only declined to quote intermediate station calling times, but indeed arrival times at the terminals. Too many hazards lay in wait. One driver told of battles with bulls and removing squealing pigs stuck between the rails. Trains were sometimes delayed "waiting for important people".

During hot summer weather, policemen down the line had to keep a sharp look-out for track-side fires from locomotive hot ash. These were rather frequent, delaying trains and sometimes resulting in claims from farmers for damaged crops. Excessive smoke was often more terrifying than the fire warranted; and this hazard remained as long as steam locomotives ran on Britain's railways.

One of the early disappointments for the directors was that their two terminal stations were on the edge instead of the centre of the two towns, but because of the barrage of opposition, they had had to be satisfied with their railway nudging the boundaries. To some extent, the service of horse omnibuses between town centre and railway terminal was a help.

So with the railway now establishing good services it was back to the drawing-board and a new Parliamentary Bill. Stephenson was asked in August 1831 to prepare plans for Liverpool which included a new tunnel over a mile long as the only means of access. Capital was earmarked and land purchased. The Company had to secure permission from the Liverpool Council and the Bill was passed on 23rd May 1832. Of the project, the *Liverpool Times* had commented, ". . . it will be a great accommodation for the public." A more central station would enable the horse-drawn omnibuses to be taken off the congested streets.

As soon as the plans were made public, astute land speculators purchased property which the railway might soon need, and the company found land prices rising. This was the kind of speculation that was to cost future railways a lot of money.

Trouble arose in constructing the tunnel, for in one section the direction was a little off course and correction took time and money. Stephenson was challenged by chagrined directors for an explanation, and the puzzled engineer discovered that his compass needle had been affected by underground iron drainage pipes.

Looking ahead, the company built a large station, called Lime Street, that hovered precariously between the pretentious and the prestigious. It contained extensive offices to serve as the nerve centre of the railway, at the same time allowing spare accommodation to rent to two other new railways with interests in Liverpool, the Grand Junction and the North Union. Its timber construction was superimposed on an iron framework, the whole surrounded by a vast slate roof. A wide ornamental frontage in dressed stone work and the spacious forecourt for private horse-drawn carriages presented a handsome and impressive entrance to the new station. Because the directors felt that its architectural merit enhanced the town, they appealed to the Liverpool Council to share the cost, and £2000 was donated.

It was on 15th August 1836, after a five-year stint, that Lime Street tunnel to the station was opened with appropriate public flourish, a memorable event in the world of railways, and adding prestige to Britain's second port.

Locomotives and waggons were prohibited in the tunnel. Carriages travelled down the slight gradient by gravity, the movement being controlled by two brakesmen riding in an open brake waggon; and they were hauled up the tunnel from Lime Street station by ropes attached to a heavy, geared counter-weight which went down a well sixty feet deep. The mind fairly boggles at the technicalities.

In Manchester, though Liverpool Road station was reasonably located, for some years the directors had sought a more central terminal. It so happened that the projected Manchester & Leeds Railway also needed a good site. Negotiations between the two railways were both acrimonious and protracted, at one stage temporarily involving the new Manchester Bury & Bolton Railway. Eventually, the Liverpool & Manchester and the Manchester & Leeds decided jointly to build a new station on a site in Hunts Bank to serve them both; this would need a new extension to the line of about a mile.

Several shareholders in the Liverpool & Manchester were originally not too happy about the idea of a railway between Manchester and Leeds for the simple reason that they also had financial stakes in the port of Liverpool; they feared the extension on to Hull which would syphon off much business shipped round the south coast to European ports. Clearly it would be an attractive proposition for merchandise to go by railway direct from Liverpool via Manchester and Leeds to Hull to cross the short North Sea route. But their narrow vested interests were not to prevail.

Cajolery, counter-proposals, excuses, hedging, threats and an ulti-
matum had been the unhappy tenor of the relationship between the
two railway protagonists arguing fiercely about sharing the costs and
facilities planned for Hunts Bank, disputes that made good stories for
the Press. One cunning ploy resulted in the Liverpool & Manchester
appointing Captain Laws, manager of the Manchester & Leeds, as a
member of its own board.

After four years of bitter wrangling, most differences had been
settled and the Act for the works was obtained on 30th July 1842. Parliamentary powers required the extension line to cross all the streets
by means of bridges or viaducts of stone, brick or iron, and the
company must make "substantial arches or culverts of brick or stone
over all gas pipes." Opposers had feared that a fiery locomotive
invading the sacred precincts of the town would jump the rails and
run amok.

This short extension with its new joint station had been one of the
most controversial projects since the line had opened in 1830; it left
the Manchester & Leeds as the principal owner of the station, and the
Liverpool & Manchester with limited rights of use.

Much detail appeared about the Hunts Bank plans in the *Manchester Guardian* on 19th August 1843. "The station, by which we
mean the lines with their sidings, turntables, and arrival and departure platforms for both companies, will be the largest in Britain . . . to
the length of 700 feet . . . the station will be covered with an iron
roofing. During the day, the station will be well lighted by skylights
in the roof, and during the night, by a series of gas lamps, fitted with
burners for the beautiful 'Rose light' . . ."

At one end of the station, the report continued, would be facilities
for horses and private carriages and for transferring carriages on and
off trains. A large covered shed would house spare carriages. Departure platforms would be about 320 feet long. At the centre of the
station would be the "station house. . . . This handsome building,
designed in what is termed the Roman Doric style, is only one storey
in height above the ground." It was being built in a warm-coloured
"parrpoint" stone, popular in the West Riding of Yorkshire, the
offices to be shared by the two railways.

In front of the station would be a refreshment room with a bar for
first- and second-class passengers, ladies' waiting room and a gentleman's saloon. A separate ticket office was allocated to third-class passengers, for whom a refreshment room with a bar would be available in
the basement. Perhaps rough working men, or shy maidservants travelling for posts as 'domestics' in wealthy households, would feel ill at
ease in the presence of distinguished gentlemen and finely adorned
ladies, and vice versa. Also in the basement would be "rooms for

porters, in which to wait and take their meals, during their hours of attendance at the station".

Stone pilasters and dressings, surmounted by elegant cornices, decorated the station frontage, in the centre of which was a large clock. Offices were built for the station-master and for parcels handling. Impressive doorways and a parapet surmounting the entire length of the building showed clearly that the railways cared for the public appearance of this prime site in the town.

The official opening of the new station for the Liverpool & Manchester line took place on 4th May 1844, by which time the Manchester & Leeds section had been in use for four months. With Lime Street at one end and Hunts Bank at the other, the Liverpool & Manchester service from town centre to town centre was at last completed. At a shareholder's suggestion, Hunts Bank station was renamed Victoria in honour of the Queen.

Among the many Press reports, the *Manchester Guardian* on 28th May 1844 stressed the new station's strategic role. "There is now therefore, one continuous line of railway communication across the country from Hull to Liverpool, and the Irish Channel is thus brought into close neighbourhood with the German Ocean."

Though the board had in hand parliamentary notices for other proposed extensions and branch lines, the Hunts Bank extension was the last new line the company built during its independence.

Other new railways were invading Manchester, none of their stations connecting by railway with the others, a feature which was to prove highly inconvenient in many other towns to passengers changing from one line to another, and to create problems for future generations of railway managements wishing to amalgamate.

Soon after the Liverpool & Manchester Railway was opened, a system of travel tickets had to be devised. On such new ground, the directors made a meal of it; each passenger had to give twenty-four hours' notice, and supply name, address, age, place of birth, occupation and reason for travelling: more a passport than a railway ticket. For each train, a waybill containing the names of all the passengers was handed to the guard. Flocks of passengers soon demolished this cumbersome routine and a paper ticket was introduced containing only basic information including the passenger's name; the booking clerk kept a counterfoil of each transaction. On the back of some tickets were heavy black printed lines as destination guides for the many people who were illiterate.

A canny merchant who used the railway six times a week in the early 1840s asked for a reduction on payment in advance for a year; the company compromised and allowed him a third reduction on six months. In 1845, annual tickets paid in advance were made available generally for the throughout journey at reduced rates, the first season tickets. Day return tickets at reduced fares were becoming popular with merchants travelling between the two terminal towns, especially in the 1840s.

To cope with goods and mineral traffic and to compete with the canals, over the years warehouses in Liverpool and Manchester were extended, and a range of equipment installed, such as cranes, hoists and weighing machines. Wharves in both towns were developed to handle large quantities of timber and coal. Exclusive use of a quay at Kings Dock in Liverpool had been secured for goods coming from ships to the railway, an excellent service for shipping merchants.

Cattle docks and pig pens at both terminals handled a heavy live-stock traffic, mainly from Ireland. Of the new facilities opened in Manchester in 1843, Henry Booth the treasurer reported to the Board: "The piggery just opened for four months was yielding considerably above 10 per cent on the outlay."

In 1843, the entire warehouse complex in Liverpool was threatened financially by a Bill presented in Parliament by the Liverpool Town Council as part of the port's fire prevention arrangements. Angry directors fought this "objectionable restriction" and petitioned Westminster vigorously. Eventually, Parliament bowed out to leave the Railway and the Council themselves to negotiate a mutual settlement. In the warehouses, men worked excessively long hours, and after dusk depended on candle-light, no small fire hazard.

Of the several workshops and locomotive sheds, the biggest at Edge Hill, Liverpool, was an unusually sturdy structure in that it had been hewn out of rock, under Stephenson's direction. Other structures at appropriate locations included carriage sheds, coach building shops, coke ovens to experiment with different grades of locomotive fuel, iron foundries, smithy, tool sheds, storerooms, lineside shelters and water tanks. This entire range was designed to meet the multifarious requirements for running the railway with efficiency and economy.

CHAPTER 9

Managing the Finances

Just as the directors had been treading virgin territory in constructing and launching the railway, so, too, were they striding a thorny path in pioneering a viable financial structure for their enterprise. They were risking vast capital, theirs and others', in an unknown realm. Most of the promoters and directors from the formative years of the line were already men of high financial standing in the shipping world, mining, heavy engineering, Lancashire cotton manufacturing, and importing and exporting. At least three had canal interests.

From the first Parliamentary Bill, the company met no real difficulty in attracting adequate capital from Liverpool, Manchester, London and Birmingham, long before interest could be earned. Now that the railway was in operation, the company sought growing revenues to justify their enterprise. Sources were mainly passenger fares and charges for goods conveyance. Services offered were far superior to the current competition, yet fares and charges had to be pitched at the right levels to be sustained and increased.

Wages for employees – trainmen, engineers, clerks, superintendents, labourers, signalling men, crossing keepers – needed to be just high enough to attract and build up the new labour force. Other financial demands, some unexpected, had to be met, such as a new track, liability for personal injury and death, and claims for loss or damage of goods in transit.

Operators of the railway, canals and roads were caught up in the universal and unceasing race of competition, that prime mover behind men's endeavours. Competition during 1831 forced canal owners and stage-coach operators to reduce their charges and improve their services; and while the railway spelled slow death for stage-coaches on the route, the increased trade generated in Lancashire by the railway also tended to bring more business for the canals.

On the turnpike roads, trustees cut rents to their lessees by as much as a half; but for two toll gates in Manchester, there were no takers, for fewer road waggons and stage-coaches were in business. Toll charges had long produced handsome revenues for the operators, but with railway competition, they began to feel the pinch.

In noting the growth of the passenger business within the first few years, a board minute recorded, "The means employed to attain this end have been principally a larger and more superior class of locomotive."

Passenger business, which started with a flourish, expanded rapidly within about a year, then remained fairly steady. But the rise in goods traffic tonnage was dramatic:

	passengers	merchandise	coal
1831	445,047	43,070	11,285
1835	473,847	230,629	116,246

Quantities of parcels and light goods were won from stage-coach services.

On 18th May 1831, fares for first class carriages with compartments seating four people were reduced from 7s (35p) to 6s (30p), and on open carriages "comfortably fitted up with cushions", 5s (25p). Open carriages were popular on fine summer days when extra trains were run. This table shows departure times from both Liverpool and Manchester published in 1835:

SEVEN o'Clock .... 1st Class Train

Quarter-past Seven o'Clock .... 2nd Class Train

TEN o'Clock .... 1st Class Train

Half-past Ten o'Clock .... 2nd Class Train

Twelve o'Clock .... 2nd Class Train

TWO o'Clock .... 1st Class Train

Three o'Clock .... 2nd Class Train

FIVE o'Clock .... 1st Class Train

Half-past Five o'Clock .... 2nd Class Train

(FARES)

By First Class Train, Coaches	Four Inside.	6s.6d.
Ditto	Six Inside.	5s.6d.
By Second Class Train,	Glass Coaches.	5s.6d.
Ditto	Open Carriages.	4s.0d.
Charges for Conveyance of	Four-Wheeled Carriages.	20s. each
Ditto	Two-Wheeled Ditto.	15s. each

Horses – For One Horse 10s. – Two Horses 18s – Three Horses 22s.

Horse-drawn private carriages on two or four wheels travelling by railway were secured and conveyed on flat waggons. The owners could travel on the train, rather like the modern Motorail service.

In the following summer, three more trains each way were added, to total twenty-four trains daily. As the Ritz in London was to be, the railway was open to all who could afford to pay, which automatically excluded most of the working populace. Even so, the directors sought to be practical, as recorded in a majority view in the Board minutes dated 27th July 1836: "A liberal policy towards the public will eventually be beneficial to the Proprietors."

During 1841, first-class carriages were fitted with window blinds, at the request of several corn merchants who presumably desired privacy and shade from the sun. Cost was negligible and customer satisfaction appreciable.

Anxious directors and shareholders realised in the mid-1830s that track improvements were essential and cost would be substantial. Locomotives were now more than twice the weight of the early ones and trains much heavier and faster, punishing the primitive permanent way. The pioneers were learning fast by experience. Within about two years, numerous rails had been bent or broken and the desperate directors sent for Stephenson. Experiments were made with various kinds of metal and different designs of rails and fittings; strength and wear and tear were carefully measured.

John Dixon compiled a detailed report for the board in June 1835 and the directors were so shaken that they made the bold and expensive decision to relay the entire line with new track.

Lavish alike with encomium and castigation as he fancied, Herapath in his *Railway Magazine* for March 1836 wrote scathingly about the track: "In many places the ballasting and dirt are almost on a level with the edge of the rails, while in others the naked blocks and sleepers present a terrifying aspect, threatening inevitable destruction to engines, carriages and passengers, should the train by any accident run off the rails. Indeed the *toute ensemble* looks like some half-finished work, reflecting the features, not of a rich and flourishing company, but of abject, pitiable poverty." A more sympathetic sentiment came in an anonymous letter, "The Directors of this line have had the disadvantage of having to contend with inexperience. . . ."

Track work proceeded and the company obtained another Act of Parliament in 1837 to raise the capital required. By the end of the year, the line had been completely relaid with new track bed and rails on a deep cushion of earth and ballast for a smoother ride and better drainage. Stone sleepers, which tended to sink in the ballast, were replaced by larchwood timber.

Even then, troubles arose. Small gaps between the ends of the rails allowed for expansion and contraction; but at Parkside the gaps were too narrow and in an exceptionally hot summer, the rails buckled badly and had to be relaid. Trial and error continued, and the technical details were widely analysed in the Press and studied by other railways to their permanent benefit. In years to come, the flat-bottom rail was to be devised to absorb temperature changes and to allow many miles of rails to be continuously welded.

The beady eyes of ambitious promoters had been riveted on the remarkable financial success of the Liverpool & Manchester, and within a decade new railways were opening in all parts of the country. Connections with other railways, notably the Grand Junction and the Manchester & Leeds, promised more revenues through direct services.

But the most significant development for the L & M, and indeed for all the new railways which were opening up at mania speed, was the introduction of third-class travel. As early as 1829, a Liverpool man had suggested running third-class trains. But smartly the directors said no! It would tempt first-class passengers to transfer to second, and second to third, with revenue losses.

Then, in 1844, the heavy hand of Parliament fell. That tireless liberal reformer, William Ewart Gladstone (1809–98), four times Prime Minister, put an end to some of the nonsense about the 'poorer classes'. All railways, it was decreed, must provide third-class travel. But that was not all. The fare must not exceed a penny a mile, carriages should be covered over against the elements, and at least one train a day must run each way with third-class accommodation at a minimum speed of twelve miles an hour. That brought the lowest fare between Liverpool and Manchester to 2s. 6d. (12½p). Some railways were already carrying third-class passengers at just over a penny a mile.

But that was still not all. Gladstone's Act, the first Parliamentary measure to exercise effective control over all railways, laid down specific measures for management and safe operation; it also included an option for the State to purchase any new railway outright after twenty-one years, but full State ownership was not to materialise until 1948.

Shareholders and directors country wide were angered at this Government interference. Some scorned it as 'The Railway Plunder Bill'. Unscrupulous railway managements ran their third-class trains, known for years as 'Parliamentary Trains', early in the morning and late at night.

Starting on 1st October 1844, dutifully the Liverpool & Manchester ran one third-class train daily in each direction and the 'lower classes' thronged in such numbers that in the following April, another was added, swelling the revenues. Many of the 'carriages', if you will pardon the sobriquet, were little more than merchandise waggons, open to the sky, and fitted with bench seats. But slowly, competition brought improvements; and of the various sections of the community to benefit from the facility, the poor gained most of all.

Though goods trains shared the same tracks, their story was a different one. From the beginning, goods traffic had not generated the volume of revenues the directors had expected. Even so, within a few years the range of merchandise carried was wide in a service that was helping to put Lancashire ahead during the Industrial Revolution, bringing wealth to local industries. Goods included coal, iron, clay, stable manure, timber, lime, slates, grain, flour, coffee, tea, sugar, dairy produce, livestock, oil tallow, wines and spirits, and manufactured goods. Growing exports and imports brought a great new impetus to the port of Liverpool.

Livestock conveyance took some off the roads. Cattle droving was a common sight at that period, some journeys taking days, with drovers sleeping rough, animals deteriorating in marketable weight or dying, and messing up unpleasantly the streets and roads in the process.

When, as often happened, severe frost closed some of the canals, goods trains rumbled along the railway one after another, which one chronicler described as "a flowing river of traffic". Occasionally, extremely long goods trains were made up, a fruitful source of earning revenue economically, and needing up to five coupled locomotives to haul them. In those days of loose coupled waggons, the clanging must have echoed far across the lonely countryside. A long train one night in May 1840 was drawn by two locomotives, *Elephant* and *Hercules*, and it was so heavy it had to be uncoupled at the foot of Whiston incline, hauled in three or four portions, then recoupled at the top. The delay must have been prolonged and the hazards unthinkable.

Competition with the canals in the early 1840s prompted a period of rate cutting. One method was to allow customers free warehousing at Liverpool and Manchester while the canals made separate charges. Some attempt was made by joint agreements between the railway and the canals, but after settlement, these would be broken, first by one side and then the other, and secret rate cuts were made behind each other's backs. To and fro, it was still war to the knife.

Led by Charles Lawrence, several directors in 1842 formed a committee "to fix the Railway rates and charges, and generally to conduct the contest with the Canal Carriers". Immediately after, they cut the railway rates. Then, the canals did likewise, followed by a further reduction by the railway; it was a ruinous way of conducting business in a reckless contest in which the canal owners did all they could to carry out their threat to ruin the railway.

To some extent they succeeded, for railway goods revenues began to fall alarmingly. It was the next year that broad agreement was reached between the Bridgewater Navigation, the Old Quay Company and the Liverpool & Manchester for the whole structure of railway and water rates. It had been a fight not to a finish but to an uneasy compromise, and a restless peace pervaded their relationships during the remaining two years of the railway's independence.

Marginal competition was also growing among the several new railways now invading Lancashire, but some benefit came to the Liverpool & Manchester by arranging with the Manchester & Leeds, partly opened in 1841, for through traffic direct between Liverpool via Manchester and the Yorkshire industrial areas. This, too, upset the canal people.

For two decades, the wealthy and influential canal companies had done their durnedest to destroy the pioneering railway; and if the L & M had not been so well fortified by its passenger revenues, which exceeded those for goods, the story might have been different. Nonetheless, the sensitive market forces of water and road competition chastised the railway's tendency to monopoly.

Careful surveillance of fuel costs had been made from the beginning, and though coal and anthracite had been tried on various locomotives, the advantages of rapid heat and little smoke from coke maintained this product as the regular fuel.

During its lifetime of fifteen years, the railway paid out numerous sums of money for personal injury and death, and for the loss and damage of goods. Directors had sought to establish a firm policy, but pusillanimous lawyers vacillated with such uncertainty that because of lack of precedents each case was argued on its merits and usually settled out of court. One which reached court in 1837 concerned a Mr Newton who was injured when his horse omnibus collided with a railway crossing gate; he was awarded £50.

Charlatans sometimes cashed in on false claims. One passenger claimed he had lost a bag worth £136; under pressure, the directors awarded him a 'donation' of £50, while disclaiming responsibility.

Legal battles between the company and merchants frequently centred on goods lost or damaged in the terminal warehouses, and the railway took out insurance against this to the tune of £20,000. On odd occasions, a cow would stray on the line and be struck by a passing train, bringing a claim from the farmer. It was not until Lord Campbell's Act of 1846 that liability for personal injury and death on railway trains and premises was clearly defined by Parliament; juries were then empowered to give verdicts, if necessary compelling railways to pay sums of money to the representatives of the deceased.

Financial losses, dangers and delays were caused many times by vandals and drunks; and on 10th August 1840 an Act for Regulating Railways included the clause, "Anyone obstructing Railways in any way so as to endanger safety of persons conveyed thereon shall be guilty of misdemeanour, or on conviction be imprisoned with or without hard labour not exceeding two years."

On the credit side, savings resulted from original ideas submitted by various people. The directors were always willing to allow locomotive builders and inventors of ancillary equipment to make tests on the line, and to adopt those of value. Suggestions from employees at any level proved useful. Henry Booth's idea for vehicle lubrication brought economies; and Melling, the railway's locomotive foreman, among various improvements designed a 'Patent Link Gearing' for locomotives. Employees' inventions, mainly modest, were patented by the company.

Useful revenues had been earned by the conveyance of Post Office mails since 1830, despite continuous rates wrangles on the way. This came to a head in 1837 during the national depression when the Post Office had the nerve to propose running their own trains on the railway free of charge to save money; they even presented a Bill in Parliament to that effect. But the directors were hardly that naïve. Led by Charles Lawrence, Henry Booth and Joseph Sandars, and supported by other railways and the ever faithful *Manchester Guardian*, the railway mounted all its resources with such fury that the following year they killed the Bill. A new agreement for mails was negotiated, giving the railway much more control of the conveyance. That showed those Post Office men where to get off.

Another Post Office venture, this time of national proportions, was to affect the railway's revenues. After a lengthy campaign, former schoolmaster Rowland Hill (1795–1879) later knighted, in 1840 introduced his 'penny post' Bill for letters, at a time when they cost ten or twenty times that. In that year, the first adhesive postage stamps were produced, with Queen Victoria's head printed in black (penny black); this was the embryo of that great new hobby of philately. Hill was later appointed a director then chairman of the London & Brighton Railway.

Increasing literacy and cheap postal rates brought more revenues to the railway; on the other hand, merchants conducted more of their transactions by post instead of by travel – swings and roundabouts.

Some shareholders disapproved of trains running on the 'Lord's

Day' and forfeited their profits earned by Sunday trains, not easy to compute. At first, no-one knew what to do with the money, until the board, which often received requests for donation to religious and charity bodies, decided to set up a fund. Sympathetic directors were particularly moved to do so by the severe winter of 1838 which left many poor people destitute. Among beneficiaries from the accumulating money were poor relief funds, provident societies, medical dispensaries and the Eye Hospital in Manchester. The directors made it clear that the money had come from this special fund and not from the pockets of railway proprietors; no feigned modesty was intended, but rather to placate those shareholders who may have thought the whole idea inappropriate anyway.

While the directors managed their financial affairs successfully and conscientiously, some of their detractors thought otherwise. Nothing invites criticism more than success, and attacking opponents accused the company of fiddling the books, or, in the language of polite society, misappropriating the accounts. Public controversy on this issue goaded the directors into angry defence; they were afraid that their reputation might be tarnished, investment fall off, or their shares deteriorate from 'bulls' to 'bears', just when new capital was needed.

Charges of impropriety streamed from the vitriolic pen of one Thomas Grahame: mishandling funds, a cover-up of expenditure and errors in published accounts. He questioned the estimates for receipts, which the directors had to admit, and claimed that the railway paid lower rates of government tax than did stage-coach operators. Grahame had published an attacking treatise as far back as 1834. He stated that the public should be protected from being fooled by a false appearance of sound finance.

Grahame conceded that "the promoters and directors having had little to guide them, except the calculations and theories of engineers, railways as general modes of conveyance being then unknown . . . all their statements were merely assumptions unproved in practice".

Such outbursts were typical of the aura of suspicion that enveloped this and other new railways. Another was made by R. Cort in one of the most smirching and diabolical accusations that could be hurled at any public company. He claimed that because of flagrant deception it was impossible to prove anything, for the simple reason that the directors kept two sets of accounts: one 'private' and the other 'public ordinary'.

While the Corts and the Grahames rampaged, sympathisers rushed to the rescue. Thomas Taylor asserted that the railway "was neither visionary nor impracticable", and compared with stage-coaches and canals had given satisfaction to the public. Honest-to-goodness Henry Booth, as company treasurer, stood at the blunt end of the financial battering, and after a year or two of public criticism, he wrote to his chairman, Charles Lawrence, on 19th October 1838:

"It was my province to give effect to the deliberations and decisions of directors, who in former days, through evil and good report, without favour from the legislature or encouragement from the public, while the risk was evident and the gain problematical, with intelligence, perseverance, and singleness of purpose pursued their work till success crowned their labours, and multitudes were eager to follow their example."

From its earliest days, the railway had been required to pay tax on its passenger business. A new rate starting in 1832 had been based on the number of carriages, whether full or empty, and had cost the company some £15,000 a year. Incensed at the severity and unfairness, a delegation of directors travelled to London to call on the Minister responsible for tax. That austere gentleman relented and it was agreed that the tax would be based on "per mile per passenger", a system which ran for ten years when it was modified to a commuted rate of 5 per cent of the total passenger revenues, to start on 1st August 1842. Prime Minister Pitt had introduced a general war tax in 1799 to finance the war against France, a temporary measure repeated in 1803 and 1805, developing into the beginnings of the British tax system; and Sir Robert Peel's Act of 1842 shook the wealthy by inflicting an income tax rate of seven pence (3p) in the £1, seen in those days as a penal imposition.

In financing the railway enterprise, shareholders were required to pay a proportion of the value they purchased, meeting the balance – the 'call' – within a specified subsequent date. Shares of those who failed to meet their calls were allocated for purchase by the railway directors or their nominees, an arrangement authorised by statute. Invariably, estimates of costs for major projects fell far short of the requirements; in fact, the original estimate for building and equipping the railway was £510,000, but Henry Booth tells us that the actual cost was about £820,000. However, throughout its fifteen years, the company was successful, not always without difficulty, in raising additional capital by issuing joint stock and obtaining loans.

Whatever the critics had to say, the figures speak for themselves. Most shares were in units of £100 (possibly £4,000 to £6,000 today); and though half-yearly dividends moved mainly between £4 and £5 (£10 per annum being the maximum permitted by statute) the shares were valued in the money markets at around the £200 mark and rarely fell below £180. At the end of the railway's independence in 1845, they had risen to about £212. In its time, the Liverpool & Manchester earned fame in railway financial circles for its remarkable achievements, while many other railways were faring far worse.

It was largely the company's handsome capital appreciation that had encouraged other railway promoters to forge ahead. Far from distributing all the profits to shareholders, the directors wisely withheld a proportion in a reserve fund for future contingencies.

Just as other railways had followed in engineering and locomotive power the pioneering pattern of the Liverpool & Manchester, so too did they structure their financing, investment and management on the L & M proved methods. The directors could well claim to have more than fulfilled their early promise, and several were invited to join the boards of other developing railway ventures.

The sad remains of the notorious Moorish Arch in Wapping Cutting at Edge Hill, Liverpool, a century and a half later. Compare it with the magnificence of that glorious opening-day pictured facing page 116.

The Leeds-York-Liverpool stage-coach passing Newton village church while a train travels on the distant embankment.

The treacherous bog of towards five miles across Chat Moss, several miles from Manchester. Distinguished engineers and parliamentarians declared that Stephenson was mad to think of building a railway across a swamp. Still standing firm, it has sunk many feet since those days. (From a contemporary drawing by Shaw.)

This beautifully symmetrical bridge was built by Charles Vignoles, erstwhile assistant to Stephenson, to carry the St Helens & Runcorn Gap Railway over the Liverpool & Manchester near Sutton. Present-day motorway-bridges do not seem to look so good!

When opened in 1844, Manchester Victoria Station boasted a 700-foot iron roofing and was the largest station in Britain. Magnificently lighted by gas-lamps, this establishment was shared between the Liverpool & Manchester and the Manchester & Leeds.

This 'mile-post' comes from Olive Mount Cutting and shows the distance from Manchester.

Original fish-bellied wrought-iron rails from the Liverpool & Manchester Railway of 1829.

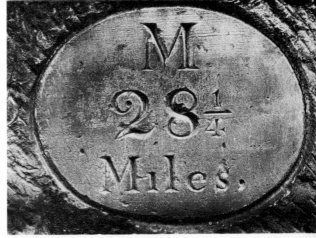

These fine prints, from the Ackermann Collection based on drawings made in the 1830s, authoritatively confirm that people and pigs really did travel by train within smelling-distance of each other. Behind the first-class

train is seen the Royal Mail Coach. In the second-class
train, two types of open carriages are shown. *Below:* a
mixed goods and a livestock train.

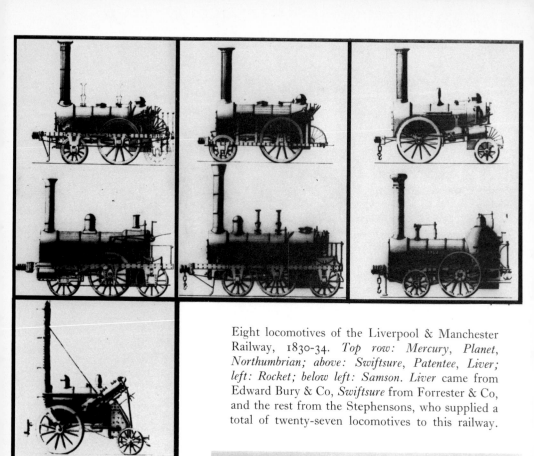

Eight locomotives of the Liverpool & Manchester Railway, 1830-34. *Top row: Mercury, Planet, Northumbrian; above: Swiftsure, Patentee, Liver; left: Rocket; below left: Samson. Liver* came from Edward Bury & Co, *Swiftsure* from Forrester & Co, and the rest from the Stephensons, who supplied a total of twenty-seven locomotives to this railway.

A station sundial of the 1830s. Inscribed "Railway Station, Manchester 1833", it remained mounted on a stone pillar above the main doorway for many years.

Souvenirs became popular almost as soon as the railways, and their fascination has never abated. This *papier-mâché* tray, about 16½ inches long, shows the grand opening of the railway at Edge Hill and was probably made in Birmingham in 1831. The plate and mugs are from the same period; the mug featuring the *Novelty* locomotive bears the marks of the years in its glazing.

Each of these travel-tickets tells its own story of the times. That for the Treasurer –
both sides are shown – was presumably for an official of the Grand Junction
Railway travelling on the Liverpool & Manchester as a reciprocal arrangement.
Hardeman Earle served as a director also for the North Union Railway and for
the L & M sat on many sub-committees.

CHAPTER 10

Social and Industrial Influence of the Railway

The metamorphosis from man and animal muscle to locomotive steam power wrought by the Liverpool & Manchester Railway did more than increase speed from walking pace to forty miles an hour, or multiply massively the number of passengers or tons of goods that could be carried together for long distances; it revolutionised the whole concept of industrial development, and a social and economic way of life that had barely altered for centuries.

Henry Booth, pioneering promoter, and the company's secretary and treasurer, disseminated widely the railway gospel according to the L & M by his considerable literary gifts. In the very first history of the railway ever written, which he published in 1830 shortly before the line officially opened, he was obviously conscious of standing at the very threshold of a great historical epoch. He captures the drama of the revolution of which the railway was the *avant-coureur*:

"Notions we have received from our ancestors, and verified by our own experience, are thrown over in a day, and new standards erected, by which to form our ideas for the future. Speed – despatch – distance – are still relative terms, but their meaning has been totally changed within a few months: what was quick is now slow; what was distant is now near; and this change in our ideas will not be limited to the environs of Liverpool and Manchester – it will pervade society at large. . . . A transition in our accustomed rate of travelling, from eight or ten miles an hour to fifteen or twenty (not to mention higher speeds), gives a new character to the whole internal trade and commerce of the country. A saving of time is a saving of money . . . the traveller will live double times: by accomplishing a prescribed distance in five hours, which used to require ten, he will have another five at his disposal . . . the quick conveyance of merchandise will infuse new life into trade and manufacturers."

This publication was distributed by booksellers from Liverpool, Manchester, London, the Midlands and Edinburgh. Containing a map of the line, details of planning, construction, locomotives, parliamentary procedures, and financial tables, this modest volume served as a veritable text book for numerous railway promoters. This, coupled with his other writings and the published works of directors and engineers, plus the constant coverage by newspapers, technical journals and society magazines, combined to provide, in Britain and overseas, a stream of intelligence about the day-to-day advance of the railway. A second edition of Booth's book was published in Philadelphia in 1831.

In the early years of the line, it was an event in people's lives to see and hear a live locomotive, and to travel on a railway train for the first time. For the town and country labouring classes, even a ride in an open railway waggon with bench seats offered a modicum of luxury compared with hours on a horse or squatting on a cart loaded with produce for the markets.

The railway let loose the travel bug in a hitherto relatively static population. It was high adventure for townsfolk to journey from their smelly dwellings into the country and to travel along the high embankment at Roby, overlooking tree tops and enjoying the fresh, scented air.

Soon, two thousand passengers were using the line daily and hordes of excited relatives, friends and sightseers crowded the terminals to see the trains away. Porters, in the course of their duties, found it difficult to bellow above the babble; and according to board minutes of 1832, a large bell was installed, to be rung five minutes before trains departed. Latecomers would come tearing along the track and try to board a moving train, sometimes with disastrous results. To combat this, barrier gates were erected at station entrances and were smartly closed when the train was ready.

Men who had been accustomed to travelling on the top outside seats of stage-coaches sometimes foolishly climbed on to the tops of railway carriages which, with rails round the roof to secure luggage, resembled their road counterparts. Several accidents prompted the directors to introduce a byelaw: "Riding on the roof forbidden". Perhaps used to jumping off farm carts while the horse was still trotting, many passengers alighted from moving trains and 'came a cropper', for the carriages were travelling faster than they had judged.

The influence of the railway on travel by turnpike roads was soon to be felt in Lancashire. Stage-coach travel had enlivened and romanticised the English scene for nearly two centuries, and the operators realised only too clearly that faster and more comfortable travelling for greater distances would soon begin to eclipse their time-honoured business.

At their peak in the 1830s, throughout Britain some 3,500 stage coaches and 700 Royal Mail coaches were in service, Manchester and Liverpool being focal points in the north-west. It is estimated that some 30,000 men were employed as coachmen, guards, jehus, postilions, ostlers and stable hands, immortalised by Sam Weller and other Dickensian characters.

Comparing road with railway, Herapath regretted the undramatic departure of Liverpool & Manchester trains from their important terminal stations, and in his *Railway Magazine* writes picturesquely, "Every one who has seen the starting of a well-horsed stage coach has doubtless felt the sensation it produces. The proud, impatient pawing of the horses, and the melodious notes of the bugle, give an air of imposing grandeur to our departing friends. . . ."

As more people deserted stage coach for railway carriage, the road operators put up a futile fight against the competing and compelling alternative; they made their coaches more comfortable and attractive, reduced fares, increased speeds and changed the teams of horses more frequently. But speed and safety on the poor roads made incompatible bedfellows.

Smiles records that in its first eight years, "five millions of passengers had been conveyed along the Liverpool & Manchester Railway and . . . only two persons had lost their lives by accident." This was an understatement, but there were far fewer injuries and deaths on the line than coach operators had predicted. Smiles continues, "Loss of life by the upsetting of stage coaches had been immensely greater in proportion."

On his many stage-coach journeys, George Stephenson had several narrow escapes. Travelling through the south Midlands, a linchpin securing the wheels broke. "The coach soon toppled over," a chronicler tells us, "and fell crash upon the road, amidst the shrieks of his fellow passengers and the smashing of glass." Shaken but unscathed, Stephenson tended the bleeding passengers and the injured driver and guard, and cut the frightened sprawling horses free from their harnesses.

For local journeys, it was some years before the more opulent classes, who could afford post-chaise travel to town in aristocratic style, became reconciled to the railway train. But sons of noble families, with less to spend and more scorning of tradition, were quickly attracted by the cheapness, convenience and sheer novelty of travel in a fast railway carriage.

Nonetheless, many people were saddened to witness the decline of the romantic stage coach. Smiles who, in a long life of ninety-two years, had travelled extensively by road and railway, leaves a colourful but realistic vignette of rolling along the rugged highways of England:

"Many deplored the inevitable downfall of the old stage-coach system. There was to be an end of that delightful variety of incident usually attendant on a journey by road. The rapid scamper across a fine country on the outside of the four-horse *Express* or *Highflyer*, the seat on the box beside Jehu [coach driver], or the equally coveted place near the facetious guard behind. The journey amid open green fields, through smiling villages and fine old towns, where the stage stopped to change horses and the passengers to dine – was all delightful in its way; and many regretted that this old-fashioned and pleasant style of travelling was about to pass away.

"But it had its dark side also. Any one who remembers the journey by stage from London to Manchester or York, will associate it with recollections and sensations of not unmixed delight. To be perched for twenty hours, exposed to all weathers, on the outside of a coach trying in vain to find a soft seat – sitting now with the face to the wind, rain, or sun, and now with the back – without any shelter such as the commonest penny-a-mile parliamentary train now daily provides – was a miserable undertaking, looked forward to with horror by many whose business required them to travel frequently between the provinces and the metropolis.

"Nor were the inside passengers more agreeably accommodated. To be closely packed in a little, inconvenient, straight-backed vehicle, where the cramped limbs could not be in the least extended, nor the wearied frame indulge in any change of posture, was felt by many to be a terrible thing.

"Then there were the constantly recurring demands, not always couched in the politest terms, for an allowance to the driver every two or three stages, and to the guard every six or eight, and if the gratuity did not equal their expectations, growling and open abuse were not unusual. These *désagréments*, together with the exactions practised on travellers by innkeepers, seriously detracted from the romance of stage-coach travelling, and there was a general disposition on the part of the public to change the system for a better."

Older people especially were sad to witness the dying days of the stage-coach and its steaming chestnuts, calling at a post in town or country, to be welcomed by the ruddy-faced innkeeper serving brimming tankards of English ale. Imagine the ladies in their bonnets, crinolines and bulging bustles at their buttocks, courteously handed down from their seats by frock-coated gentlemen in chimney-pot hats; a hurried change of horses, the sound of the cracking whip and the post-horn, the burly driver settles the capes of his coat round his shoulders, and the coach grinds off into the distance in a cloud of dust. . . .

Though the stage coach and its social order vanished from the roads of Britain over a century ago, the timeless charisma of the 'good old days' when the world rolled along at a leisurely pace, has been kept alive by generations of Christmas-card artists to the unfailing delight of the recipients. Symbolically, railwaymen today still know railway carriages as 'coaching stock'.

The expansion of the stage-coach industry during the late eighteenth century had been made possible largely by the driving energy of Thomas Telford and John Macadam who built many good roads, adding to a system that had seen little radical change since the Roman occupation.

When the Liverpool & Manchester Railway arrived, many stage-coach builders turned their skills to building carriages for the line, until the company began to build their own; they also built vehicles for other new railways coming on the scene. This railway and others owed a considerable debt to the coaching industry in terms of carriage design and in organising passenger services.

Just as the directors had taken care to design passenger carriages to appeal to a discerning public taste, so too did they see that their major structures were pleasing to the eye. Notable examples were the Sankey Viaduct, the Moorish Arch and the two new stations – Lime Street in Liverpool and Victoria at Hunts Bank in Manchester. Other railways followed this lead as part of the policy to persuade the public to accept railways as a whole. As the century progressed, the country's best architects were commissioned to build main stations, some of which remain as representative of the finest buildings of the great Victorian era, by implication as solid and dependable as the Bank of England. Grecian columns, Italianate flamboyance, the stately home and the English castle were popular design ingredients. Smaller stations resembled country villas or Tudor-style half-timbered cottages.

In the 1840s, the new stations in Liverpool and Manchester matured steadily as centres of public interest, for they attracted investors in inns, restaurants, hotels, shops, and stages for the dying coach industry: all reciprocative to the railway business.

When the Liverpool & Manchester Railway entered the labour market for the range of abilities and skills required, most of the needs were of the menial kind. This new source of work gave fresh opportunities to ease the miseries of the labouring poor who, at any rate in the two main towns, endured a slum life in a background of squalor and crime. In the early 1830s, labour uprisings were troubling the Government, and it was fortunate that the large amount of new employment, directly in the new railway and from the consequential expansion which began in the coal, iron and manufacturing industries, did much to quell the upsurge.

In a mammon-orientated era, more and more employers were doing better for their work people and in the conditions of those days, the Liverpool & Manchester directors were better than many. Henry Booth, the treasurer, consistently revealed humane sentiments. In describing the factories and works served by the railway, he referred to the workers and "that eternal round of labour and care, of abundant toil and scanty remuneration, of strained exertion and insufficient repose, which, through day and night, through seed time and harvest, through years of civilisation and ages of barbarism, have been the condition and tenure to which the existence of so large a portion of mankind has depended."

He considered that the effect of the railway would be decidedly favourable. "It has frequently been a matter of regret, that in the progress of mechanical science, as applicable to trade and manufactures, the great stages of improvements are too often accompanied with severe suffering to the industrious classes of society. . . ." And contemplating the railway, he expostulated, "What a source of occupation to the labouring community!"

While some directors shared his social conscience, money must be made and shareholders' dividends paid. By today's aims of a thirty-five-hour week, the long hours worked by the 'railway servants' were shattering. Station and warehouse men had to work from six in the morning till ten at night, or even longer, earning a tiny bonus for extra time. Objections by the men in the 1840s reduced the hours at the Wapping terminus in Liverpool to around fourteen or fifteen a day, these menial workers rarely earning more than £1 a week.

Office clerks were paid about £100 to £130 a year, and a head clerk, £200. As business increased, lad clerks were engaged at 5s (25p) a week. A nice social distinction was made between manual workers paid at a weekly wages rate, and office staff, superintendents, and others 'higher up' at an annual salary rate, a practice in railways and other industries still perpetuated. Locomotive drivers could earn over £2 a week and firemen somewhat less; both were paid extra for certain special trains.

Booth, in his full role of secretary and treasurer, was the highest paid officer. In 1834, he received a salary increase from £750 to £1,000, and four years later to £1,500. Assistant engineers, superintendents and foremen were paid roughly between £100 and £300 a year according to ability and responsibility.

Provided the railway workers behaved themselves, employment in the railway was fairly regular.

By 1832, George Stephenson had brought a nucleus of about sixty "steady and sober" enginemen from his native Newcastle and the north-east, and these men trained others in the arts of coaxing the temperamental steam locomotive. To maintain high standards, the board formed a sub-committee in 1834 to approve the hire of every driver and firemen. A new agreement required enginemen freshly appointed to give three months' notice of leaving, and to deposit £10 (about five weeks' wages) as security for good conduct. One objective was to discourage them from scurrying off to other new railways being built in Lancashire and elsewhere.

Men were sometimes hired or fired depending on the level of railway business handled, and employees were often sacked for misconduct, being drunk, breaking the operating rules, and causing accidents. As a financial measure, in 1835 the directors proposed a reduction in enginemen's pay and the men's reaction was that they would leave the railway *en bloc*. Booth was directed to write to each man giving him the chance to change his mind or quit. Final though that sounded, invidious negotiations rumbled on for several months; then on 8th February 1836, most of the enginemen stayed away from their work, or, in popular parlance, they went on strike. Their main complaints were about excessive hours and damage to their clothing from the open footplates.

Train delays and loss of revenue immediately followed, but the vacant places were soon filled by men from the company's own mechanical workshops. Within days of the stoppage, both the *Liverpool Times* and the *Manchester Guardian* commented:

"The engineers on the railway still remain out, but their places are well supplied, and some three or four of them who left their work contrary to agreement have been sent to study practical mechanics on the rotatory engine at Kirkdale House of Correction, commonly called the tread-mill." As elsewhere in industrial England, the management firmly held control.

Running costs were temporarily increased, partly from accidents and delays caused by inexperienced enginemen. The company was convinced that this was better than giving in to the men. "The directors," said *The Times* on 27th June, "have taken care that their present enginemen should all enter into agreements of service, and they have every reason to believe that the strict measures adopted in this first display of insubordination will tend powerfully to secure discipline and good conduct hereafter." And that proved to be the case.

Drivers on the Liverpool & Manchester were the genesis of a new breed of railwaymen; physically strong and robust, they were of independent character that was nurtured by the personal responsibility of driving their trains in the face of frequent difficulties and dangers.

Trainmen were given a lively literary ride via the quill of Herapath in the *Railway Magazine* dated March 1836. Here is an extract:

"I shall never forget the impression made on me once when ascending the Whiston inclined plane. I was outside the carriage last before the mail, with my back towards the engine, and noting down the time of our passing the quarter-mile posts. We shot by the station of the auxiliary engine, a dirty-looking place at the foot of the plane, with great velocity, and before we had ascended half a mile our speed had diminished nearly three-fourths. The former engine now slowly moved into our track, and then pursued us with the swiftness of an arrow.

"Here the effect began. The red hot cinders every now and then dropping from the grate, the immense volume of steam issuing from the chimney, together with the black faces of the men, and the flying velocity of their engine, I could not help observing to the guard who attended me, looked as if his Satanic Majesty had just sent two of his imps with the instrument of torture vomiting with fire and smoke . . . to which the deep grunting of our own engine, now distinctly audible from our slow motion, seemed to typify the moans of despair."

Hard taskmasters though they were, the Liverpool & Manchester people deserve credit for a number of innovations which eased the burdens of their workers. They built railway cottages, presaging the era of railway terrace houses; in them they housed policemen, level crossing keepers, station men, mechanics, clerks and others. Most were simple structures of timber or local stone, had two or three bedrooms, and unfinished interiors and dirt floors, common in cottages of the period. Rents varied. One with a small patch of ground at Sutton was 3s. 6d. (17½p) a week, and a "wood cottage on the line", 2s. (10p).

Bonuses were paid to 'servants' for accident-free records, long and faithful service, good conduct, and care of equipment. When business was good, bonuses were more liberal.

Bearing only moral obligations, the board on many occasions gave financial aid to employees absent from work because of illness or injury. Medical expenses were paid for those seriously injured on duty; one labourer laid up for nearly four months in 1840 was paid half his usual wages. As treasurer, the liberal Booth usually paid out such expenses at his personal discretion.

From the beginning, the Liverpool & Manchester did not hold itself liable for the dependants of an employee killed on duty, but in practice the treasurer made discretionary payments from a special benevolent fund the company had created. Not until after the company had lost its independence did the Government step in humanely concerning deceased employees' dependants. A director named Hardman Earle proposed that employees should be encouraged to join a benefit society on small regular payments; a number did so and were able to qualify for sick benefit.

To induce employees to put something by for a rainy day, the directors in 1832 and again in 1841 tried to create an employee savings bank. Understandably, the most thrifty man had little to spare from his meagre wages, and the scheme seems not to have got off the ground. But not many years later, the larger railways adopted this suggestion and the idea bore fruit; regular deductions were made from employees' wages and sums could be withdrawn at will in times of need, the deposits earning interest. From those early beginnings, the British Rail Staff Savings Bank has evolved with employee deposits in the late 1970s running to over twenty million pounds.

Another 'good employer' move in 1843 was the setting up of a circulating library and reading room which the literate few could enjoy. But clearly the directors wished to avoid their servants' innocent minds being tarnished by 'undesirable material', for they personally approved all the books and periodicals to be stocked. Railway libraries were to thrive elsewhere and to mature into some of the finest literary collections of their kind in Britain today.

Against the criteria of the day, the directors sought to be fair and reasonable employers, a necessary *sine qua non* in maintaining an efficient and economical railway system. Wages in other industries in the county tended to rise because of the reasonably good wages the Liverpool & Manchester paid and other new railways were inclined to follow suit.

In addition to providing employment on the line itself, the railway purchased all kinds of materials and equipment such as paint, oil, rolling stock, machinery, rails, timber, and bricks, iron and stone for its many buildings and structures; their suppliers increased their work forces and expanded their businesses.

Expansion of the coal-mining industry was promoted by the railway on several fronts. Large amounts of fuel were used for locomotives, stationary engines and other machinery. Better services for coal carrying stimulated other coal-using industries, particularly the steam-powered looms in the Manchester area and fuel delivered to Liverpool for the large number of ships coming into and out of the port and which were rapidly converting from sail to steam power. The railway coal services also contributed to the coastwise shipping of fuel deliveries and to its exports.

Because of the railway's cheaper and faster services, prices of coal and food for the populace decreased; the prompt delivery of agricultural products reduced the waste from deterioration and more people could enjoy fresh fruit and vegetables. Workers in Liverpool and Manchester who could afford it moved into the healthy countryside in which to bring up their families.

Social reform in Britain was considerably influenced by the Liverpool & Manchester, other railways inspired by its lead and the striking development in trade and industry which the new railways nourished as they straddled the country. The Industrial Revolution, which had begun around 1750 and was now being thrust ahead by the railways, brought its own complexities which combined to prompt social and political changes. Combination Acts of 1799 and 1800 had made trade unions and meetings of men to discuss wages and working hours illegal. Though this was repealed in 1824, it was not until 1871 that trade unions were to be granted legal recognition.

The Factory Act of 1833 provided for the appointment of factory inspectors, of great significance to the Lancashire cotton mills where men lost fingers and limbs in the unfamiliar machinery; and the Act of 1847 limited the working day to ten hours. Of the several Reform Acts, that of 1832 prompted the formation of the National Association for the Protection of Labour, and gave the vote to "£10 householders"; this was to be extended to workers in towns in 1867 and to country labourers in 1884. The 1832 Act ended an aristocratic government in which both Houses of Parliament had been controlled virtually by members of the great landed aristocratic families. It ushered in the dawn of an industrial democracy that is still witnessing radical changes.

Social and political reform, which had really taken off during the lifetime and with the aid of the pioneering railway, was largely inspired by Quakers, Church leaders and humanitarians in high places; and was continued by liberal-minded parliamentarians such as Lord Palmerston, Gladstone and Lord Shaftesbury.

One thing is certain: the increased travel for poorer people widened their horizons, gave them a brief if envious insight into the good life, and enabled them to mingle with social classes usually outside their daily experience. Well-entrenched social barriers began to break down. With a subtle inevitability, all this influence oiled the engines of the emerging democratic processes in an Age of Reform that was to shatter Victorian complacency. There was no turning back the clock. Railway bosses were quick to notice these changes and one of them once remarked that the great mass of people must necessarily remain in humble employment and that class distinctions must continue. This calls to mind a lyric, one day to be sung in a Gilbert & Sullivan operetta:

> "When everyone's somebodee
> Then no-one's anybody!"

A new experience opened up to people along the Liverpool & Manchester route, more so as connecting railways were introduced – "going to the seaside", notably to Southport and Blackpool. The fashionable and phenomenal habit of people converging regularly on the seaside in large numbers was a unique by-product of railways. Town dwellers, escaping from the miserable surroundings and smoky atmosphere, sped wide-eyed through the countryside by steam train to the edge of the land, to see the open sea for the first time, to listen to the lapping waves, and to gaze at ships small and large sailing off into the sunset. They returned to their slave labour conditions in better heart, with something new to talk about.

Extra revenues were earned by the railways as the social patterns changed. At the resorts, new businesses were started by the far-sighted. Hotels and playhouses were built. Large Victorian homes were converted to boarding houses and property prices soared. Eating places blossomed forth, from the plebeian whelk stall to the plushy restaurants served by waiters in tails, luxurious in a setting of red velvet upholstery and glittering chandeliers.

Time for the early Victorian travellers, though not exactly anyone's guess, was still nonetheless rather haphazard. L & M directors at first were content to time their train departures half-hourly. It was not until the 1840s when more connections were being made with new railways that their time-tables needed honing down to minutes. Local times taken from sundials, which varied longitudinally across Britain by as much as half an hour, were the vogue and, indeed, in several legal disputes concerning missed connections, carried the force of law. As an example of variations, Glasgow time was about seventeen minutes behind that for London, with a still greater difference between the east and west coasts.

Lost connections caused by time variants resulted in many complaints, and some law suits, by angry passengers who had been left stranded for hours, sometimes at a junction, 'miles from anywhere'. From these pressures, the directors in June 1844 presented a petition to Parliament for the adoption of a "universal time". Three years later, the rapidly extending Midland Railway added its powerful voice; this was supported over the years by other railways; industry and commerce, which also desperately needed a common time, joined the assault.

Though hard to believe now, it was not until 1880, by which time all the L & M directors who had campaigned for it must have died, that a Bill was to be passed: the Statutes (Definition of Time) Act. And for the first time in history, Greenwich Mean Time, transmitted from the famous Greenwich Observatory in London, became the legal standard time for all the railways and for Britain generally. Following an international conference to be held in Paris thirty-two years later, GMT with the aid of wireless telegraphy formed the basis of world time, adapted to a zonal system. Standard time stems from a brilliant and visionary piece of initiative for which the Liverpool & Manchester Railway is not always awarded its quantum of credit.

A great new railway literature began in the early years of the Liverpool & Manchester, modestly at first with its own published time tables which other private printers reproduced, a field in which George Bradshaw (1801–53) made his name. From about 1833, the time tables were supported by a proliferation of pamphlets and booklets, many with illustrations and maps, which described the countryside, towns, villages and stately mansions to be seen from a railway train. They pioneered a segment of publishing that never seems to lose its popularity.

Quite soon after the railway had opened, resourceful manufacturers started to produce all kinds of articles featuring the railway – models, handkerchiefs, table cloths, railway adventure games and jigsaw puzzles. Also a curious piece of music was composed, inscribed to the directors, and bearing an illustration of the *Rocket*. *Punch* appeared in 1841 and in vigorous caricature castigated railways for inefficient management and the poor treatment of their workers. It brought to the notice of affluent Victorians the shocking realities of life for the poor which they may have thought existed only in novels. Credit goes to Herapath and his provocative *Railway Magazine* in helping the whole country to be aware of the railway revolution that started in Lancashire.

Another revolutionary innovation, consolidated by the Liverpool & Manchester Railway and essential for the nineteenth-century canals, was the compulsory purchase of land. This was totally alien to the privileges wealthy landowners enjoyed, and accounts for much of the fierce parliamentary opposition the Liverpool & Manchester had faced in its formation. Its complexities were somewhat simplified by the Lands Clauses Consolidation Act of 1845 (whose powers were to be amplified by the Compulsory Purchase Act of 1965). It was no accident that the 1845 Act was passed in the same year as the Railway Clauses Consolidation Act for the construction of railways, with which it was closely associated.

Apart from the immediate influence of the pioneering Liverpool & Manchester Railway on the social, travelling, trading and industrial life of Lancashire and beyond, its greatest direct contribution was to prove to the civilised world the speed, safety, efficiency and financial viability of the railway concept itself. Under the incredible drive and native talents of George Stephenson and the dedicated work of a handful of directors, the world of railways had been established for the centuries ahead.

Striking a philosophical chord, W. H. Lecky was to write in 1865: "It is probable that Watt and Stephenson will eventually modify the opinions of mankind almost as profoundly as Luther or Voltaire."

CHAPTER 11

End of the Railway's Identity

Those railway promoters who had been waiting on the sidelines studied carefully the progress of the Liverpool & Manchester; passenger and goods business had met most expectations, dividends remained steady and share prices were high. As new lines opened which connected with the L & M, the pioneering railway became more and more involved with joint arrangements in which the trains of one company continued on the tracks of another for longer distances.

A funny thing happened to the L & M directors on the way to success. In an ironic *volte face*, they found themselves as early as 1831 resisting a proposed new line with much the same ferocity that canal owners had fought their railway in the 1820s. It came as a shock for them to learn that the Manchester, Bolton & Bury Canal & Railway Company was seeking parliamentary powers to build a railway between Clifton, some five miles north-west of Manchester, and Liverpool, to be called the North Line. Such a closely competitive venture was bold indeed. Charles Lawrence the chairman and his co-directors hired engineer Charles Vignoles to represent them in Parliament in opposing the Bill. Turned down in 1833, it was resurrected the following year when the L & M directors mounted all their skill and strategy, learned the hard way, to kill off the enterprise. Strong public and newspaper support was gained and the North Line never really had a chance.

A similar project was rumoured during 1836, and the *Manchester Guardian* on 25th June quoted the *Liverpool Times*: ". . . there is not the slightest necessity of a new line. The fares of the present railway are very reasonable; the speed of travelling is very great; the management is excellent; the conduct of persons employed by the company is civil and obliging; and there is the greatest readiness to rectify anything that may be amiss. . . . It is absurd to ask for liberty to drive off the road a company which has expended upwards of a million in money in trying an experiment of the greatest public importance which has not yet received any sufficient remuneration." The company's chairman, Charles Lawrence himself, could hardly have written a more fulsome eulogy!

The first line to branch off the Liverpool & Manchester was the Kenyon & Leigh Junction Railway of 2½ miles which opened in 1831. It ran directly northwards to the Bolton & Leigh Railway which had been opened on 1st August 1828; though under eight miles long, technically this was the first public railway to run in Lancashire. It was built by Stephenson and worked partly by one of his locomotives and partly by stationary steam engines, mainly for minerals and crops. The short Kenyon section gave direct links between Bolton and both Liverpool and Manchester.

Also in 1831, the Warrington & Newton Railway of nearly five miles running southward opened, the L & M initially supplying locomotives and waggons. To the north, Wigan, another important Lancashire town, was connected to the L & M at Parkside by the Wigan Branch Railway of seven miles which opened in 1832; connecting with it was the Springs Branch of three miles serving local collieries. In the Bill for the Wigan line, Parliament had decreed that it must be built under the direction of the Liverpool & Manchester engineers. Ambitiously looking northwards, in 1834 the Wigan line amalgamated with another projected railway, the Preston & Wigan of some fifteen miles; they formed the North Union Railway Company and opened to Preston four years later. In 1834 another line called the St Helens & Runcorn Gap Railway of seven miles was opened southward to the River Mersey to become one of the busiest colliery lines in Lancashire. Though it crossed the L & M over a viaduct, spurs connected both railways.

Opening on 31st May 1838, the Manchester, Bury & Bolton Railway was well located in Manchester and, in association with the Liverpool & Manchester, parliamentary powers were secured the following year to build a short line to connect their two stations. Pushing further north, the Lancaster & Preston Junction came to life on 26th June 1841, and within six years a new railway to Carlisle was to link Lancashire close to the Scottish border.

Agreeable propositions were made from time to time by colliery owners within the vicinity of the Liverpool & Manchester line for building short branches for coal traffic. New business came to the L & M, but always after hard bargaining. Owners of the land needed for the line demanded their pounds of flesh; in fact, a Mr Unsworth managed to squeeze from the L & M an annual payment of £300 plus free railway conveyance of his own coal for the six miles to Liverpool.

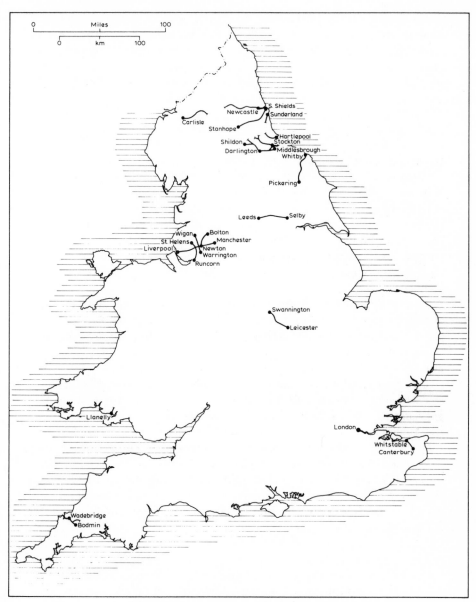

Railways in England and Wales 1836

All these direct new links with the Liverpool & Manchester increased its business and enhanced its standing in the railway world. They also involved the directors in complicated negotiations with the other lines for payments for the use of their track, vehicles, locomotives, engineering services, warehouse rents and wages for employees. Such deals had no precedents and were settled through often bitter and acrimonious arguments. Trials of strength saw the L & M win some and lose others. As more connecting and competing lines were built and entanglements grew, the directors found themselves embroiled in the scheming politics of railways.

Closest ally of the L & M was to be the new Grand Junction Railway which opened throughout on 4th July 1837 between Birmingham and Warrington, to form Britain's first trunk railway; the route skirted the tiny village of Monk's Coppenhall where a new station was built, taking its name from Crewe Hall, the country seat of Lord Crewe. Another new line of importance to the L & M was the Manchester & Birmingham Railway which was completed to Crewe in 1842.

Prompted by the initiative and example of the Liverpool & Manchester, a railway network was now busily threading its way throughout Lancashire and around Britain, rapidly building up the country's trade and commerce. Some, however, were unconnected with others and used different rail gauges.

George Bradshaw, the time-table expert, published in 1849 a list of selected new lines opened during the years 1832–48. Some dates may vary slightly from other sources because several railways opened, then had to close temporarily to meet problems; some were opened experimentally, and others had an 'official' opening ceremony which may have been before or after the date opened for public traffic, passengers and goods. Most of the following details are extracted from Bradshaw's list, omitting those we have already described and spanning the independent lifetime of the Liverpool & Manchester Railway Company:

1830	Canterbury & Whitstable
1831	Edinburgh & Dalkeith, part, with cable and horses
1831	Glasgow & Garnkirk, part
1831	Dundee & Newtyle, with cable and horses
1832	Leicester & Swannington
1834	Bodmin & Wadebridge, Cornwall
1834	Leeds & Selby
1834	Dublin & Kingstown
1835	Newcastle & Carlisle, part; completed 1839
1836	London & Greenwich, part; completed 1838

1836	Ffestiniog, Wales, world's first narrow-gauge railway at 1ft.11½ins.
1837	Paisley & Renfrew
1837	London & Birmingham, completed 1838
1838	London & Southampton, part; completed 1840
1838	Great Western, part; completed to Bristol 1841
1838	Sheffield & Rotherham
1839	Midland Counties, (Derby, Nottingham, Leicester, Rugby), completed 1840
1839	Eastern Counties, part
1839	Birmingham & Derby Junction
1839	Ulster, part
1840	London & Brighton, part; completed 1841
1840	Birmingham & Gloucester
1840	North Midland (Derby to Leeds)
1840	York & North Midland
1840	London & Blackwall, with cable haulage
1840	Glasgow, Paisley, Kilmarnock & Ayr
1841	Great North England (Darlington to York)
1841	Bristol & Exeter, part; completed 1844
1842	Edinburgh & Glasgow
1842	South Eastern, part; completed London to Dover 1844
1844	Yarmouth & Norwich
1844	Newcastle & Darlington
1844	Dublin & Drogheda
1844	Bristol & Gloucester
1845	Maryport & Carlisle

Most of these new railways benefited enormously from the pioneering experience of the Liverpool & Manchester in construction, motive power, rolling stock, operation, management and financing which the L & M was glad to share. Even so, far too many were coming into operation far too soon with too much near-duplication, bringing some close to ruin. Excited by the astonishing success of the L & M, promoters had plunged into the railway business with the expectation of making money fast, a veritable cornucopia. This was fine for those lines serving the great industrial centres and ports of Britain; but in sparsely populated areas, much money was lost. Most promoters met the same obstruction from canal interests, landowners and Parliament as suffered by the L & M.

So feverish was the activity in new railways and so numerous the accidents and financial disasters that the Government intervened with Acts of Parliament in 1840 and 1842. They gave the Board of Trade, the late Huskisson's old department, power to appoint railway inspecting officers, who were recruited from the Royal Corps of

Signals, to form the Government's own Railway Department. No new public railway was allowed to be opened until the inspecting officers had examined it and signified their official approval. They were also required to investigate accidents and report their findings, and to make remedial recommendations.

As new railways were projected for Lancashire, L & M directors desperately campaigned to protect their preserves; two other railways – the Grand Junction and the North Union – joined them to form a vigilante committee, of which the L & M directors were the catalysts. Their joint brief was to oppose what they described as "uncalled for and competing lines". Meantime, the L & M itself was planning its own additional lines and soon its own monopoly slip was showing. Its activities brought a sharp rebuke from the Government in a lengthy document entitled, "Report of the Railway Department of the Board of Trade on Schemes for Extending Railway Communication in Lancashire and Adjoining Districts, 1845". In a nutshell, it showed the Board of Trade as determined to resist the tendency of the Liverpool & Manchester Railway to build a monopoly, because this would be damaging not only to the private interests to be served by newly projected railways, but harm the general welfare of the travelling and trading public in the county.

So, to fight off competition and make economies, some railways began to think of amalgamation, the first of which had been the Wigan Branch and the Preston & Wigan in 1834; L & M directors had thoughts in this direction, too.

Elsewhere, ten years later the largest and most important amalgamation took place: the North Midland, Midland Counties, and the Birmingham & Derby Junction railways joined to form the great Midland Railway Company which, during the next seventy-nine years, was to grow into one of the most powerful railways in Britain.

This incredible financial feat was master-minded by George Hudson (1800–71). In modern neology he was first a whizz-kid, then a fly-boy, amassing a fortune on the way. Rotund and be-whiskered, George hob-nobbed with nobility, travelled with royalty, supped with ambassadors, borrowed from the wealthy, fiddled the books, bought a stately home, was welcomed in London's most exclusive clubs and surrounded by sycophants.

In 1849, his dark and greedy deeds caught up with him and, as a Member of Parliament, he was called to the House to give an account of himself. That precipitated his final disgrace and downfall. Later, he was sent to prison and at seventy-one died in comparative poverty. This apocryphal character of corruption and gigantic frauds had "loomed larger than life-size from the gloomy shadows of history", and greed had ended his rapid apotheosis.

Just how did it all start? A farmer's son turned draper's assistant,

Hudson had been left a fortune by a great uncle in 1827, which later led him to railway investment. In 1833, he met George Stephenson by chance at Whitby, Yorkshire. He was impressed by the success of the Liverpool & Manchester Railway and he used the engineer on many railway projects; Stephenson helped to make him a rich man. Over the years he acquired several railway directorships, enabling him finally to achieve his masterstroke of creating the Midland Railway, with himself as its chairman. He had been appointed Lord Mayor of York in 1837 and a Member of Parliament for Sunderland in 1845. At one stage, he controlled nearly a third of all the railways in Britain and was dubbed, 'The Railway King'.

Hudson may have cast his greedy eye on the Liverpool & Manchester, but a smarter man, Captain Mark Huish, beat him to it. Despite the Railway King's massive frauds, by 1844 he had demonstrated the value of amalgamating smaller railways into larger groups to remove competition, to enable trains to run for longer distances, and to achieve financial viability; for this, the railways of Britain owed him a great debt. Hudson had manipulated George Stephenson in several ventures; but they quarrelled, and the temperature between them rapidly fell from cool to cold.

While Hudson was busy creating the Midland Railway, Charles Lawrence and his fellow directors were considering the future of the L & M which was small and vulnerable compared with many other railways. General industrial and economic factors and the growing competition from new lines penetrating their territory, meant that the only way to survive was to join another influential railway. An anonymous letter in the *Railway Times* in 1843 suggested an amalgamation with the Manchester & Leeds and the Hull & Selby; another letter there said that the only way the L & M could survive the competition was by an amalgamation. Other publications contributed to the debate, predicting that the L & M could be completely overwhelmed or gobbled up by a large and voracious railway animal.

But without public prodding, the L & M had its own ideas which the board discussed at a meeting on 26th August 1844. Chairman Charles Lawrence favoured the Grand Junction with which there were already close ties; this would open up services from Liverpool and Manchester, over the Grand Junction to Birmingham, then to the metropolis on the London & Birmingham Railway. Happily, agreement was unanimous, for this was the best way to maintain joint competitive power against rivals.

Already, L & M directors knew that the formidable Captain Mark Huish was a power to be reckoned with; Huish had arrived on the Liverpool scene in summer 1841 when appointed as secretary and manager of the Grand Junction Railway. A forceful character highly skilled in negotiating financial deals and traffic agreements with other railways, he was reputed to be a railway political in-fighter. Some years later, a distinguished chairman of a leading railway company was to describe him as an "intriguing web-weaving protocoller".

In the early 1840s, railway amalgamation fever was in the air and rumour was rife. At the same time, railways generally were being rapidly accepted by the public. The royal accolade had been bestowed on 13th June 1842 when Queen Victoria (1819–1901), a young mother aged twenty-three, made her first railway journey. Travelling from Windsor Castle to London, she rode in the Great Western Railway's luxurious royal saloon. In the following year, Her Majesty persuaded the Duke of Wellington to accompany her on a trip on the South Western Railway. As an eye-witness of Huskisson's fatal accident the day the railway opened, Wellington had borne a strong prejudice against all railways, and it had taken the 'Iron Duke' thirteen years to regain his lost nerve.

Nerve was now needed by Lawrence and his fellow directors as they manipulated their strategy against the ambitious Huish. Several meetings were held between the two railway companies during 1844. First, the Grand Junction asked the L & M directors to name their price for the entire line. Astutely, the directors refused and invited the Grand Junction people to say how much they would pay.

Why not a working union, suggested the Grand Junction, to give the benefits of a full amalgamation, but each company to retain its own identity and separate capital? Then the two railways could be managed by a joint committee composed of directors of both companies. No, this was not acceptable; it was full amalgamation or nothing. After a long battle of wits, no doubt with poker faces on either side, broad agreement was reached for an amalgamation, to be achieved by a mutual exchange of shares at agreed prices.

Two hurdles still lay ahead: one was to persuade the shareholders of both companies, and the other was to secure the essential Act of Parliament. In a softening up exercise, L & M directors circulated their shareholders on 5th December 1844, "Combined capital may easily accomplish what individual resources would have hesitated to undertake; while the interest of the associated companies will be best served by affording the amplest accommodation to the trade and commerce of the port."

At that time, Grand Junction dividends were higher than those of the L & M, and some shareholders were accused of wanting to sell just for this reason. Even so, almost unanimous support was given by the shareholders and on 10th December a special general meeting of the proprietors was called. Here, a full commitment was undertaken: "Resolution: Unanimously That the additional agreement of the Directors for the Amalgamation of this Company with its projected Branches and Engagements (including the Bolton & Leigh and

Kenyon & Leigh Junction Railways, and the North Union Railway, with its Branches and Engagements), and the Grand Junction Railway Company into one consolidated Company, on the terms above stated be and the same is hereby adopted and confirmed by this Meeting."

At other meetings of the protagonists, details of the proposed amalgamation were hammered out. Closer co-operation was further assured when it was agreed to appoint Charles Lawrence, chairman of the L & M, as deputy chairman of the Grand Junction, and for directors from the amalgamating companies to join the board of the new company. For some time, the proposal for the L & M to amalgamate with the North Union had been in negotiation and the preliminary terms were settled in 1844. But at the last minute, the North Union backed out.

Ready for the main amalgamation, Clay, Swift & Company were retained to prepare the legal content of the Bill which was placed before the House of Commons in April 1845. Inexorably, the end of the independence of the world's great pioneering railway was drawing nigh, but the directors secured a good share in the management planned for the new company which reflected the capital values of the respective companies. Directors of the new board would be required to own shares to the value of not less than £500, giving each a sizeable financial stake. Period of office and rotation of departure from the board were settled. Two directors with canal interests were retained.

It so happened that at this period the L & M had several petitions before Parliament for extensions of the line; only one was processed to completion, the building of a new tunnel between Edge Hill and Waterloo goods station which was completed within four years. The remainder were abandoned or postponed.

Some opposition to the amalgamation Bill was met in Parliament, particularly concerning monopoly, and Sir George Clark held that it would be against the public interest. Opposition mounted during the various committee stages and in early August, the directors' hopes of early success began to fade. Naturally, they were anxious for a speedy acceptance, for much finance was involved. Following the success of the Midland Railway the previous year, many other railway Bills were going through Parliament and this may well have helped the Lancashire project. Petitioners' counsel battled on and on 8th August 1845, the Bill was approved. A new railway company was born, but without a new name, for it was called the Grand Junction Railway.

A major clause in the Act specified ". . . that from and immediately after the passing of this Act and the several and respective Persons and Corporations who immediately before the passing of this Act were proprietors of Shares in the Capital or Joint Stocks of the Liverpool & Manchester Railway Company, and the Bolton and Leigh

Railway Company, or either of them, and their executors, administrators, successors and assigns respectively, shall be and they are hereby united and incorporated with the Grand Junction Railway Company."

No reference is made here to the Kenyon Junction & Leigh Railway of 2½ miles, for it had been recently sold to the Bolton & Leigh Railway for £38,750.

Among the six L & M directors appointed to the board of the new company of fifteen named in the Act were Charles Lawrence, Joseph Sandars, John Moss and Hardman Earle; two of the fifteen represented canal interests. Henry Booth joined the new management team.

The new Grand Junction Railway Company was fortunate in taking over L & M locomotives, for they were of a higher quality than any other batch in Britain.

After the amalgamation, the Liverpool & Manchester Railway lost its name, its independence and its identity, but never to this day its world-wide historical significance. From its inception in the 1820s and through its fifteen years of life, the promoters, directors, George Stephenson and his teams and the work force had started virtually from scratch in a little-known environment of technology and operational management; and investors had demonstrated their faith by taking a high financial risk.

Many fundamental technical, commercial and administrative innovations which were subject to prolonged experiment by the Liverpool & Manchester Railway directors and engineers remain in steam locomotive railways to this day. The leaders attacked a series of unforeseen and growing problems with intelligence and courage. Always, they were ready and willing to try out new ideas, from whatever source. No detail was too minute for individual attention. It was the patient and persistent scrutiny of every facet of the entire project that made the venture such a success. From a cautious beginning, both passenger and goods trains were now running at speeds the world had never seen before. Comparatively, it was a safe railway; and financially it was a success by any commercial standards.

Certainly, the Stephensons had made their world reputation with this short Lancashire line and, thanks to the orders they received for new locomotives after the brilliant performance of the *Rocket* at Rainhill, the Stephenson locomotive works at Newcastle at the time of the L & M amalgamation employed over 800 men. And this "Grand British Experimental Railway" dragged sluggish industrial Britain literally steaming and roaring into the nineteenth century.

It also launched that crazy and desperate period which historians have long known as the 'Railway Mania', which gathered frightening momentum from the Grand Junction amalgamation in 1845, to reach its feverish peak, then burnt itself out by about 1848. The Grand

Junction had been the most significant amalgamation after the formation of the Midland Railway the year before.

Though the ambitious Captain Mark Huish now headed the new Grand Junction Railway, judging by the pattern rapidly developing in different parts of the country, further amalgamation still seemed to be the key to greater success. And on 16th July 1846, the Grand Junction amalgamated with the London & Birmingham and the Manchester & Birmingham railways to form the London & North Western Railway Company; Huish was appointed as chairman, a post he was to hold until 1859. With many other absorptions and extensions, the L & N W R maintained a distinguished and aggressive independence with its headquarters at Euston in London, for another seventy-seven years. Meanwhile, the constituent Liverpool & Manchester line, key route though it was, subsided into relative oblivion as a small cog in a massive machine.

Noting how the L & M had begun to build its own locomotives from 1841, the Grand Junction followed suit by opening its own locomotive building works at Crewe in 1843. The works was founded by Francis Trevithick, son of the famous Richard who had invented the steam locomotive; and after the formation of the L & N W R, he was appointed that company's locomotive superintendent.

First, the Grand Junction and then the L & N W R were in at the height of the Railway Mania; and during the boom years of 1845–48, about 650 Acts of Parliament were passed for new railways, or expansions of those already in operation; and in the peak year of 1846, 272 Acts went through. Many projects never saw the light of day and some were quickly in financial ruins to be taken over by stronger railways. Promoters with rolls of plans queued up at Westminster or parliamentary agencies, and the enormous legislation clogged the parliamentary procedures. In a short time, large fortunes were made and lost. Well-to-do families were left destitute, wealthy respected men were ruined and a number committed suicide.

Always at hand with a shaft of irony, the *Illustrated London News* published a verse in 1845:

> "Railway Shares! Railway Shares!
> Hunted by Stags and Bulls and Bears –
> Hunted by women – hunted by men –
> Speaking and writing – voice and pen –
> Claiming and coaxing – prayers and snares –
> All the world mad about Railway Shares!"

During 1844, Brunel, who was still building the Great Western Railway, wrote to a friend, "Here, the railway world is mad. I am really sick of hearing proposals made. I wish it were at an end." And

Railways in England and Wales 1848

to his friend Charles Babbage, "Things are in an unhealthy fever here, which must end in a reaction . . . All the world is mad!" George Stephenson had expressed himself in similar terms. Samuel Smiles reprehends Parliament for imposing inadequate checks and says that Members of Parliament in the Commons and the Lords were as much interested in the boom "as the vulgar herd of money-grubbers. The railway prospectuses now issued – unlike the original Liverpool & Manchester . . . were headed by peers, baronets, landed proprietors, and strings of MPs . . ."

Some order emerged from the chaos. Such a plethora of complicated legislation for new railways had accumulated that departmental officers were swamped with paper work and could hardly keep track of events. That is why the Government in anticipation passed the Railway Clauses Consolidation Act on 8th May 1845; its stated objective was "to consolidate into one Act certain provisions usually inserted in Acts authorising the making of railways".

After the Government itself, Members of both Houses of Parliament and the many other speculators had had their fingers burnt, the fever of the mania gradually cooled off and a long period of more sensible railway development followed.

Looking back sadly, in the autumn of 1845 it was 'curtains' on the world stage of railways for the Liverpool & Manchester Railway as an independent company. Those who had backed and built it had shown a venturesome spirit, shrewd business sense, and an unbounding willingness to learn the intricacies of running a railway. In doing so, they had acquired a wealth of unique knowledge which was to benefit the world.

CHAPTER 12

The Liverpool & Manchester Men Promote World Railways

In any objective assessment of railway history, George Stephenson towers as the genius who perfected the crude locomotive of his day, had the practical conception of railways for meeting an urgent transport need, and the skill and dedication to build locomotives and railways for many parts of Britain and the world. In every sense, he stands unchallenged as the Father of Railways, and his name, coupled with the *Rocket*, is safely enshrined in English folklore.

Other men, too, had the vision to see the enormous potential, and the faith and wealth to back him, and often to exploit him; and it was the pioneering Liverpool & Manchester Railway that gave him the unique opportunity to settle, once and for all, that railways had at last arrived. In the process, Britain was firmly established as the laboratory of the 'iron road'.

Many eminent men of genius have 'lived before their time'. George Stephenson was not one of them. In the fundamentals, everything was right for him. After the wars of the early 1800s, Britain was emerging as the richest country in the world, her empire was expanding, and her industrial revolution was sweeping her ahead of any other country. Money was there to invest, men to work, and an abundance of fuel, timber and iron products waiting; surging industry and trade were crying out for something better than canals and turnpike roads. On top of all this, his only son quickly matured as an ineffably gifted engineer in his own right, to share the burden. George Stephenson was the man of the moment, the man of destiny: the right man in the right place at the right time; and he rolled up his sleeves and got on with the job. It is as difficult for the work-a-day historian to gain a real insight into this remarkable genius as to probe the creative artistry of Shakespeare, Rembrandt or Beethoven.

In tackling the Liverpool & Manchester Railway, Stephenson was fortunate with his backers, especially Charles Lawrence, Joseph Sandars, John Moss and Henry Booth. As the opening day approached, Booth waxed prophetic:

"But we must not confine our views to London, or Liverpool, or Manchester; there can be no question that foreign countries will adopt the Railway communication, the one great step in mechanical improvement and commercial enterprise. France and Germany and America have already their railways . . ." (Much overseas development had been stimulated, first by James Watt's stationary steam engines, Trevithick's early locomotives, and Stephenson's Stockton & Darlington Railway opened mainly for coal in 1825). ". . . and the Pasha of Egypt may be expected to follow close on the heels of his brother potentates. The country of the Pyramids, of Memphis, and of Thebes, shall then be celebrated for Railways and Steam Carriages; the land of the proud Mameluke or the wandering Arab, of sphynxes and Mummies, will then become the theatre of mechanical invention, science and the arts. The stately Turk, with his turban and slippers, will quit his couch and his carpet, to mount his Engine of fire and speed, that he may enjoy the delights of locomotion. . . . The Loco-motive Engine and Railway were reserved for the present day. From west to east, from north to south, the mechanical principle, the philo-sophy of the nineteenth century, will spread and extend itself. The world has received a new impulse."

How right he was! And judging by the prolific literary output of this gifted company treasurer, he obviously revelled in phrases as much as in figures.

After the L & M amalgamation, Booth served the Grand Junction Railway for a year, and when it was absorbed into the London & North Western Railway in 1846 he became its company secretary for the northern division, and a director of the board after two years. During his directorship, he was presented with two financial sums, donated by hundreds of subscribers, totalling £8,400, a fortune at the time. Retiring in 1859, he died ten years later at the ripe old age of 83. Following a close association with pioneering railways for some thirty-five years, he had done more than most in promoting world-wide the basic elements of the Liverpool & Manchester Railway. That his services were well appreciated by Liverpool is evidenced by his statue, holding the screw coupling he invented, placed in St. George's Hall, Liverpool, which is one of the finest modern examples of classi-cal architecture.

Other Liverpool & Manchester men, including Lawrence, Sandars and Moss, and its shareholders, invested money in several other new railways, including the Midland Counties. The 'Liverpool Party', as these men were known, spread widely the knowledge gained with the now absorbed L & M by invading other boardrooms.

But the gospel according to the Liverpool & Manchester chapter was preached most effectively by the nucleus of construction and loco-motive engineers who had been most closely involved. Apart from many colliery railways and the Hetton Railway using his locomotive, Stephenson was commissioned to build a six-mile railway between Canterbury and the tiny port of Whitstable, later known affection-ately as the Crab and Winkle line. Busy elsewhere, father handed over to son and the line was opened on 3rd May 1830, part stationary engine and cable to cope with heavy gradients and part by the Step-henson locomotive *Invicta* which is still preserved in Canterbury. On the opening day, it was driven by the young Edward Fletcher (1807–89).

As an apprentice at the Newcastle Works, Fletcher had assisted with the *Rocket*, both in its building and at the Rainhill Trials. Eventually, he moved to the North Eastern Railway, became the loco-motive superintendent 1854–82, and built many fine locomotives, based on his L & M experience, especially those for the York–Edinburgh expresses, one of which is still preserved. Performance of Fletcher locomotives was described as "majestic, dominating and powerful".

While finishing the L & M, Stephenson took on a sixteen-mile railway to connect the Swannington coal-mining areas with the growing town of Leicester. Local people, still interested in canals, failed to raise the capital and Stephenson had no difficulty in persuad-ing the 'Liverpool Party' to subscribe. Without this aid, the line might well have been delayed for some years. Promoters of other railways in the Midlands went to see it at work. Again, son Robert was the engineer and the line was opened with several Stephenson loco-motives on 17th July 1832.

When the question of gauge had arisen, George said, "Make them the same width [as on the L & M]. They [other new railways] may be a long way apart now. Depend on it they will be joined together some day."

This railway launched Robert, in his late twenties, into a long and distinguished railway and civil engineering career in his own right, as well as many more commissions for his father.

In May 1833, the Stephenson locomotive *Samson* at a level crossing on the Leicester line scattered a farm cart loaded with eggs and butter, following which George had the locomotive fitted with a steam-blown whistle. From those days onwards, warning whistles, horns, hooters and sirens intoning various sounds were to acquire a fascination of their own.

While building the Leicester line, Robert convinced his father, both of them experienced colliery men, that the locality offered much coal-mining potential. George persuaded Joseph Sandars of the L &

M and another old friend Sir Joshua Walmsley to join them, and the partners purchased an estate at Snibston adjoining the Leicester railway near Coalville.

Now that the L & M was in operation, in 1831 George bought a stately country house, Alton Grange, near Coalville, so as to supervise the colliery sinkings. Leaving their modest house in Upper Parliament Street, Liverpool, for the last time, he and his wife Elizabeth climbed into their high gig with the faithful pony Bobby in the shafts and journeyed in easy stages to their new home.

The colliery venture proved highly successful and George had the pleasure of despatching the first train of coal to Leicester, where the price of fuel was dramatically reduced. His younger brother James joined him at the colliery, also James Campbell who had experience of the Liverpool & Manchester and later was resident engineer on a number of new railways, the hilly and tunnelled Matlock and Buxton line being the most problematical.

Living locally near the colliery, Stephenson, remembering his own poverty-stricken youth, took a keen personal interest in his workers. He paid fair wages, built a village of workers' cottages each with a small garden, had a church and church schools erected to educate the miners' children, and a chapel for dissenters.

The colliery and other rapidly growing commitments induced Stephenson in May 1833 to resign as chief engineer of the Liverpool & Manchester Railway but he was retained in a consultative capacity. He had been commissioned to build the first trunk railway, the Grand Junction, between Birmingham and Warrington for which Joseph Locke conducted the survey. Locke so impressed the directors that they wanted him to be in sole charge which led to unpleasant wrangling between doyen and pupil and they parted with ill-will. The jealous parent never really enjoyed seeing any of his railway children grow to fledglings, spread their wings and fly off from the Stephenson nest. As a compromise, Stephenson was given the southern end of the line and Locke the northern. By sharing out the route, the Grand Junction had the services of a promising young engineer without seriously offending the respected master. Even then, Stephenson had trouble with the directors; because he delegated too much to inexperienced assistants, mistakes were made and costs underestimated, and in August 1835 he withdrew, leaving his former articled pupil and son of an old north-east friend, in sole command.

From his experience with this railway and the Liverpool & Manchester (he had been in charge of the *Rocket* on that fateful opening day), Locke went on to build locomotives with great mathematical accuracy and he introduced the technique of standard components. Alone or with partners, he built at least sixteen railways, among them the London & Southampton, Sheffield & Manchester, Lancaster &

Preston, Greenock, Paisley & Glasgow, Lancaster & Carlisle, East Lancashire, Scottish Central, Caledonian, Scottish Midland, also Greenock Docks. He designed an improved track for heavier loads. When only twenty-one in 1826 he had been sent by Stephenson to survey a railway between Leeds and Hull.

After an exploratory visit by Robert Stephenson to Spain, Locke built the first Spanish railway – the Barcelona & Mattaro line of seventeen miles. In France he built three railways – Paris & Rouen, Rouen & Havre, and Mantes, Caen & Cherbourg; and in Holland, the Dutch-Rheinish Railway. From 1838 he was a Fellow of the Royal Society, and was President of the Institution of Civil Engineers in 1858–9. By 1847, still comparatively young, he was a wealthy man and bought Honiton Manor in Devon; in that year, he was elected a Liberal Member of Parliament for the local borough, holding it to his death in 1860. He was fifty-five.

Locke delivered important railway papers and received honours at home and abroad. To his erstwhile home town of Barnsley in Yorkshire, his widow presented Locke Park in which his statue, still standing, was erected. He had also made an endowment to his old grammar school there. Stephenson-trained, this one man alone did much to establish railways on the Liverpool & Manchester paradigm.

Vignoles was another. Before joining the Liverpool & Manchester Railway and George Stephenson, fiery-tempered, Irish-born Charles Vignoles was already bound for an illustrious career. Soon after graduating from Woolwich and Sandhurst as an army officer, he went to America, was engaged as a surveyor and met businessmen who were already planning new railways. In 1832 when thirty-nine, he became engineer for Ireland's first railway, the Dublin & Kingstown, after Stephenson and Locke had surveyed its prospects. He became engineer or consultant for dozens of new railways in Lancashire and elsewhere in Britain, designed an improved rail and frequently appeared as a civil engineering witness for railways at parliamentary committees.

His most shattering experience was as chief engineer of the projected Manchester, Ashton-under-Lyne & Sheffield Railway, an appointment he had secured in competition with Joseph Locke who shared the work. The line pierced the Pennine range at about a thousand feet above sea level with a single bore, Woodhead Tunnel, at just over three miles, then the longest in the British Isles. Spanning rugged and moorland territory the railway took seven years to construct, against Vignoles' estimate of four. Costs far exceeded his estimates and the railway never recovered from its financial adversities; frequent angry exchanges with fretful promoters were wearing.

Because capital came in slowly, the then wealthy Vignoles committed the tragic error of financing the line himself and inducing friends and relatives to buy the shaky shares. Costs rapidly mounted, in time beyond his entire fortune and he was forced to resign as engineer. The board of directors took him to court in Liverpool and his diary for 15th January 1841 exposes the sad story:

"This day the Court of the Exchequer gave judgement against me . . . by which decision a great number of my friends will be utterly ruined. Good God! that men who I had served so faithfully, and for whose railway I had done so much, should act like this! . . . We are half distracted at the frightful prospect before us all!"

His total losses exceeded £80,000, millions by today's standards; some of his relatives and friends and other influential investors were declared bankrupt and one was sent to prison in York Castle. Tragic episodes of this nature, for engineers and investing speculators, were common in those pioneering and mania days, from which the Liverpool & Manchester Railway had emerged unscathed. Joseph Locke took over the Pennine line and picked up the pieces; four miles were opened in 1845, the rest following in stages.

It took family man Vignoles – amateur artist, poet and prolific diarist – about two years to recover solvency and freedom from debt; such a trauma that would have broken a weaker character. Such must have been men of iron! Among his outstanding works overseas were the first railway in Switzerland, railways in Spain, consultancies in Europe and surveying a route in Brazil. Several times, he visited Russia for civil engineering projects and helped with the new railway between Warsaw and Terespol. At the age of seventy-seven, in 1870 he was elected President of the Institution of Civil Engineers and died five years later at Hythe, Hampshire, surrounded by his wife, children and grandchildren.

Without being too extravagant with the adjectives, Daniel Gooch (1816–89) was another incredible product of the Liverpool & Manchester and the Stephenson stable. After working on Stephenson locomotives at the Newcastle Works for the L & M, he designed two locomotives in 1836 in a gauge of 5 feet 6 inches for the projected New Orleans Railroad in America. For financial reasons, however, at a late stage the order was cancelled and the locomotives were shipped back home from New York.

Bitten by the wide-gauge bug, Gooch wrote to Brunel who was building the Great Western Railway in the wide gauge of 7 feet. In 1837, Brunel, then thirty-one, met the young Gooch in the Manchester Railway office and appointed him to take charge of locomotives for the GWR. On reaching Paddington in London, Gooch was appalled at the poor quality of machines the GWR had purchased ready for the partial opening of the railway the following year. He managed to persuade his master to buy the two returned from America, which were then specially converted in the Stephenson

Newcastle Works from 5 feet 6 inches to 7 feet. They were named *North Star* and *Morning Star* and saved the GWR from serious trouble and delay in opening the line. *North Star* was listed in the Newcastle Works as No 150 and in the GWR stable as No 1.

Based on his L & M and Newcastle experience, Gooch went on from the Stephenson idiom to develop his own design improvements. At the GWR Swindon Works, opened in 1843, he built splendid locomotives and laid the foundation for a series of outstanding GWR locomotives, such as the 'Kings' and 'Castles', some of them later to create world speed records.

Daniel Gooch resigned as locomotive superintendent from the railway he so loved and, using one of Brunel's mighty steamships, the *Great Eastern*, in 1866 he laid the first successful cable across the Atlantic; on completion, he despatched the first electric telegraph message to America. That year, he received a knighthood for his services. Covered in public glory, Sir Daniel returned to the Great Western Railway as its chairman.

Daniel's brother Tom was also a Stephenson pupil. He was the engineer's right hand man during the construction of the Liverpool & Manchester and made practically all the drawings. He became resident engineer of the Bolton & Leigh Railway, and later of the Stephenson-built Manchester & Leeds. Tom was succeeded as secretary to Stephenson by Frederick Swanwick who was afterwards resident engineer on the North Midland Railway. Each of these young men had been in charge of a locomotive on the day the L & M had officially opened.

Timothy Hackworth (1786–1850) worked as locomotive foreman of Stephenson's Stockton & Darlington Railway opened in 1825. Setting up on his own, he built locomotives at his Shildon Works near Darlington, the most famous with which he was associated being the *Royal George*. While working for the Stephensons at the Newcastle factory, he learnt much about the Liverpool & Manchester; and though his *Sans Pareil* failed miserably at the Rainhill Trials, it saw some service on the L & M. Hackworth built locomotives for other railways in Britain and overseas. Jointly with Robert Stephenson, he supplied locomotives for Russia's first railway between St Petersburg (now Leningrad) and Pavlovsk.

One of the leading civil engineers associated with the Liverpool & Manchester from its formative years and a judge at the Rainhill Trials was John Urpath Rastrick (1780–1856). This engineer from Northumberland had patented a locomotive as early as 1814 and had experimented with Stephenson's first machine at that period. He surveyed or built several railways in Britain, including part of the London & Brighton jointly with Sir John Rennie and frequently supported new railways at parliamentary committees. In 1829, his works

Models of signals mounted on permanent posts as used on the Liverpool & Manchester Railway about 1834. They slowly replaced 'policemen' with hand-signals.

Above left: Joseph Locke, who helped Stephenson to build the Liverpool & Manchester, became one of his most famous protégés and almost out-shone the master!

Above right: Daniel Gooch, another Stephenson pupil, a local boy who joined the great Brunel and climbed to the top as chairman of the Great Western Railway.

The one and only 'Railway King', the legendary George Hudson. A legacy led him to the new railways which he expanded at a rapid rate; he used Stephenson, hobnobbed with royalty and the titled, and became Lord Mayor of York, an MP, a millionaire – and a fraud, leading him to prison and poverty. Yet he contributed so much to the railway world.

Captain Mark Huish, a forceful character and manager of the Grand Junction Railway, after a few years of campaigning, took over the Liverpool & Manchester in 1845 by amalgamation of the two companies.

Excursion-trains were run by the Liverpool & Manchester very soon after the railway was opened. Thomas Cook ran his first excursion in 1841 (as illustrated in this artist's impression), to build a worldwide business.

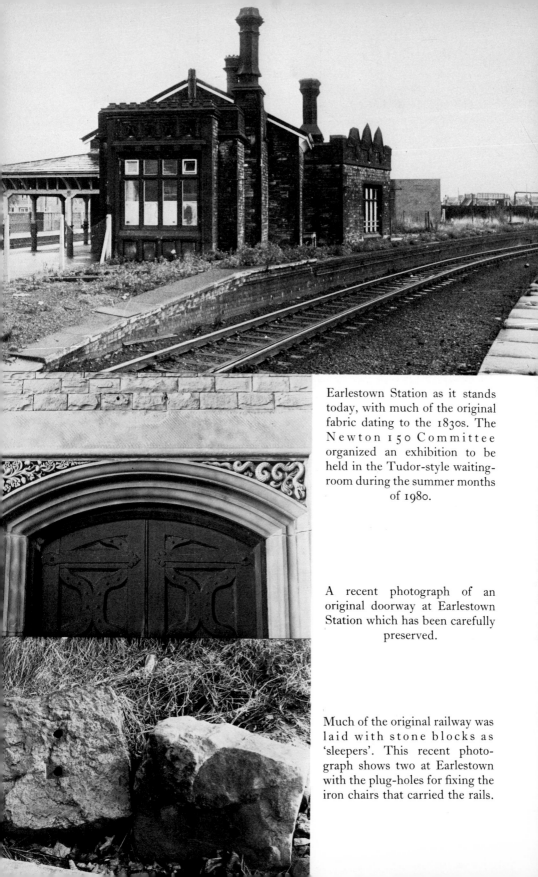

Earlestown Station as it stands today, with much of the original fabric dating to the 1830s. The Newton 150 Committee organized an exhibition to be held in the Tudor-style waiting-room during the summer months of 1980.

A recent photograph of an original doorway at Earlestown Station which has been carefully preserved.

Much of the original railway was laid with stone blocks as 'sleepers'. This recent photograph shows two at Earlestown with the plug-holes for fixing the iron chairs that carried the rails.

After lording it majestically for some century and a half, the time came to say
goodbye to dear old steam in British Rail timetables. This 'last steam-train'
storms out of Liverpool Lime Street on Sunday 11th August 1968 to make way for
the new technology. Praise be – for the railway preservation societies!

The Lion in chains, bound by road from her home at Merseyside County Museum, Liverpool, in April 1979, for the famous Vulcan Works at Newton-le-Willows, to be prepared for her several public appearances in 1980. Having supervised the loading, popular and widely-known Tony Quirke of British Rail's Liverpool Division, who is manager of the Rocket 150 project, is delighted that this fine old lady of 1838 vintage is still in the running.

This model of the *Rocket* won a first prize in the Lord Mayor's Parade in Liverpool in June 1979. Built by railway engineers at nearby Wavertree, it toured to publicize the 1980 celebrations.

The boiler for the replica *Sans Pareil* by Hackworth being made at Crewe Works in 1979 ready for Rainhill in 1980.

Michael Satow's reproduction *Rocket* on a demonstration-run in Kensington Gardens, the Albert Memorial being almost lost in the steam. On the left, Norman St John Stevas, Minister for the Arts, with John Bellwood, chief mechanical engineer of the National Railway Museum, York.

in Worcestershire, Foster, Rastrick & Company exported a locomotive the *Stourbridge Lion* to America for testing, but it was not
very successful. He also sent *Delaware* and *Hudson* for the Delaware
& Hudson Railroad. Rastrick abandoned locomotives and developed
successfully his heavy engineering works at Stourbridge.

One of Stephenson's greatest supporters for the steam locomotive
from its darkest days was Nicholas Wood who first worked for him at
Killingworth Colliery when only sixteen in 1811. He rose to be chief
engineer of the colliery, had seen Stephenson's progress from obscur-
ity, and at one time had young Robert as his apprentice. After judging
at the Rainhill Trials, Wood was involved in various railway projects
and for some years was engineer of the Liverpool & Manchester when
it was in public operation. Using his L & M experience as a basis, he
presented many impressive technical papers on railway development
and was elected a member of the Institution of Civil Engineers.

John Braithwaite, who had shared the *Novelty* at the Rainhill
Trials, went on to build railways and was engineer to the Eastern
Counties Railway; his partner, John Ericsson, emigrated to America
in 1839 where he earned fame as an engineer.

Of the several firms who built locomotives for the Liverpool &
Manchester to L & M specifications, a number supplied thousands of
machines to numerous railways at home and abroad. Among them
were Fenton, Murray & Jackson, Leeds; Edward Bury, Liverpool;
Mather, Dixon & Co, Liverpool; Haigh Foundry, Wigan; Hawthorn,
Newcastle; Todd, Kitson & Laird, Leeds; and B. Hick & Sons,
Bolton, whose Soho Works there still flourishes as Hick, Hargreaves
in industrial engineering. Charles Tayleur & Co. of Newton-le-
Willows built eleven in the Vulcan Foundry for the L & M, and
others for Europe and America; but Tayleur was fortunate in having
Robert Stephenson as his partner from 1832. The Vulcan works is
currently part of the General Electric Company.

Sharpe, Roberts & Co. of Manchester built one for the L & M,
twenty for the Grand Junction, and large numbers for other railways
including some for France and Germany. In later years, the company
moved to Glasgow, teamed up with another to become the famous
North British Locomotive Company supplying locomotives throughout the world. Though Edward Bury had built only one for the L &
M, the company allowed him to conduct extensive experiments on the
line and his firm built hundreds for railways in Britain and overseas
and he became locomotive superintendent for the London & North
Western Railway, parent company of the L & M.

From all this activity, railway lines were spreading rapidly across
Britain and shocked empty slopes of ground into new busyness. They
brought new towns, new power plants, new collieries and new factories to regions nobody had ever noticed on any map, set into

seething life new resorts, expanded property development, and shifted masses of people to live in new places to make new lives for themselves and their families. What had been proved by the Liverpool & Manchester was being brilliantly confirmed.

Adding further to the Liverpool & Manchester influence, its directors and engineers were frequently called to Parliament as witnesses concerning new railway projects, services which they gladly gave.

Busy at the centre of the railway revolution, the two Stephensons travelled far and wide. They took the railway from Chester to the Isle of Anglesey on the Chester and Holyhead line for ship links with Ireland, from which tiny Holyhead grew into an important port. Bangor was reached in 1848; and to cross the Menai Straits, Robert built the first tubular bridge of unique structure, the trains being completely enclosed in a tunnel of iron.

George's marathon had embraced many lines – the Norfolk railways, Scarborough to York, Manchester – Macclesfield – Stoke-on-Trent, the Manchester, Buxton & Midland Junction, Midland Counties, North Midland, Trent Valley, and the Manchester & Leeds which was the first railway to cross the bleak Pennine Range. His many viaducts were majestic. He surveyed a route for his son to build from Newcastle to the Scottish border at Berwick-on-Tweed and examined a route on to Edinburgh; and jointly with G. P. Bidder he engineered the London & Blackwall Railway. For many other railways he was active as surveyor, engineer or consultant. Needing to be close by Parliament for committee investigations, in 1836 George had opened an office in Duke Street, Westminster, and the fees rolled in. A year later, he moved to 30 Great George Street. And who can blame him if the great man found the address irresistible?

Overseas, too, his output was prodigious. His services were commissioned in Spain, France, Germany, Belgium and Holland. He travelled spartanly by road until the railways came, for months at a time, sometimes taxing his health. In 1835, father and son had been invited to Belgium by King Leopold to advise his engineers about their first railways. By 1840, George had handed over most of his current work to his son so that he could enjoy his friends and potter in the garden.

While with the Liverpool & Manchester, he had spent many evening hours in candle light with his young assistants, talking railways incessantly; and he started several mechanics' institutes. In 1847, he was elected founder president of the Institution of Mechanical Engineers – which delighted him. He had refused many other offers of public honour, including a seat in Parliament.

In his later years, by which time he was accepted and indeed fêted in high society, he moved from Alton Grange in Leicestershire to Tapton House near Chesterfield, Derbyshire, where he had other valuable coal mining interests. His faithful pony Bobby also retired, to nuzzle contentedly among the clover, then died in 1845 aged about 20. That year, George's second wife died and he married again early in 1848. Seven months later he died and was buried in Chesterfield. By then, the intricate network of railways in Britain was rapidly approaching six thousand route miles, which is more than half the mileage in use today.

In the early 1820s, Stephenson had forecast a national network and he lived to see his great dream come true. He was 67. Of great physical strength and endurance, he was the supreme architect who had drawn the first bold lines across Britain on which others were to elaborate, and has often been described as the most famous engineer who ever lived. His life's work certainly places him high among the world's greatest benefactors, and it was the Liverpool & Manchester Railway that had launched his world career.

Son Robert inherited his father's enormous wealth. Though happily married, Robert remained childless. Of his vast engineering output, suffice to add that among his other great works were the London & Birmingham Railway, the High Level Bridge over the Tyne at Newcastle, a tubular bridge over the River Conway in North Wales, and the Royal Border Bridge spanning the Tees at Berwick. In Canada, he built the Great Victoria Bridge, a tubular iron railway structure, to cross the St Lawrence River at Montreal: at about two miles, then the longest bridge in the world.

Of the locomotives Robert built for Canada and America, his *John Bull* served as a basis for extensive locomotive building in America, and from it Matthias Baldwin built what grew to be one of the largest locomotive works in the world. As well as sending locomotives to several European countries, Robert visited Denmark, Norway and Sweden to plan or lay out new railways. He advised engineers on tunnelling work for railways through the Swiss Alps and built two bridges to cross the River Nile in Egypt where he again met the tired Brunel on a health tour. He was also consulted about the proposed Suez Canal which eventually opened in 1869.

In character, Robert was cautious and experimental. Both the Stephensons shied away from many tempting speculations and normally invested in only sound railways that they were themselves building. Of great personal charm, Robert, like his father, drew on his great wealth to help the needy. But ruthlessness was there when needed. Calculating assets, earnings and dividends, he was reputed to have been the first railway-engineer millionaire.

His most serious setback had been in the 1830s when consultant engineer to the heavily graded Stanhope & Tyne Railway using a mixed bag of power – locomotives, horses, gravity, and fixed engines. Of it, the traffic manager said, "It was like a lot of fiddlers playing at a concert; if one made a mistake it spoiled all the rest!" Robert had invested heavily in the line, lost his money and swore it would never happen again.

He followed his father as president of the Institution of Mechanical Engineers, and in 1855 was elected president of the Institute of Civil Engineers. Other honours were showered upon him at home and abroad. He rejected a knighthood but accepted a seat in Parliament in 1847 to represent Whitby. Robert delivered many technical papers in which he always spoke warmly of the Liverpool & Manchester that had brought him youthful success and had launched railways upon the world scene. Though his greatest compliments were reserved for his revered father, he acknowledged at a public meeting in Newcastle: "The locomotive is not the invention of one man but of a nation of mechanical engineers".

Hard work, extensive primitive travel and heavy cigar-smoking took toll of his indifferent health and he died in 1859, four days before his fifty-sixth birthday and twenty-seven days after his friend and competitor Isambard Brunel. He survived his father by only eleven years, and was buried in Westminster Abbey alongside his fellow-pioneer, Thomas Telford, who had so searchingly investigated his father's work on the Liverpool & Manchester Railway. Statues of both father and son were erected at Euston station in London. At the close of the Stephenson era, Britain's railway network was almost nine thousand route miles.

Both the Stephensons, and indeed other pioneers, conducted their business by personal contact, extensive travel and massive correspondence. What would they not have given for a telephone or a typewriter? But these administrative contrivances were locked away in an arcane future.

Early rapid growth of the railways illustrating the concentrated achievements of the pioneers is reflected in the following table:

to decade ending	route miles in use
1840	1484
1850	6084
1860	9069
1870	13563
1930 (peak decade)	20445
1980	11100

Gangs of railway navvies, first seen in large numbers on the Liverpool & Manchester, were an essential element in railway building. They were usually engaged by contractors responsible to the engineers. They worked hard, lived rough, and drank rough, their brawls at nearby inns terrifying the locals, especially on pay nights which were a saturnalia of riot among the Irish, Northumbrians and other ethnic groups. Sometimes they erected crude shelters of timber or turf as sleeping quarters in the lonely countryside, on occasion being supplied with tents. Gangs were often sent to Europe to work on railways in which British engineers were involved. If the navvies worked, the engineers worked harder still. After toiling on the line from the Manchester and Liverpool to Wigan in 1830, Charles Vignoles showed the strain of it all in his diary: "For three nights, none of us went to bed, and when all was finished every one was completely knocked up. I have, however, accomplished my task; but it has left me full of nervousness, and I am reduced to a skeleton."

Railway contractors regularly went bankrupt. Others made money. During the pioneering period, Samuel Morton Peto (1809–89) learnt much from the Liverpool & Manchester and grew to be one of the greatest railway contractors of the Victorian Age. Alone or with partners, as well as railways in Britain, he constructed lines in Norway, France, Russia, Algiers, Australia and Canada. Peto, Brassey & Betts erected Robert Stephenson's bridge over the St Lawrence River, and built locomotives at Birkenhead for the first railway in Finland. A devoted Baptist, Peto gave generously to the deprived poor and received a knighthood. His father erected Nelson's Column in Trafalgar Square, London, in 1840–43, and Peto senior could have justifiably challenged, "Follow that, lad!" And he did.

In considering the Liverpool & Manchester and other early railways, the pioneers were young, vigorous, starry-eyed; they built the railways literally with their own bare hands and sent the steam locomotive thundering across the world on iron rails. Most of these fellows were in their twenties and thirties; Henry Booth was in his thirties when he joined the first promoters of the L & M. Even slow-starter George Stephenson was only thirty-three when he built his first locomotive. Those who became famous were not to be flattered by fashionable portrait painters until their older years; hence, we are left with an impression of austere, stern old gentlemen adorned in Victorian side-whiskers, cravats and frock coats which, in their day, were the very latest in sartorial elegance. Even photography, which became popular later in the century, shows the static sitters tense and grim for the long exposure that was required. But when young, most met a girl, fell in love, married, set up home and had children, intimate details of which are inappropriate here. Thankfully, many left memoirs, letters and diaries in which they bared their burdened souls.

One unique contribution which the Liverpool & Manchester Railway made to railways around the world was a standard gauge of 4 feet 8½ inches between the rails. George Stephenson had recommended uniformity; and anticipating a network, he had insisted on it determinedly wherever he could, both at home and abroad. His son, protégés and associates supported his policy. Despite this, a surprisingly large variety of gauges proliferated, ranging from about four feet to seven. As examples, the Dundee & Arbroath was 5 feet 6 inches, the Garnkirk & Glasgow 4 feet 6 inches, and the Eastern Counties and the London & Blackwall 5 feet. But the greatest deviant was Brunel's Great Western Railway at 7 feet, swinging out west from London to Gloucester, Bath, Bristol and Exeter.

Inevitably, the Government intervened and a Gauge Commission was appointed in 1845 to investigate and to make recommendations. At the enquiry, Robert Stephenson was asked whether his father had advocated 4 feet 8½ inches. "No," he replied, "it was not *proposed* by my father. It was the original gauge of the railways about Newcastle-on-Tyne, and therefore he *adopted* that gauge."

Distinguished railway directors and engineers wrangled bitterly for about a year, then the Commissioners decided on 4 feet 8½ inches. But whatever the mighty Commissioners thought, they really had no option: the decision made itself. What had been done so extensively could not now be undone, even though arguably the Liverpool & Manchester was not the ideal long-term standard gauge. But this gauge could accommodate relatively much sharper curves than a wider one.

An exception was made by the commissioners for the GWR and its associated lines. What a savage and costly blow this was to Brunel and Gooch who then had to lay a third rail to take rolling stock of other railways. Over many years the change was gradually made to 4 feet 8½ inches. Costs for the track conversion and the scrapping of locomotives, carriages and wagons brought the ailing GWR almost to its financial knees. It was not until 1892 that the conversion was completely made. Incidentally, the first underground railway in London (Paddington-Farringdon) opened in 1863 with steam locomotives, was laid with three rails to accommodate two gauges, largely because GWR rolling stock had been used. The wide gauge had been one of the brilliant Brunel's most disastrous errors.

Though the first railway in Ireland was of 4 feet 8½ inches, years later 5 feet 3 inches was adopted, different from the rest of the British Isles; this made it impossible for standard gauge English rolling stock ever again to run on Irish metals. Amen to that!

Eventually, the Liverpool & Manchester gauge was accepted throughout Europe (except Spain, Portugal, Finland and Russia), in America, Canada, Australia, the Middle East, Mexico, China, Japan and elsewhere, though some countries have more than one gauge. Much of the track in Southern Africa is 3 feet 6 inches.

Supposing the Rennies had built the Liverpool & Manchester in their proposed gauge of 5 feet 6 inches? Though a fascinating hypothesis, the historian's mind boggles at the world-wide implications.

Numerous visitors to the Liverpool & Manchester from abroad and massive overseas correspondence swiftly promoted the railway concept. The French Consul and the Turkish Ambassador were intrigued to see the locomotives. In 1828, three promoters of the proposed Baltimore & Ohio Railroad arrived, and three years later offered a cash prize in dollars for the best American locomotive, Rainhill fashion. Earlier, an American visited England from Philadelphia which was to develop as a great centre for railroads. Jonathan Knight, an engineer of the Baltimore & Ohio, noted in his diary that the L & M was "the first great theatre for the display of such machinery", meaning locomotives; and John B. Jervis of the projected Delaware & Hudson Railroad recorded that the L & M must be "regarded as opening the epoch of railways, which has revolutionised the commercial and social intercourse of the civilised world".

In 1828, George Stephenson had invited a young American engineer named Horatio Allen to inspect railway projects and locomotives; Allen returned home with notes and sketches to build railways. In his diary, Allen cited the Liverpool & Manchester as "one of the greatest curiosities of the Kingdom." Stephenson's locomotive *America* ordered for the Delaware & Hudson which arrived in New York in January 1829 was the first steam locomotive to be seen in that country.

A Boston (USA) civil engineer wrote to Charles Vignoles in June 1830: "I should like very much to have a run on your Manchester and Liverpool railway; but the accounts show with what frightful velocity you move. Will it do to go at the rate of 15 or 20 miles an hour?"

About that period, Vignoles received a letter from his friend Major Wilson from Philadelphia: "Professional men in America are indebted to Britain for what is valuable both in railroads and canals; and the late results of the Liverpool and Manchester road have given an increased interest and impetus to similar enterprises in this country." Americans still say 'railroads', a term that was common parlance among the early English pioneers.

Shortly after the Rainhill Trials, a Massachusetts businessman wrote: "We have been called on to receive, in astonishment, the accounts which are given, of recent experiments in England, upon the capacity and adaptation of Steam Carriages, as a self-moving power over Rail Roads. This invention promises to produce a new era in the business and arrangement of society."

American Press reports featured such glowing phrases as "novel experiment," "grand experiment," ". . . it will yield a golden harvest to its spirited proprietors, and immediately benefit a vast population," ". . . the ability of this invention to accomplish mighty results, beyond the dreams of those who were regarded as almost infatuated only twelve months ago." Following Britain, young, thrusting transport-hungry America bounded swiftly ahead of any other country in the world with her railways. Undoubtedly, the dynamics of a common heritage, language and literature were key factors in her accomplishments.

Another country aided by the influence of the Liverpool & Manchester was India, for capital was subscribed both in Liverpool and Bombay for the projected Great Peninsular Railway to tap the vast cotton-producing areas; interested Lancashire cotton mill owners also lobbied in London for financial support.

Men with money in the Liverpool & Manchester invested in many railways overseas; one was the new line to serve Paris and Rouen of which, on the recommendation of English railway directors, Joseph Locke was appointed engineer. From their European projects, British promoters and investors had earned several million pounds by the mid-forties, some of them selling out with handsome capital gains. Inevitably, from the intelligence garnered from the pioneering Liverpool & Manchester, engineers in Europe, Russia and America soon began to build their own steam locomotives and railways.

Today, British Rail are still exporting unique skills and revolutionary technical equipment competitively to America and to many other overseas countries. But the talented technocrats were not too proud to take time off from their laboratories and chart rooms to celebrate in 1980 the modest railway that started it all.

Examining old documents and peering through the misty, far-off years, it is difficult to conceive in depth the world-wide impact and influence this short line of thirty-one miles wielded during its fifteen years of independent existence; but it will remain for many generations as a great railway to remember, and a reason to honour the incredible men who created it.

CHAPTER 13

The Line's Place in the Network
(1845–1980)

After the Liverpool & Manchester Railway had been amalgamated in 1845 with the Grand Junction which, in turn, was absorbed the following year by the London & North Western under the ambitious Captain Mark Huish, the men responsible for building up the pioneering line could sit back, safely embraced in the arms of a powerful company. From the wings, they could watch the rise and fall of other small companies as the fury of the mania raged and burnt itself out.

The old line was now better fed and nurtured by the parent company which, starting in 1846 with some three hundred and fifty miles of route, was swiftly to take over many other railways and to build new ones. In time, it stretched its hungry tentacles to serve North Wales, Buckinghamshire, Bedford and Huddersfield. By extensions and joint agreements with other railways, the Nor' West trains in later years penetrated into competitors' territory as far as Swansea, Shrewsbury, Hereford, Birkenhead, Blackpool, Peterborough and Nottingham. Eventually, the prestigious Oxford and Cambridge line via Bletchley came into its net.

For many of these services, Liverpool and Manchester were crucial centres. At the end of its career of nearly seventy-seven years, the Nor' West, self-styled the 'Premier Line', had grown to 2,149 miles and, like its pioneering constituent, remained a predominantly passenger railway.

During its sojourn, the Nor' West constructed several new branch lines connecting with the Liverpool & Manchester, which brought the old line new business. Vast marshalling yards were laid out, including one at Edge Hill. Lime Street station, its Liverpool terminus, was considerably enlarged in 1851, its iron structure being the first of its kind. In the 1880s, it was again rebuilt, and modernised yet again recently.

Originally, directors of the Liverpool & Manchester and other new railways were mainly merchants, manufacturers, bankers and shippers; and the more shares they held the greater personal power did they wield. Times changed. Techniques developed. Competition became more cut-throat. And gradually jejune 'railway governors' whose amateur blunders often proved disastrous, were replaced by specialist directors with technical and mechanical skills, commercial nous, financial flair, and a deep understanding of the growing railway industry. In that thrusting period, it was survival of the fittest, and natural selection produced a stronger railway animal.

Among many technical innovations in which the Liverpool & Manchester shared, was the gradual introduction of the electric telegraph for signalling trains and exchanging communications. After the celebrated American Samuel Morse (1791–1872) had invented his alphabetical code of dots and dashes in 1837, the Morse Code in later years began to come into general railway telegraphic use. Station clerks, signalbox and other staff operated the instruments, many of which remained in active service until the 1930s when this author worked one in Hanley station booking office, Stoke-on-Trent. Towards the end of the nineteenth century, that new-fangled gadget, the telephone, over many decades, steadily superseded them.

Among the numerous businesses that grew with the railways was the bookstall service. From 1848, two stations on the Liverpool & Manchester line were served by W.H. Smith – Liverpool Lime Street and Manchester Victoria. Young William Henry Smith (1825–91) was making his name and soon secured exclusive rights at Nor' West stations. During the 1860s and 1870s, he opened new bookstalls on Liverpool & Manchester stations at Edge Hill, Earlestown, Newton Junction, Patricroft and Eccles.

Other firms' bookstalls were notorious for their salacious publications – in modern jargon, porn. Devoutly religious, Smith maintained high standards which earned him the aphorism 'The North Western Missionary' and further contracts with other railways. Elected a Liberal Member of Parliament, he rose to cabinet minister. Today, the sixth W.H. Smith (Lord Hambleden) is a director of the company. WHS have a distribution depot at Broad Green near Liverpool which is served by a private siding from the Liverpool & Manchester line.

About mid-century, reading was growing in popularity and railway bookstall literature often featured the pioneering line. By then, about two-thirds of children were receiving daily education, a better standard than any other country in the world. Most of the schools were sponsored by Quakers, churches, charities and benevolent employers. The Education Act of 1870 brought compulsory elementary education for all children, most of whom began working at twelve or thirteen.

Late in the century, the Liverpool & Manchester line saw more promise with the proposition by Manchester man Sir Edward Watkin that a tunnel should be built under the English Channel to take trains through between Manchester and Paris. The idea was shelved. First considered in 1802, the tunnel has been on and off ever since. It was very much on again in 1966 and digging began, only to be abandoned by the Government, and to remain as a pipe dream for the distant future.

Throughout the nineteenth century, steam power, which had revolutionised the Lancashire looms, heavy industry and shipping, stood as the power in the land. From the time Trevithick's first steam carriage had run on the street, steam-operated road vehicles carried passengers and goods in growing numbers. Even the first attempts at flight were steam-powered. Though the Wright Brothers using petrol engines in 1903 sped America to the aerospace lead, William Henson of Chard in Somerset, as early as 1842, had built a primitive 20-foot wingspan flying machine powered by steam. Alas, its weight prevented it from climbing into the sky.

When Otto, Benz, Daimler and other nineteenth-century inventors developed the internal combustion engine, it shared with steam identical principles: pressure behind a piston rod inside a cylinder created rotary movement.

If Newcomen or Watt had applied their inventive skills along another route, for example plying steam jets to wheel flaps waterwheel fashion, or directing pressured steam through a simple spiral screw or turbine, the history of the Liverpool & Manchester Railway, and indeed all transport, might well have been entirely different.

In the early years of the Liverpool & Manchester, travel in isolated compartments was, for nervous ladies, a frightful ordeal. When they were molested, they could not call the guard. Screaming was useless. As more railways came, passengers were increasingly exposed to thugs, thieves, confidence tricksters and card-sharpers. Innocent young ladies were ravished and sometimes murdered. For decades, most railways resisted pressures from Press and public for some system of summoning the guard, on the supposition that trains would often be halted trivially. A Board of Trade enquiry into a murder on the North London Railway in 1864 resulted in a system of passenger communication being recommended. Some railways had already fitted a rope running outside the carriages; when pulled by a distressed passenger, it rang two bells: one on the locomotive and the other in the guard's van. A succession of brutal attacks prompted Parliament to demand a proper emergency system linked to the train braking which forward looking railways had already fitted. The modern 'communication cord' (some are handles) makes a partial train braking only, otherwise a train might be stopped on the Forth Bridge, in a tunnel, on a lonely moor or just short of a station.

Continuous automatic brakes on passenger trains and interlocking between points and signals were made compulsory by the Regulation of Railways Act 1889; it also enforced the 'block signalling system' to replace the time interval method originally practised on the Liverpool & Manchester.

During the century, new railways brought much wasteful duplication of lines, and many towns had two or three stations unconnected with each other; and when the Cheshire Lines Committee opened its line between Liverpool Central and Manchester Central (both terminals since closed) via Warrington, adding to the Lancashire & Yorkshire Railway route via Wigan established in the 1850s, three separate routes served the two terminal cities. All three routes are, however, still busy, the Liverpool & Manchester being the shortest.

During the second half of the century – the 'Champagne Years' – several significant innovations made travel more welcome. Station catering facilities were followed by luxurious Pullman dining cars on some routes and the Anglo-Scottish sleeping-car trains. Corridors between the carriages with lavatories also made travel more comfortable. Upholstery was improved, though third-class travellers still had to suffer hard unsympathetic seats of bare wood.

Dating from the pioneering years, winter travel in draughty four-wheeled carriages with iced-up windows had been a misery, especially for the elderly and children. Coats and blankets kept out some cold. Then along came hired footwarmers filled with hot water, and in due time under-seat radiators heated by steam from the locomotives were installed.

Primitive lighting by tallow candles and oil lamps tried out on the Liverpool & Manchester and used on other railways, for many years just about enabled literate passengers to peer at their newspapers. Next came gas lighting, hailed as "the greatest invention of artificial light", some gas-lit carriages surviving until the 1930s. Gas lighting was introduced at some of the larger stations in the 1880s, and was puttering away at a few stations into the 1970s. Electric lighting in trains first appeared in 1881, but the change to this power for trains and stations generally was a long, slow metamorphosis.

Speed and comfort progressed in parallel. Even in the 1830s when the Liverpool & Manchester was jogging along at 10 or 20 miles an hour, fast trains had been foreseen, as expressed in a contemporary pamphlet: "We shall, one of these days, hear of a man breakfasting in London, dining in Manchester, supping at Leeds or York, and sleeping in Edinburgh! Then may the ardent and anxious lover, the object of whose idolatory is in the distant part of the Kingdom, 'fly on the wings of love', not in imagination only, but find himself really and corporally in the presence of his mistress by the potent agency of a railway and locomotive engine, with a rapidity that almost outstrips his ardour; thus realising the poetical extravaganza:

> Ye Gods! annihilate Time and Space
> To make two lovers happy."

Such journeys were possible by the time the Liverpool & Manchester Railway celebrated its fiftieth anniversary in 1880; the event was organised in lavish style by the Nor' West, an impudent railway company for publicity on any pretext.

Other days of old were recalled in 1888 when the St Helens & Wigan Railway was launched. Lord Derby did the public honours and strongly recommended the new line to investors. His Lordship was gracious enough to admit the relentless opposition his distinguished great-grandfather had waged against the projected Liverpool & Manchester Railway over sixty years earlier, and applauded the vast development in railway enterprise since those distant days.

The boot was on the other foot when, in the 1880s, Manchester campaigned for a ship canal. Liverpool, naturally anxious about its port revenues, asserted protectively that the railway facilities were adequate. Eventually, Manchester won. Opening in 1894, the Manchester Ship Canal of 35½ miles took great sea-going ships through green fields and suburbs to the very door of Manchester, and is now listed as one of the great ship canals of the world. The town had been created a city in 1853 and her sister in 1880.

Liverpool had the distinction of launching in 1893 the world's first elevated electric railway. Its familiar sight and sound above the city streets vanished with its closure in 1956, the city environs now being well served by a network of electrified railways. Yet surprisingly, despite the progress of the steam locomotive, the stationary engine with haulage cables remained in use for Wapping tunnel until 1896.

Regular railway traveller Queen Victoria, who had observed at close quarters the revolutionary developments, died in 1901, ending the great Victorian Era. She was succeeded by King Edward VII.

By the turn of the century, a recent invention was making inroads into the passenger traffic on the railways, especially in towns and suburbs. The electric tramcar had arrived. A route, with unconnected sections which prevented through journeys, opened between Liverpool and Manchester, but it ran well to the north of the pioneer railway line, which diluted its competitive power. Even the humble bicycle whisked away some short-distance passenger business; this British invention of 1879, featuring pedal cranking and chain-driven rear wheel, was to emerge as the common man's way of getting to work and enjoying leisure outings.

But worse was to come. In the early 1900s, motor cars and vehicles to carry passengers and goods began to make their sporadic appearance. At first, directors of the larger railways regarded motor cars as toys for the indulgent wealthy. World War I (1914–18) changed their attitude. War needs had promoted fast progress of motor vehicles; and when the débâcle was over, numerous surplus motor lorries were purchased, some by ex-servicemen using their gratuities to start one-man businesses to carry passengers or goods.

Exactly as had happened with railways, little businesses amalgamated into big businesses commanding large fleets of buses and lorries, even if most did have solid rubber tyres. Manchester and Liverpool and the towns between steadily filled up with motor vehicles of all kinds, sharing the congested streets with horse-drawn vans and carts. Petrol was 1s 6d (7½p) a gallon.

Mammoth railway amalgamations were completed in 1923. The 120 separate railway companies were grouped into four main line railways: London Midland & Scottish, London & North Eastern, Southern, and Great Western which proudly retained its historic name. The Liverpool & Manchester line, along with its parent company the Nor' West, was absorbed into the LMS.

A few years were occupied in settling down; then the new companies combined to fight, by every means at their command, the swiftly swamping road competition. Robert Bradshaw, powerful Bridgewater Canal man of the 1820s, must have rolled over in his grave to enjoy a secret chuckle.

Desperately, in 1926 the LMS – dubbed wickedly by its competitors ''ell of a mess' – called in Josiah Stamp as chairman. His father had been a bookstall manager for W. H. Smith & Son at Wigan station. During a distinguished career, Stamp received many honours at home and abroad, was knighted and later made a peer.

But he was not too big to appreciate the historic significance of the small railway that had started it all. In 1930, the LMS staged a magnificent week, 13th–20th September, of centenary celebrations of the Liverpool & Manchester Railway in the presence of enormous cheering crowds, redolent of 1830.

Highlights included the *Lion* (described in the next chapter) and other veteran locomotives, carriages and waggons, displays of relics, historic illustrations, decorated streets, a railway fair, miniature railway and countless souvenirs. The star that stole the show was the full-sized replica of the *Rocket* built in 1911 at the Nor' West Crewe Works. At night, an illuminated electric tramcar depicting the *Rocket* in coloured lights, rumbled and squealed along the streets. Other attractions included sports, brass bands, vaudeville, ballet, special church services, fireworks *et al*.

Scenes of the historic opening day were re-enacted. Characters in period costume impersonated George Stephenson, the Duke of Wellington, William Huskisson, railway directors and 'railway servants'. A town crier bawled out the announcements and the Railway Queen was crowned to a fanfare of trumpets. The Lord Mayors of Liverpool and Manchester travelled along the line on a celebratory train, and unveiled a plaque at the original terminal in Liverpool Road, Manchester.

Among those who attended or took active part were the Earl of Derby (whose ancestor had tried to filibuster the railway promoters); Josiah Stamp; Viscount Churchill, Great Western chairman; William Whitelaw, London & North Eastern chairman (whose grandson is a Member of Parliament of the same name); and Ashton Davies, a former Lancashire railway clerk who had risen to vice-president of the LMS.

"Let us now praise famous men," wrote Stamp in an epigrammatic foreword to the centenary programme. "We pay homage to the memory of men of valiant vision who . . . brought their great design to pass in the face of cunning and incredible opposition, and proved, as pioneers and reformers have ever proved, that cunning is the dark sanctuary of incapacity, and that opposition is the father of opportunity.

"We also celebrate the perfection of their machine, clothed in romance and endowed with an individuality by a century of workers 'who are perished as though they have never been'. . . . George Stephenson towers above them like a Colossus of Rhodes. . . . He deserves a centenary all to himself. But George Stephenson was fortunate in being associated with men who became known as the 'Liverpool Party'. . . ." One contributor to the programme acknowledged, "The L&MR was the genesis of the LMS."

Of transport competition, Stamp observed, "Now, after a hundred years, men are asking themselves whether railways in their turn are not to be dispossessed by the motor and the aeroplane." By the 1980s, trimmed certainly. But still far from dispossessed.

When the celebrations were over, it was back to work. To fight off road competition, the railways invested heavily in more road transport passenger vehicles, and steadily replaced their horse-drawn vans and drays with motor lorries. Both in and out of Parliament, they campaigned persistently for a 'square deal'. In 1934, they formed Railway Air Services Limited and set up a modest internal airline network in which both Liverpool and Manchester were connected with other leading cities; but the outbreak of World War II (1939–45) demised a promising venture.

Enjoying a final fling before the war shattered Europe, the railways went madly into the high speed business; and on 3rd July 1938, a London & North Eastern Railway train, hauled by Nigel Gresley's

Pacific locomotive *Mallard,* reached 126 mph to make a speed record for steam in Britain, and probably in the world. Locomotives were then commonly thirty times heavier than the *Rocket.*

At the height of steam, many expresses still carried names; the *Merseyside Express* linked London (Euston) with Liverpool; Manchester and London were served by the *Mancunian,* a historic reminder of the occupation of the site by the Romans in AD 76 who named it Mancumium: only a minor literary miss, but what is a couple of ems between friends – and Romans? Ethnically, Mancunian still survives alongside Liverpudlian and Cestrian.

After playing a valiant part in the war effort and surviving devastating aerial bombing, the railways were soon deeply entangled in party politics. War leader Winston Churchill for the Conservatives was rejected by the electorate in favour of Socialist Clement Attlee. Consequently, the railways in 1948 were nationalised, along with most of Britain's inland transport.

Though the small pioneering line was to be all but lost in a massive bureaucratic machine, its dramatic story popped up in the Press from time to time.

Typical was an illustrated article in the former *Picture Post* in 1947 while the political hyperbole still raged. It begins about Chat Moss: "Newspapers said it was lunacy. Parliament said it was worse. George Stephenson had laid an iron rail over a swamp. He had cut through a mountain of red sandstone. He had burrowed for a mile and a quarter beneath a city. Amid a nation-wide atmosphere of wild excitement he built the Liverpool & Manchester Railway between 1825 and 1830."

During the post-war period, some branches connecting with the Liverpool & Manchester line had been closed. Several wayside stations were also closed as improved road vehicles served by the new roadways proved more efficient and convenient. Among them were Collins Green 1951, Lea Green 1955, Astley and Seedley 1956, Ordsall Lane 1957, Glazebury and Huyton Quarry 1958, Cross Lane 1959, Kenyon Junction 1961. Weaste had been closed in 1942.

Under his chairmanship of British Rail (1961–65), Dr (now Lord) Beeching closed numerous uneconomic stations, marshalling yards, goods stations, coal depots, workshops and lines. He also introduced many improvements. He brought in modern marketing techniques on the precept that seats and wagon spaces are as much a product as toothpaste or cans of beans but are far more perishable.

In 1969, a new British Rail subsidiary, Transport Systems and Market Research Limited (Transmark), was formed. It has since operated in about fifty different countries and is selling British Rail technology widely, bringing prestige and valuable exports to the native land of railways, the beginnings of which are traced to the Liverpool & Manchester pioneers.

At last, steam, which had served so well, was being swiftly phased out, as promised in British Rail's modernisation programme of 1955, to be replaced by diesels and electrics. In the light of new technology and the natural reluctance of men to work any longer in the dirt and grime of coal, it was inevitable.

However, steam was not to say goodbye to the Liverpool & Manchester line without a fuss; and on the last journey in 1968, a great assembly of well-wishers and steam enthusiasts clicked their cameras feverishly to capture this last great historic moment. Venerated coal-burning steam was replaced by oil-burning diesel, based on German engineer Rudolph Diesel's engine of 1893, a power seen by British Rail as an interim stage to the wider introduction of electrification.

Except for the Rheidol Valley narrow-gauge line from Aberystwyth, steam in British Rail time-tables was in its last gasp when, on Sunday 11th August 1868, BR with a sense of occasion ran a special named *Farewell to Steam* from London. Loaded with officials, Press men and enthusiasts, it arrived at Lime Street station, Liverpool, to a tumult of glamour that these occasions happily inspire. On that memorable day, enthusiasts must have felt they had died a little inside. Steam was dead. Long live diesel and electric!

In the next important phase, both Liverpool and Manchester benefited from one of Britain's largest electrification schemes. It was opened in sections to minimise service disruptions. A full electric service direct from London (Euston) and along the old Stephenson routes of the London & Birmingham and the Grand Junction railways connected with Liverpool Lime Street and Manchester Piccadilly (formerly named London Road) starting on 18th April 1966. When the scheme was finished, both cities were served by electric trains also with Birmingham, Wolverhampton, Coventry, Stoke-on-Trent and Northampton. Robert Stephenson's old station at Euston, which had 'growed like Topsy', was completely rebuilt and opened by Queen Elizabeth II on 14th October 1968. British Rail described it as "a station which ranks with the finest of modern termini in any continent and which is an appropriate gateway to the 100 mph electric services".

Improved services between Liverpool and Manchester and the north and Scotland began on 6th May 1974, the day the main-line electrification was extended to Glasgow. In the 1980s when the Advanced Passenger Trains serve the Anglo-Scottish route, travel is expected at 150 mph, a speed which even the visionary George Stephenson in his most phrenetic flights of fancy never dreamed.

Nowadays, the pioneering line, an established Inter-City route, continues to serve travellers, traders and industry as Stephenson and his directors had planned. The ten busy intermediate stations are Edge Hill, Broad Green, Roby, Huyton, Rainhill, St Helens Junction, Earlestown, Newton-le-Willows, Patricroft, and Eccles. Earlestown took its name from Hardman Earle, then chief engineer of the L&NW Railway. The carriage and waggon works there, used by the L&NWR from 1853 were closed by British Rail in the 1960s.

Current passenger services consist of local diesel multiple-unit stopping trains; diesel locomotive-hauled expresses direct to and from Liverpool, Manchester, Leeds, York and Newcastle; direct services between Manchester and North Wales via Earlestown and Warrington. Manchester and Liverpool are also connected with the south coast by through trains. Freight using the line is predominantly traditional coal.

Edge Hill has lost its status as a main marshalling yard but has a diesel-locomotive service point, and depôts for waggon repairs and coal concentration. Another depôt opens there in the early 1980s for the new Advanced Passenger Trains. Lime Street station was remodelled and resignalled in good time for the celebratory year. Over the line nearby stands part of Liverpool University, and in quiet moments students in Lecture Room "A" can hear the faint rumblings of the trains below.

Two short sections totalling towards four miles are already electrified. One is between Lime Street and Edge Hill for trains to and from the south and London; the other is between Earlestown and Newton-le-Willows, this short section being used mainly when engineering work affects the nearby west-coast electrified main line.

Electrification is being extended to Parkside Junction in the early 1980s to a length of about 15 miles. Plans are in hand to electrify the remainder of about 14 miles to Manchester Victoria in later years; this will ensure for the pioneering line a long life to come.

CHAPTER 14

The Great Celebrations of 1980

Whenever future historians tackle the Liverpool & Manchester Railway, one thing is certain: the 150th anniversary celebrations of 1980 will rank as one of the most memorable years for this pioneering line. Notions began to take shape early. Even in 1975, Michael Satow and Lyn Wilson, while still managing the Stockton & Darlington Railway celebrations, were visualising events for 1980. Correspondence was exchanged with the Merseyside County Council, Greater Manchester County Council and local museums; financial support was outlined. Satow, a professional engineer, was then designing and building parts for a full scale working reproduction of the *Rocket*, to steam in 1979 and 1980.

No celebrations of real substance could be mounted without British Rail. In good time, BR showed tremendous enthusiasm and by 1978 had formulated the principal rail events, and appointed Tony Quirke of the Liverpool Division as project manager Rocket 150, charged with co-ordinating all the related activities. All BR affairs were promoted and marketed under the brand name of Rocket 150, and about a million pounds was allocated for local and national support, an investment to bring handsome returns.

An information and central booking office was opened in Rail House alongside the historic Lime Street station in Liverpool; tickets for the main Rainhill event of May 1980 were available a year ahead, by which time enquiries and early bookings had already been received from America, Australia and Japan. Even before the tickets were printed, over one thousand pounds in remittances had reached Rail House, with such requests as, "Please reserve for me four tickets . . ." which were duly honoured. An agent in London booked a party of about two hundred millionaires from Switzerland. An elderly enquirer in Australia wrote that he had attended the centenary in

1930.

To manage all the major events, a joint committee was formed comprising British Rail and the two county councils, the latter undertaking the financial support of non-rail events. In addition, several local committees were formed from local communities to stage-manage their own events within the general programme. For example, two groups in the Merseyside county – Rainhill and Newton – organised an extensive programme of related events and were supported by their local authorities; another group, the Edge Hill Railway Trust, was responsible for the Wapping cutting rail trail and other Edge Hill interests. The Liverpool Road Celebrations Joint Advisory Committee took command of related activities at the Manchester end.

Extra trains were scheduled from main centres in Britain for the principal events; and to catch a whiff of history, British Rail planned to run steam-hauled special trains on Sundays in 1980 from 1st June to 17th August between Edge Hill and Manchester Victoria: additional to normal services.

Steam is bound to have a great year in 1980. For several years, British Rail have authorised about one thousand miles of their track on which the railway societies and other owners can run their vintage locomotives and carriages, subject to appropriate insurance and inspection for public safety. In recent times, enthusiasm for steam locomotives has grown at an astonishing pace; now, there are about five hundred societies, some with their own paid staff, stations, track, workshops, locomotives and carriages: a large proportion founded since 1955, the year British Rail decided to phase out steam. Capt. Peter Manisty RN (Retd), chairman of the Association of Railway Preservation Societies, estimates that there are some two million railway enthusiasts in Britain, of whom about half a million are active members of the societies.

Over five hundred steam locomotives are today preserved by the societies, museums and other bodies, together with carriages, wagons, signalling equipment, and every other kind of railway relic that recreates the glorious past. Without this magnificent stock from which to draw, the railway celebrations would be much less spectacular. Steam preservation is far from the prerogative of the middle-aged or wealthy. Many young men, and girls too, who barely remember the steam age, are excited by the thought, sight, sound and smell of the steam locomotive; they don overalls at the weekend to wield paint brush, polishing rag and oil can, and work away for the sheer love of it, always ready for a public showing.

Ever since Queen Victoria's time, members of the Royal Family have displayed a lively interest in railways. Currently, the Duke of Edinburgh is Patron of the Transport Trust, its president being ardent railway preservationist Sir Peter Allen, former chairman of

Imperial Chemical Industries. Sir John Betjeman, the Poet Laureate, is president of the Midland & Great Northern Joint Railway Society. To mark the railway anniversary, the Association of Railway Preservation Societies has arranged its Second Symposium of Railway Preservation for 13th September 1980 in the Reynold's Hall, Manchester. A liberal proportion of railway officers will be present, signifying the close co-operation between business and hobby.

Conscious of the extra public interest in steam during 1980, between the spring and autumn railway societies and other owners will be running steam specials on their own private railways and on British Rail from bases as far apart as Wales and East Anglia, Devon and Scotland. Casual observers will see magnificent specimens of vintage locomotives and carriages, including such gallants as the *Flying Scotsman, Sir Nigel Gresley* or the *Duchess of Hamilton*, thundering through the quiet countryside, and may find themselves stopping to look with something akin to the enchantment experienced by Lancashire folk as the *Rocket, Dart* or *Arrow* rumbled along the rails in the 1830s. Those enthusiastic stalwarts and stewards of steam history will bring much nostalgic pleasure to an appreciative public. Anticipating the value of nostalgia in the travel market place, British Rail in 1978 launched their new steam specials with the advertisement, "Full Steam Ahead – for All the Family!"

At a time of high unemployment in the north-west, the Government, local authorities and trade and industry welcomed the celebrations as a unique opportunity for proclaiming to Britain and the world the facilities and potential of the region. Whatever the long-term industrial benefits happen to be, a surge of new commerce and trade was sweeping ahead on the crest of the railway nostalgic wave. For miles around, extensive bookings began early in 1979 for hotels, restaurants and sales stands. By March 1979, the internationally renowned Adelphi Hotel near Lime Street station was fully booked for the Rainhill Trials period in May 1980. Built originally in 1826, the Adelphi accommodated actress Fanny Kemble and her mother on 14th September 1830 ready for the official opening of the railway. Several times extended and rebuilt, the Adelphi can cope with gatherings of a thousand people.

For such a massive influx to the north-west, countless shopkeepers and traders dealing with the major events will be open from early morning to late at night as the cash tills ring up sales ranging from ice cream to camera film.

From 1978, manufacturers were busy making souvenirs and mementos by the hundred thousand – cut glass, textile goods, trays, badges, medals, models, T-shirts, paintings in limited editions, and commemorative medallions and ingots in bronze, copper, silver and gold. Priced at £540, the Birmingham Mint offered a presentation

case containing a set of thirty solid sterling silver ingots depicting celebrated locomotives. Hornby produced a model *Rocket*, and another
manufacturer offered a model of the *Rocket* fitted inside a bottle.
Wedgwood designed a superbly hand-engraved glass tankard, illustrating the *Rocket* and the emblem which had been specially created
for the joint management committee.

Special pictorial commemorative stamps were designed by the Post
Office to celebrate the anniversary year. They were for issue in March
1980, special covers for Post Office franking being available at the
Rainhill Trials re-enactment in May. Special frankings were also
arranged for the "opening of the railway" event at Liverpool Road
station in Manchester during September, and again on 10th November, the 150th anniversary of the first contract for mails arranged
between the Post Office and the Liverpool & Manchester Railway.

For more than a year, business corporations of various kinds, especially in the north-west region, took the opportunity to incorporate
the themes of the celebrations into their commercial advertising cam-
paigns.

Few major events in recent years have been backed by such a magnitude of publicity razmatazz as attended Rocket 150. International
coverage had been assured by two years of advance planning. Press
conferences, Press statements and visits to the sites organised by
British Rail were reinforced by a steady stream of advertisements
published by numerous firms and industries as part of their own marketing strategies for products and services. Local authorities and local
committees also published their own events. Regular news items
appeared in the Railway Preservation Societies' monthly newsletter
which is edited by Michael Crew, a Leeds schoolmaster.

Using their highly sophisticated resources, British Rail conducted a
general advertising and publicity campaign for over a year in advance
of the main events; leaflets and brochures were supported in May
1979 by the main BR poster for display in Britain and overseas. One
leaflet was headed, "The greatest programme of railway events ever
planned will operate throughout 1980." Press visits to principal
events and exhibitions produced a continual crop of news stories;
many newspapers and magazines published special feature articles.
Some published special supplements, a notable one consisting of
thirty-two pages was published by the *Manchester Evening News* in
March 1979.

For October 1979, the *Daily Express* organised a Rocket 150 competition jointly with British Rail, the prizes including free rail travel
tickets and seats in the stands at the Rainhill Trials. Other newspapers mounted similar competitions. In the autumn 1979, British
Rail published an illustrated commemorative booklet to retail at
£2.40. BR also promoted the events overseas through their own travel

centres – seventeen in Europe, three in America and two in Canada. Both the North West Tourist Board and the British Tourist Authority made wide use of their network of home and overseas publicity services; BTA also appointed in 1978 a publicity officer for the celebrations to use "every event or occasion likely to draw visitors from overseas."

News and feature items frequently transmitted by radio and television for over a year swelled the volume and left few people in ignorance of the celebrations to come; clearly, something worth seeing was happening in the north-west.

Henry Booth and Joseph Sandars, with their considerable pamphleteering skills and limited means, had alerted the world in the 1820s and 1830s; but what would they not have done for a satellite or two, or just simply a telephone line!

Contiguously, the several museums involved and the railway societies added their considerable quota of advance promotion. Such massive media coverage would remind the world that not only was Great Britain the crucible of railways, but that the Liverpool & Manchester was the prototype for the world. Certainly, the wide range of events and attractions extending for more than a year, amply justified the promotional work of the organisers. Throughout Merseyside and Greater Manchester, the range of associated activities involved schools, and all kinds of sporting, leisure and social pursuits; on the arts side there were music, dancing and the theatre. Brass bands would be well in evidence.

In planning the celebrations, British Rail decided to postpone the main event – the re-enactment of the Rainhill Trials – from the true historic starting date of 6th October 1979 to 24th, 25th and 26th May 1980; this would co-incide with the spring holiday, concentrate the main events within the one year, and be more convenient both to organisers and visitors. However, the correct historical date was marked on 6th October 1979 by the opening of an exhibition at Rainhill station near Stephenson's celebrated skew bridge and site of the original trials. Selected for display were historical relics, photographs, documents, drawings and a full-scale replica of Thomas Brandreth's 1829 *Cycloped*, the horse-operated machine that had been disqualified. Schoolboys and masters of New Heys School at Allerton near Liverpool built the replica, supported by the sponsorship of British Insulated Callender's Cables. On Rainhill station is to be seen a large notice board proclaiming the *Rocket*'s success of 1829. Finding nothing exceptional at the station, visitors have been known to exclaim, "Oh, is this *the* Rainhill?"

Visitors will be more impressed by Liverpool Lime Street and Manchester Victoria stations which were both cleaned up for the celebrations to reveal the rich brown tones of the stone frontages.

Opening at Easter 1980 for the summer months, an exhibition was to be staged in the Tudor-style waiting room at Earlestown, a station built by the Liverpool & Manchester Railway about 1835. Organised by the Newton 150 committee, it features particularly the nearby Vulcan Works in which Charles Tayleur and Robert Stephenson, in partnership, built locomotives for the Liverpool & Manchester and many other railways at home and abroad. In January 1980, a British Rail main line electric locomotive was to be named *Vulcan Heritage* at Warrington Bank Quay station.

Exhibitions and displays were arranged at local museums and public libraries. In London, special attractions were high-lighted in the Science Museum, the centrepieces of which were two of the original locomotives which had run at the Rainhill Trials in 1829: *Rocket*, and *Sans Pareil* and a *Novelty* cylinder, all bearing the scars of time.

The Science Museum was responsible for staging in London in 1979 the very first event of note for the celebrations. Along nearly three hundred yards of railway track laid near the Albert Memorial and opposite the Albert Hall, public demonstrations of Satow's reproduction *Rocket* in full steam were made; it hauled an open third-class carriage of the period daily between 11am and 7pm from Saturday 25th August until Sunday 2nd September. John Bellwood, chief mechanical engineer of the National Railway Museum at York, the locomotive's permanent home, recruited volunteer locomotive crews from the railway preservation societies. They were assisted by a maintenance crew from Locomotion Enterprises. Large crowds were fascinated by the tiny locomotive chuffing away in the West End; and the wide publicity so generated was of much value ready for the celebrations of 1980.

Legitimately related to the celebrations, at Shildon near Darlington the one remaining building of Timothy Hackworth's original locomotive works was restored as a museum by the local authority; there, Hackworth had built his *Sans Pareil* for the Rainhill Trials of 1829. Almost opposite is Hackworth's original cottage, which the Queen Mother had opened as a museum in 1975. Hackworth's descendants, the Youngs, who assiduously propagate the memory of their pioneering ancestor, were delighted in 1979 when British Rail named a class 86 Inter-City electric locomotive *Sans Pareil*. Other electrics in this class were named *Novelty, Planet, Phoenix, Goliath*, and *Comet*, recalling the originals that are steeped in the history of the Liverpool & Manchester Railway.

Superb arrangements were made by British Rail for staging the re-enactment of the Rainhill Trials. The same stretch of line, some nine miles from Liverpool, as used in 1829 was selected. Scaffolding Great Britain Limited were commissioned by British Rail to build nearly thirty stands, each about thirty feet apart, at a cost of half a million pounds, with a total seating capacity of 50,000. Location of the stands was restricted by the suitability of the adjacent land available for renting. Erection was to begin in February 1980, ready for the first cavalcade on Saturday 24th May.

Stretching for a mile, most of the stands were for the north side of the line, all at £6 per seat; the other stands, at £7.50 and £10 per seat, were located on the south side which was better for spectator photography, especially if the sun were bright. Sites for sales stalls were offered by British Rail at a rental for all kinds of merchandise, including souvenirs and literature.

About a dozen huge marquees were booked for the site to serve refreshments; Travellers' Fare, the station and train catering division of British Rail, was granted an exclusive concession to slake the thirsty and to feed the hungry. Several hundred toilets were provided. At strategic points on the site, space was allocated for hundreds of Pressmen and broadcasters from many countries in the world. A BBC 2 television team was scheduled to transmit the trials live; earlier the team had made a documentary film of the railway including the building of the three reproduction locomotives – *Rocket, Novelty*, and *Sans Pareil* – for transmission late in 1979. Copies of both films were expected to be sold for extensive use overseas.

So essential wherever large crowds assemble, public services of the usual range were organised; in attendance would be first aid staff, ambulances, doctors, nurses and missing-child finders. Appropriate police forces, fire brigades and hospitals were kept in the picture. Local authorities jointly with the AA and the RAC prepared for traffic control. Parking space was booked to accommodate about ten thousand cars at £1 a time, for each of the three days, and for two hundred coaches.

Some travel agents and hotels bought in advance blocks of Rainhill tickets and were able to offer the public the convenience of a package holiday; these were in great demand by visitors from overseas.

Rarely does British Rail close a busy working line; but on this unique occasion, for three days the route will be used exclusively for the great cavalcade and spectator trains. Expresses from and to Liverpool would be suitably diverted. Continuous shuttle services of diesel multiple unit trains will run from and to Liverpool and Manchester to Rainhill. They will start before nine in the morning to allow ample time for spectators to get to their places, and finish around ten at night.

British Rail promoted the three-day Rainhill Trials as a 'once in a lifetime railway extravaganza'. Never before will there have been such an incredible assembly of locomotives and carriages; and each passing year may well make a repeat performance on such a spectacular scale extremely unlikely. But who knows?

Of the three full scale working reproduction locomotives – *Rocket, Novelty* and *Sans Pareil*, Michael Satow, using Locomotion Enterprises Limited, built the first two. He and Lyn Wilson, then a lecturer at Durham University, while managing the Stockton & Darlington Railway celebrations of 1975, had formed that company, partly to promote the interests of *Locomotion No 1*. which Satow built and drove at Shildon for the Darlington event. Satow is a steam enthusiast, an industrial archaeologist, and honorary adviser to the Rail Transport Museum in India. Trained as an engineer at Loughborough, he made his career with Imperial Chemical Industries and retired some years ago as managing director ICI (India) Ltd. (In 1976, he showed this author in his workshop at Ormesby near Middlesborough some parts he had made ready for the *Rocket* replica).

It was that well-known steam enthusiast Bill McAlpine of the civil engineering and construction company who commissioned Satow to build a replica of Braithwaite & Ericsson's *Novelty*; he was acting on behalf of Flying Scotsman Enterprises of which he is a director. Another commission for Satow was to build three replica open third-class carriages, in original Liverpool & Manchester style, for the cavalcade; the sponsors were Filtrate Limited who had supplied lubricating oil for the original *Rocket* in 1829. Industry had made some contribution to the construction costs of the two locomotives and three carriages; the occasion was used to develop the Locomotion Enterprises Limited workshops at Springwell, Tyne & Wear, utilising, in collaboration with the Government's Manpower Services Commission, unemployed youths to undertake the work. Satow confessed that having spent so much time in intensive research into Stephenson the man and Stephenson the engineer, he began, in a most eerie sense, to feel the ghostly presence of the railway genius himself.

The reproduction *Sans Pareil* was assembled by the Hackworth Locomotive Trust from parts made mainly by apprentices at British Rail Engineering Works at Shildon near Darlington, works at Harwich, Swindon, York and Doncaster also being involved. Its boiler was built at BRE Works at Crewe. Ron Ellis, a plater there, worked on the boiler early in 1979; he confessed that it was a mystery to him how the pioneers had coped, "How they managed to get the jobs done in 1829 with their equipment baffles me!" After twenty years at Crewe, this was Ellis' first experience of steam construction. Nearby, the workshops echoed to the clatter of the construction of a High Speed Train. Some of the building costs of *Sans Pareil* were underwritten by Cecil Attwood on behalf of Dufay Paints Limited of Shildon.

All the three reproduction locomotives were fitted with safety devices that were additional to the originals, to make them safe for modern operation, and acceptable to British Rail's inspecting engineers.

For this greatest of all locomotive cavalcades, two refined old ladies in retirement were hauled gently from their comfortable resting places for a face lift and an injection of life-giving steam. L & N W R No. 173 2-2-2 *Cornwall* is among the oldest working steam locomotives in the world, and a superb machine of its day. She was built in Crewe Works in 1847 by Francis Trevithick, son of the famous Richard, when he was locomotive superintendent of the L & N W Railway. Some time later, she was rebuilt. Her unique visual feature consists of two enormous driving wheels of 8 ft 6 ins diameter, higher than the ceiling of a modern suburban house.

Until the turn of the century, *Cornwall* hauled expresses on the Liverpool & Manchester and other lines, but she had not steamed since the 1930s; in fact, when she was on her way to London Euston for the centenary of the London & Birmingham Railway in 1937, this author photographed her passing through Bletchley, Buckinghamshire, where he then worked. After being admired by countless visitors from around the world at the former British Transport Museum at Clapham in London, she was transported by road in 1974 to her first home at Crewe. At Bridgnorth in 1979–80 she was stripped right down and rebuilt, ready for a full head of steam to show her paces at Rainhill, resplendent in L & N W R livery of black, lined in yellow, pale blue and vermilion, work of the Severn Valley Railway.

Yet, this charming old lady is sure to be upstaged by *Lion*, built in 1838 at Leeds by Todd, Kitson & Laird, for the Liverpool & Manchester Railway; *Lion* is claimed to be the oldest working steam locomotive in the world and is certainly the most lively and realistic direct link with the pioneering railway. An 0-4-2 with two inside cylinders of 14-inches diameter and 18-inches stroke, she has driving wheels of 5-feet diameter and weighs about 27 tons; those are her vital statistics. Main visual features include a tall chimney, striped boiler and a sparkling copper dome over the firebox. Fuel is carried in a four-wheeled tender.

Her life story would make a chapter. Suffice to say that she was passed successively to the Grand Junction Railway, the L & N W Railway, the Mersey Docks, and up to the 1920s worked in a less dignified stationary capacity operating as pumping engines. In 1930, she hauled a replica train in the centenary celebrations of the Liverpool & Manchester Railway in Liverpool, spent some years being admired on a pedestal at Lime Street station, then was sent off to Crewe for safe keeping during World War II.

As befits a great and beautiful lady she went into films, was featured in several, and was the star in the Ealing Studios *Titfield*

Thunderbolt of 1952 for which she hauled a train for hundreds of miles. In April 1979, she was conveyed by road from her home at Merseyside County Museum, Liverpool, to Vulcan Works, Ruston Diesel Limited, at Newton-le-Willows to be put in working order. Her programme includes display at Steamport Transport Museum in Southport, then in May 1980 she is expected to travel under her own steam for a great performance at Rainhill. She is bedecked in a bright livery, with boiler cladding of highly polished strips of timber that are bound by shiny brass bands, green wheels, black framework, and hauls a green tender.

Turning now to the most spectacular and stirring event of the entire celebrations, the three-day programme for the re-enactment of the Rainhill Trials begins with the three reproduction locomotives, *Rocket, Sans Pareil* and *Novelty*, each hauling three period carriages loaded with passengers clad in period costume. Three of the carriages were built by Locomotion Enterprises, two come from the National Railway Museum of York, two from Liverpool Museum and two from Tyseley Steam Museum near Birmingham; the latter four belong to the N.R.M., York.

This batch is joined by *Lion* and *Cornwall* and the steam entourage makes one trip each way along the Rainhill level, starting from the east (in 1829 from the west). On its second return journey, it is joined by one of the greatest collections of locomotives ever seen together: about thirty steam locomotives, nine diesel electrics, two electrics, one diesel multiple unit, one 125-mph High Speed Train (already in service), and one 150-mph Advanced Passenger Train (due in public service in the early 1980s). Specimens of ancient and modern carriages and waggons are also scheduled for the cavalcade.

Among the steam locomotives in the early selection for the cavalcade were some much-loved favourites: *Hardwicke, Lord Nelson, Flying Scotsman, Sir Nigel Gresley, Leander, Princess Elizabeth, Hagley Hall, Cheltenham, Clan Line, Duchess of Hamilton, Green Arrow*, "Spinner", L & N W R tank, Lancashire & Yorkshire Railway saddle tank, MR Compound, LMS Goods, MR "Jinty", LMS Black Five, Somerset & Dorset 2-8-0, LMS 2-6-0 *Mickey Mouse*, BR 2-6-0 and BR 2-6-4 tank. In making this selection, British Rail took several factors into account: general condition, should be predominantly LMS, its predecessors and standard BR; a few from lines other than the LMS; tank engines to be limited because of low water capacity; proximity to Rainhill and availability from rail-connected home bases. GWR locomotives were limited by loading gauge profiles.

British Rail had commissioned Michael Satow for Locomotion Enterprises Limited to organise the transport and control of the three replica locomotives and his three period carriages to and from the site. It fell to Tony Quirke to cope with the rest of the cavalcade in a complicated schedule that took nearly two years to organise; rolling stock would come by road and rail from railway societies, museums and other owners from all over Britain. Locomotives had to be scheduled for prior inspection by BR engineers, appropriate insurance by the owners, and the taking of water and coal on the journeys.

Such backroom administrative accoutrements will interest few of the entranced and applauding spectators. On each of the three days, fifty thousand people (this author will be there) will be seated in the stands, which are uncovered. Thousands of others will find their own viewing points along the line from bridge parapets, windows and walls of houses and other adjacent properties, and by standing on motor vehicles.

People in their positions during the morning will see the shuttle service of diesel trains from Manchester and Liverpool disgorging packed passengers and returning empty for more. They will observe television camera crews and Press photographers waiting for action. Then, soon after one o'clock, the cavalcade will begin to move out of the sidings at Bold near St Helens Junction in a railway spectacular that will occupy nearly four exquisite hours, historic details being recounted dramatically over the loudspeaker system by popular steam-lover Alan Pegler.

As the three replica locomotives pant and puff along with their tiny trains, many spectators are sure to sense acutely something of the real-life drama of the original Rainhill Trials, when the future of the steam locomotive and the Liverpool & Manchester Railway hung desperately in the balance. In 1829, people were watching in wonder the genesis of a great new revolution; this time, onlookers will be fascinated that such tiny locomotives and primitive carriages and wagons could have survived as the paradigm of the great railway systems of the modern world.

Larger locomotives in the cavalcade, throbbing and steaming with latent power inhibited only by the slow pace, will reveal the progress to greatness the pioneers began; and their proud drivers will wave to the crowds and sound their whistles and sirens in salute. On this mundane stretch of line, the re-enactment of the historic scene will echo the past through a loophole in time, and bring to life a few hours of the glorious past of this great little railway. Railway society members and other enthusiasts will feel warmly rewarded by the privilege of just being there, enjoying the happy thought that the preservation societies and museums did so much to make such a magnificent cavalcade possible. Visitors should be able to return home far and wide, satisfied that British Rail in its lavish publicity did not overstate its case.

Many local people who take their railway for granted may well wonder what all the international fuss is about; but when the celebra-

tions are finally over, perhaps on their next journey through Olive
Mount Cutting (widened for four tracks in 1871), under Rainhill
Skew Bridge, over Newton and Sankey Viaducts, past the old Tudor-
style waiting room at Earlestown, across Chat Moss with its wastes of
rich black fertile soil on which the railway track has steadily subsided
sixteen feet since first laid, then into Manchester Victoria with its fine
stone frontage, the travellers will spare a reflective moment for
George Stephenson and the railway promoters who made their
journey possible. It remains as the most notable piece of railway in
world history.

Those unable to attend the grand cavalcade of steam will be able to
see locomotives and other rolling stock on display at Spekeland Road
in Liverpool during June and at Liverpool Road station yard in Manchester the following month through to 14th September.

Enthusiasts with a penchant for archaeology were catered for by
the Edge Hill Railway Trust Limited which organised a visitor centre
and rail trail at the historic steam terminus at Edge Hill. Opening to
the public was planned for April 1980. Attractions included an
inspection of excavations at the site of the rope-winding engine house
in Wapping Cutting, the nearby engine sheds which often housed the
Rocket, and boiler houses and stables excavated in the sides of the
cutting. The North West Industrial Archaeological Society jointly
with Merseyside Museum conducted a 'dig' on the site. In the station
building, which has been restored and cleaned by British Rail, is an
exhibition illustrating the history of the line, and a large-scale
working model of the Edge Hill terminus as it was in 1839. Diligent
research in the area reveals a liberal number of original relics and sites
on the railway, offering scope for photography, sketching and note-
taking. Financial aid for the Trust came from the Merseyside County
Council, from industry and from individuals for restoring and maintaining this historic site for future generations.

Turning now to Manchester: "Station sold for £1" is a headline that
is sure to catch the eye. "The first passenger station in the world, at
Liverpool Road," reported *Rail News*, the BR staff monthly newspaper, in October 1978, "has been sold for £1 to the Greater Manchester Council." With the promise of £100,000 from British Rail, the
Council undertook to restore the buildings and land, to form an
extension to the North West Museum of Science and Industry.

The buildings were already listed for preservation for their architectural and historical merit. Having been opened in 1830, the station
faded from the passenger scene when the line was extended in 1844 to
the new Victoria station, and begins a new life in 1980.

Anniversary activities at the Manchester end were organised by the
Liverpool Road Celebrations Joint Advisory Committee, which
received a grant of £40,000 from the Greater Manchester Council.

The GMC also authorised the spending of £35,000 to build a temporary rail connection into Liverpool Road Station, to replace the track that had been removed after the former goods depot closed in 1975. In a festival to run for eight weeks in the autumn 1980, many steam locomotives were to be displayed, among them the three replicas, and the original *Lion*. Planned events included a boat rally and steam boat trips on the River Irwell, a traditional funfair, drama and music concerts, exhibitions of railway painting and photography, film shows, model railways, with trade stands and railway society stalls.

On Sunday 14th September 1980, a celebratory train with historic locomotives and a vintage flavour was scheduled to run from Liverpool to Manchester to mark the 150th anniversary. Many visitors for this event were expected in both cities to which British Rail arranged to run special trains.

At the end of an impressive and spectacular year, the events will be seen as a fitting tribute to those great visionary pioneers. We railway enthusiasts will have revelled in nostalgic railwayana, acquiring talking topics, new friendships, photographs for the albums, tape recordings for family and companions and a renewed interest in a fascinating hobby. And why not! Merseyside and Mancunian people may walk a little taller having discovered, or rediscovered, the historic significance of the line that joins their two great cities and threads through their towns and villages; and railwaymen themselves may have acquired a little more pride in their great calling. Repeating the pattern of the 1830s, trade, industry and commerce will have been rejuvenated at a time when it was never more needed in the economy of the north-west region.

On returning home, visitors from around the world will treasure their souvenirs selected from the mass of commemorative miscellany, to be happily reminded of a unique experience, not the least of which will be the discovery that the so-called reserved British really do know how to enjoy themselves.

As to the pioneering line itself, its long-term future is assured; and if coming generations of preservationists maintain their devotion and enthusiasm, the line may yet see its two centuries celebrated in 2030. For it seems that Britain's railways will continue serving the public as long as the iron wheel – joined in holy wedlock by Stephenson, honeymooned at Rainhill and settled down on the Liverpool & Manchester – remains happily married to the iron rail.

Bibliography

ACWORTH, W. M., *The Railways of England* (John Murray, 1889)

AHRONS, E. L., *The British Steam Railway Locomotive 1825–1925* (Locomotive Publishing, 1927)

ANDERSON, MATTHEW, (Ed.), *The Liverpool & Manchester Railway Centenary: Book and Programme* (Liverpool Organisation 1930)

BAINES, THOMAS, *History of the Commerce and Town of Liverpool* (Longmans, 1852)

BOOTH, HENRY, *Liverpool & Manchester Railway* (Wales & Baines 1830, reprinted Frank Cass, 1969)

BOULTON, W. H., *The Railways of Britain – their History, Construction and Working* (Sampson Low, 1950)

CARLSON, ROBERT E., *The Liverpool & Manchester Railway Project, 1821–31* (David & Charles, 1969)

CARTER, ERNEST F., *Britain's Railway Liveries: Colours, Crests and Linings 1825–1948* (Burke, 1952)

CHURCH, WILLIAM C., *The Life of John Ericsson* (Sampson Low, 1890)

COLEMAN, TERRY, *The Railway Navvies* (Pelican, 1965)

DEVEY, JOSEPH, *The Life of Joseph Locke* (E. Bentley, 1862)

DONAGHY, THOMAS J., *Liverpool & Manchester Railway Operations 1831–45* (David & Charles)

ELLIS, C. HAMILTON, *Nineteenth-Century Railway Carriages in the British Isles* (Modern Transport Publishing, 1949)

FRANCIS, JOHN, *A History of the English Railway* (Longmans, 1851)

HOLT, G. O., *A Short History of the Liverpool & Manchester Railway* (Railway & Canal Historical Society, 1955)

LAMBERT, RICHARD S., *The Railway King 1800–71* (George Allen & Unwin, 1934)

LEE, CHARLES E., *The Evolution of Railways* (*Railway Gazette*, 1937)

LEWIN, HENRY G., *Early British Railways: A Short History of Their Origin and Development 1801–44* (Locomotive Publishing, 1925)

MARSHALL, C. F. DENDY, *Liverpool & Manchester Railway Centenary History* (Locomotive Publishing, 1930)

NOCK, O. S., *The London & North Western Railway* (Ian Allan, 1960)

PAINE, E. M. S., *The Two James's and the Two Stephensons* (G. Phipps, 1861)

REILLY, JOHN, *The History of Manchester* (John Grey Bell, 1861)

ROLT, L. T. C., *Red for Danger* (Bodley Head, 1955)

ROLT, L. T. C., *George & Robert Stephenson* (Longmans, 1960)

SIMMONS, JACK, *The Railways of Britain: An Historical Introduction* (Routledge & Kegan Paul, 1961)

SIMNETT, W. E., *Railway Amalgamation in Great Britain* (*Railway Gazette*, 1923)

SMILES, DR. SAMUEL, *George Stephenson and his Son Robert* (John Murray, 1868)

STRETTON, CLEMENT E., *The Locomotive Engine and its Development* (Crosby, Lockwood, 1892)

TREVITHICK, FRANCIS E., *Life of Richard Trevithick* (E. F. & N. Spon, 1872)

TUCK, HENRY, *A Railway Shareholders' Manual* (Effingham Wilson, 1845)

VIGNOLES, O. J., *Life of Charles Blacker Vignoles* (Longman, Green, 1889)

VEITCH, GEORGE S., *The Struggle for the Liverpool & Manchester Railway*, (*Liverpool Daily Post*, 1930)

WALKER, JAMES SCOTT, *An Accurate Description of the Liverpool & Manchester Railway* (J. F. Cannell, 1830)

WARREN, J. G. H., *A Century of Locomotive Building by Robert Stephenson & Co* (Andrew Reid, 1923)

WHISHAW, FRANCIS, *The Railways of Great Britain and Ireland Practically Described and Illustrated* (Simpkin, Marshall, 1840)

WHISHAW, FRANCIS, *Analysis of Railways: Consisting of a Series of Reports of the Twelve Hundred Miles of Projected Railways in England and Wales, Now Before Parliament* (John Weale, 1837)

WOOD, NICHOLAS, *A Practical Treatise on Rail-Roads* (Hurst, Chance, 1825, revised 1831)

YOUNG, ROBERT, *Timothy Hackworth and the Locomotive* (Locomotive Publishing, 1923)

"A TOURIST", *The Railway Companion* (Wilson and Fraser, 1833)

ANNUALS

Railway Directory and Year Book (IPC Business Press)

Jane's World Railways (Macdonald & Janes)

Railway and Steam Enthusiasts' Handbook (David & Charles)

Railway World Annual (Ian Allan)

INDEX

INDEX